WORKING WOOD 3

THE CABINET MAKER'S WORKSHOP

An Artisan Course
With Simon James

Artisan MEDIA
INSPIRING CRAFTSMANSHIP

Published 2014 Artisan Media Ltd
Ty Mawr, Clwt y Bont, Caernarfon,
Gwynedd. LL55 3DH
United Kingdom

Author - Simon James
Photographer - Dave Brown

Printed in the USA by Unitedgraphicsinc.com
ISBN: 978-0-9569673-1-2

About the author

Simon James, lives and works in the foothills of Snowdonia National Park, in North Wales. After several years abroad, he returned to his home county of Gwynedd, with his wife Joy and three teenage children, where the whole family re-built a 300 year old farm house which is now their family home.

Simon has a 'no nonsense', practical approach to woodworking which he admits, is largely due to his father Jesse's influence. Jesse James, also-re built a farmhouse, "The Bunkhouse", 50 years previous. Having made a living as a mountain guide, even now at 83, he is still ridiculously fit. Simon also inherited an interest in industrial chemistry, and all manner of other scientific interests, which led to a degree in Mining Engineering, and then to employment at a gold mine in Ecuador.

In spite of his engineering background, he started married life as an apprentice carpenter, with a certain Steve Fisher, who had a reputation for attention to detail that suited Simon's engineering approach to carpentry and joinery. In his spare time, he made tables, gates and built kitchens and cabinets entirely from scratch. This soon became a full time business, undertaking commissions from a string of wealthy clients.

Working out of a small workshop, his reputation for quality workmanship grew to the point that he took on apprentices, instilling the need for genuine care and attention to detail in every project. Teaching and training became a passion, leading to an educational degree in Design and Technology, where he naturally specialized in woodwork. He then went on to teach woodworking, amongst other things, in Romania for five years, before returning to Wales around 10 years ago. Simon brings a fresh perspective to teaching woodwork, one that is very firmly based on the skills and techniques from the past, but with a passion to communicate them clearly to a modern audience, and often with some fresh new insights. Always with a pragmatic approach, to find the best way to work with, and integrate, a few modern machines with traditional hand tool methods.

Acknowledgements

Well, after so much work, it's marvellous to be at the stage of thanking people for their input and support. Firstly, I'd like to thank my family for putting up with my frequent absence from family life, late nights of work and weekends in the workshop. To my wife, Joy, especially for her support and understanding that this book has taken more thought, time and effort than any 'normal' job. To Matt, Jess and Josie, for encouraging me to spend more time with my wife and family, and less time at work, and for putting up with my frequent absence from family activities.

To Dave and Lynwen Brown, my colleagues, for their unending dedication to working as an interdependent team and for their determination, encouragement and sheer effort in bringing this series out. Dave's attention to photographic detail has made this book more than just an educational manual, and even now, I thoroughly enjoy just flicking through the fantastic photographs.

I'd like to thank Phil Edwards for his encouragement and technical editing skills. Working with Phil is a riot, and I'm usually laughing to myself even before he answers the phone. Also to Ifan Bates, for his design and layout work, and for juggling all the usual work to fit in such a large and demanding project. I would like to thank Tez Chainey from Sparsholt, for the gift of a box full of molding planes, all those years ago, that got me started in the wonderful world of hand made moldings. And finally, to two fine craftsmen, Steve Fisher and Paul Gander, for pointing me in the right direction in the early days.

Foreword

I first met Simon, naturally, at a woodworking show – I was there demonstrating my planes and he and Dave walked up to the bench while I was talking to a customer. He jumped straight into the conversation and we chatted away enthusiastically for ages. I could tell he was passionate about his woodworking and the keenly angled questions he poised were a breath of fresh air. One topic we talked about was how we got into woodworking and the books we used to gather information from. I told him how I found most books only contained part of the information that was necessary, assuming the reader knew a certain amount about a subject and that I had to search multiple sources to attain a full and rounded knowledge. He agreed, having found the same thing. He mentioned that he was writing a book and I was very excited when later he got in touch and asked if I would be involved.

If you have worked your way through *Working Wood 1&2* then you have already built a firm base of skills and techniques. In this book you will find a feast of new methods, a myriad of jigs and tricks that will open your eyes to new ways of achieving your goals while providing many "why didn't I think of that" moments along the way. Of particular interest to me are the many new and specialised tools that are introduced throughout the chapters – I guarantee you will find something special that will change the way you work for the better! There is also invaluable advice on how to maintain and sharpen these tools – tools with curved cutting edges require a different approach and using the methods described will allow you to achieve this with confidence. Being able to keep your tools in top condition means they will always perform efficiently, and your work will reflect this. And the jigs that you will find in these pages will allow you to use your tools in ways you would never have imagined.

We are very fortunate with our chosen vocation – very rarely is there ever only one way to perform a particular task. I guarantee that when you reach the end of this book you will come away with a head packed full of ideas and techniques and that will allow you to work faster, more accurately and to achieve your goals. And most of all to enable you to enjoy your craft in the way that feels most comfortable to you. So what are you waiting for? Turn the page and get started... the feast awaits.

Phil Edwards - Plane maker

Contents

Introduction

Welcome to Working Wood 3

This part of the Artisan Course is deliberately very different from the previous and forthcoming volumes. Rather than just starting on a new project and teaching new skills, this book presents a concise summary of the key tools and items of workshop equipment required to make solid wood cabinets. Launching into a complex cabinet making project without getting your workshop, bench and tools fully prepared for the task would be like starting the hundred meter hurdles with your laces untied. Statistically, we know that in woodworking, and probably in the majority of the things we do, most of the successful projects are preceded by detailed planning, good organization and adequate training of all those involved. In line with this ethos, this book is all about preparation. There are no cabinet making projects just yet (though there are numerous very useful things to make). Instead we'll look at some important new tools, some new sharpening methods and devices, a range of new woodworking techniques and also a set of workshop jigs and devices. We'll also look at glues, wood finishes and many other elements of

Introduction

what it takes to get properly organized for making cabinets using traditional methods. Though proudly traditional, the methods and practices described are in fact fully compatible with a modern workshop equipped with machinery and power tools. Following soon in this series, I will be presenting methods of work where wood machining processes are harmonised with hand tools, and particular matched sets of hand and machine tools together create a wider range of options than considering any tool in isolation.

Knowledge, skill and pragmatism are the key ingredients that will give you the opportunity to enjoy making the most of your creativity.

"Woodworking is an expression of creativity, immersed in a world of possibilities and variety..."

A simple, shop made 'hold down'. I only use these devices because they really work!

Pragmatism not nostalgia

My philosophy of working wood is centered firmly on pragmatism, not on nostalgia or Western traditions. Woodworking always has been, and always will be, a very practical subject. As an art, a craft or a trade, woodworkers apply common sense, skill and ingenuity to get the job done. There are so many different ways to work wood, from whittling a tree with a sharp flint to making the most of your immense investment in machines, and in all of this there is very rarely one, single, 'best' way to carry out an individual operation. Adopting a pragmatic approach means finding out what works best for you. To save re-inventing the wheel, it's always better to find out what your preferred method of work is by studying the methods used by others, and in some ways, this part of the course gives you that opportunity. You can choose which jigs and devices you think will be most useful to you, and look at the specialist planes section, all the time weighing up if the methods appeal to you.

Hand tool furniture making should never be a chore, a bore or a tedious grind. It shouldn't wear you out either. If you know your hands are not as strong as they used to be, get a local wood shop to surface plane, thickness and crosscut all your stock and materials before you start. In the past I have stubbornly hand planed so much timber that my hands were barely usable for a couple of weeks after. Machines are great for donkey work, so make the most of them as appropriate. I'm a big fan of my electric routers, but I have to say I have more fun and satisfaction in a single day using a bunch of lovely old wooden molding planes than I would have in a year of efficient machine routing.

Just ask yourself...

What aspects of working wood do you most enjoy? Is it being able to tear into your stock, and against the clock, finish the project in record time? For me, woodworking is an expression of creativity, immersed in a world of possibilities and variety, enjoying the satisfaction of making something useful, beautiful or original. I think you can achieve all three. I never stop learning, and I'm fascinated by the challenges of working with natural materials, the contrasting colors, grain patterns and the incredible structural versatility of timber. Whether I choose a machine for a particular operation, or just get on with using hand tools, is not chiseled in stone. I enjoy variety, the peace and quiet of hand tools, the versatility of specialist planes and the undeniable efficiency of my band saw and mortising machine.

Where do we go from here?

The one enduring mantra from the foundation course presented in *Working Wood 1&2* that is worth a mention here is this: The principles of accurate layout, use of sharp tools and good technique, underpins every diverse craft in the vast realm of wood work. These elements are the basics, to which you must cling on to, never depart from and only add to, not replace.

However, once you get past the basics, you then need to make some choices. Are you training for a profession that you will successfully develop into a means of earning an income, or do you just really enjoy working with wood? If you had the time, knowledge and resources, where would you want to be in a few years time? A boat builder, instrument maker, timber framer, model maker, furniture designer and maker? I just love working with wood but I also enjoy a real challenge, so I would quite happily build boats, furniture or guitars, and enjoy every bit of it. So, in a predominantly 'hand tool' wood working course, is there any need to specialize? I would argue that there really is, even at this stage.

"...once you get past the basics, you then need to make some choices."

There are three shop made devices in the photo that are invaluable to me.

My first, purpose built workshop, under construction.

The specialist

There is an old saying where I'm from which in some ways has a ring of truth in it: "A Jack of all trades and a master of none". I have to agree that to be a really good 'all rounder' does somehow deny the opportunity to become a true 'master' of any specialist area. I find it interesting to consider this in reverse, because it's a belief that I hold to even stronger. Could it be that no highly polished specialist could also claim to be a really good 'all rounder'? It's debatable; we all have our strengths and weaknesses in different areas.

Even if you are very keen to specialize in one particular area, there is a lot to be said for having a pragmatic understanding of a broad range of different trades, processes and materials. To get the most out of this course, it's really your responsibility to read around the subject - why not delve into the physics of mechanical leverage and tensile strength of materials; the structure and composition of tool steel; the finer points of the iron-carbon equilibrium diagram, or even the geometrical principles of Gothic Arches? I have an engineering background, but that in itself does not deny me an understanding of working with natural materials. It does however steer me away from the Krenovian end of the spectrum, where 'understanding wood' goes way beyond simple physics!

Perhaps like a lot of guys and gals, alongside a diverse range of interests, I always enjoy learning new skills, new techniques and interesting solutions to technical problems or challenges. I don't actually mind making a few mistakes along the way, and I'd much rather have a go than wonder if something would have been possible. I also enjoy the sheer technical challenge of complex joinery.

With a simple jig you can often make light work of an otherwise difficult operation.

This is a selection of some of my general purpose and specialist planes.

Simple tools but stunning results, there's nothing nostalgic about that!

I have always had the need to gain as much knowledge as possible in whatever field of work I've been involved in, so I'm definitely on the 'Jack of all trades' end of the spectrum. This approach could put me in the 'all rounder' camp, which I think suits me fine, as I have never claimed to be a specialist in any one particular field.

However, as far as course structure goes, some degree of specialization is unavoidable. As we learn more about working wood, we need to work smarter, not harder. This means narrowing our horizon for a season and becoming well practiced in a particular field before we move on to the next. In the Artisan Course, we are going to sequentially look in detail at a series of specific, specialist areas, chosen in order of 'usefulness' to the everyday wood worker.

The area of specialization that we are going to look at in more detail first, is one that I consider gives the woodworker the broadest skill set - the art and craft of cabinet making. I am using this term in a rather archaic sense, because I am not referring to fitting together flat pack, veneered chipboard kitchen units! I am talking broadly about the course structure here, and not about this book in particular, which is dedicated to getting organized and ready for the work to come. We are going to look at how solid wood has been, and still can be, used to make fine examples of functional furniture, fit for any kitchen, hallway, or office.

Now these fine furniture pieces could possibly be made with a handful of tools, but before the advent of machines, the cabinet maker's workshop was kitted out with a whole lot more than just a few tools. A system of work was established over time, that allowed the likes of Chippendale to run a very successful and productive furniture making enterprise.

In reality

I have a huge amount of respect for craftsmen of this era, for their care, determination, skill and sheer effort in creating exquisite furniture. However, there is a myth here that needs to be busted: The craftsmen working for Mr. Chippendale did not need the same artistic flair and virtuoso talent of the master for their own day to day work. Indeed, they were highly skilled, but general production of the beautiful furniture was all achieved using patterns, jigs, workshop aids, craftsman-made gadgets and some specialized tools. They were specialists, and they had their own range of holders, guides and special devices. Boat builders did not have these things, they had their own measuring rods, layout templates and cutting jigs. Violin makers did not have this equipment, they too had their own very different and very specialized devices.

So, we are heading for some very nice cabinet making projects in the next series, but right now, let's make sure we have the specialized 'stuff' that is going to make the future work enjoyable, straight forwards, and well within reach for all of us.

Section 1
Chapter 1 Your workshop

Your workshop may be where you earn a living, a place for evening retreat and solitude, or somewhere you just like to hang out, have fun and make things. I have always had a workshop of some description, and over the years, every one has been a place of enthusiastic activity, sometimes for earning a living and other times a place of creative relaxation.

Storage and access: This is the balancing act!

I am not a naturally tidy worker. I leave tools on my bench that I may not need for a while, offcuts and so on, and keeping the decks cleared is something I have to really work at. As we beaver away in our workshops, sheds or yards, we sometimes loose sight of the fact that we are in an environment that we have control over - perhaps the only one! If the place is untidy and disorganized we have nobody else to blame.

Getting organized in the first place requires a methodical and disciplined approach. However, keeping your shop in order may take an ongoing sense of determination and purpose. The benefits of working efficiently are sometimes lost through the tyranny of the urgent -"I'm too busy to organize my shop!".

I enjoy nothing more than working in a tidy, organized workshop, but in the past I have definitely been in the 'too busy' camp. The real question here is this: How can you make the most of what you have got, and arrange your shop in such a way that work can actually be enjoyable, with the minimum of frustration?

Quite apart from tools and materials storage, the environment you work in is a big deal and to be brutally honest - it really is under your control. It's well worth standing back to check if you are making the best of what you have got. Be fully prepared to make big changes if you need to, and open minded enough to accept that the way things are in your shop, right now, does not need to have any bearing on how things could be. Before looking at any other aspects of getting set up for making cabinets, we'll cover some general workshop requirements, which I hope, will help you make the most of what you've got.

Space

At the risk of stating the obvious, the space you need is directly proportional to the dimensions of your finished work, whatever that may be. A violin maker can manage with reasonably small workshop and a boat builder needs a long, high shed.

This is the first aspect of organization I want to look at. I am convinced that the potential for efficient work increases in proportion to the space you can use, if you need to. I have worked in many tight shops, with every cubic inch of storage utilized to it's maximum and I've often used the flat table of the radial arm saw for layout, the rafters for temporary part storage and the gaps between workbenches for jig storage. Being short of space is far from ideal, and as we give our full attention to the particular job in hand, we end up working as though we had blinkers on. Stop, step back and ask yourself some important questions:

How much space have I got, and how much space do I need? Am I using the space I've got to it's best advantage?

To answer these questions, you need to ask yourself what you intend to do. If you intend to make a living, you need a very different approach than if you just enjoy making furniture for yourself or maybe occasionally for friends.

If you have enough space to arrange all your tools, jigs, and work in progress, without your shop feeling cluttered, it's a luxury! As a bare minimum, you need storage for everything you have, at least so you have the possibility of keeping the decks cleared.

Boat building takes a lot of space. I'd love to give it a go some day as I live by the sea and I enjoy sailing.

Hang as much as you can off the walls.

I have racks of short pieces. All the really short off cuts go straight into the wood stove.

A place for everything

A place for everything? Now this could take a lot of effort. Bite the bullet and just do the best you can. Get stuff stowed, hung up, stored, racked out, stacked, arranged and generally fitted in everywhere you can. Aside from this goal, as far as possible, you need to work ergonomically, so have your most used tools and jigs closest to hand. Don't ever get so set in your ways that you are not prepared to change things around if it seems like a good idea.

Time spent hunting for anything (pencils are my No.1 problem), is quite simply time wasted. I don't enjoy hunting for pencils, but every now and again, I simply can't find one!

Storage of materials

This is not such an issue if you don't intend to keep a good stock of materials. If you generally buy materials just before you need to use them, pretty much most of what you have could be work in progress.

I like to have wood 'in stock', and generally have several pieces being built at the same time. I also like converting locally grown lumber into usable stock. I have wood in all stages of seasoning which is a short way of saying I have wood stacked pretty much all over the place.

I am a persistent hoarder of short pieces, as I can't bring myself to saw up and burn anything over 10 inches long. The rails on narrow cabinet doors can be about 10 inches, which is the way I look at small pieces.

I use the space above my machines for wood storage, but in any workshop, the layout is going to dictate where the best places for wood storage will be. Long lengths are sometimes more trouble than they are worth. I've sometimes tried to deal with long lengths in small spaces, where the simple solution was to cut them in half, or thirds.

TOP TIP: *Don't store any wood in such a way that it either sags in the middle or sags at the ends. Keep it as straight as you can until you take it out to saw it up.*

Ask yourself if you really need to keep long lengths? I rarely need anything with a finished length of more than four feet, so I cut to length in multiples of three and four feet. This takes care of most cabinet work I carry out. My racks have 8 to 10ft lengths at the most, and materials 3 to 4ft go into a stillage, or onto a shelf if they are not work in progress. If you have an intended purpose for materials, get them down to the right length at the earliest opportunity.

You can see how I store plywood - vertically, with dividers for different sections. This allows me to sort through, choose and pull out what I want easily.

TOP TIP: *If you are going to buy seasoned rough sawn lumber, buy the closest size you can, to the finished size you need, plus say a quarter of an inch or so. Once you start ripping deep cuts to get two thin boards out of one thick one, the chances of the wood cupping increases dramatically. Also, plane off equal amounts from each side of your rough sawn board as this will even out the stress in the wood fibers.*

In my yard I have slabs of tree seasoning, interesting woods and logs of walnut, cherry, holly and ash, planked or ready for planking. I have pitch pine out of old Welsh chapels, old barn roof purlins, rafters from my own house and pine panelling boards, ½" thick, 16" wide in single boards. I would not part with any of it, as someday, I know I'll use it all to make things.

I have a mixture of sapele, maple, walnut and a few more besides. Most of this rack is oak.

For safety, the vertical rack is divided into sections by short steel 'arms'.

"Ask yourself if you really need to keep long lengths?"

My layout table is where the planning and marking out happens.

I use a thin plywood cover sheet to protect the table top

Layout table

This is a piece of kit that is very useful indeed, it's second only to my workbench. I need to physically arrange parts in front of me in order to choose good faces, see the arrangement, mark the joinery out etc. I have at times had to work without a proper layout table and it's been irritating at the very least! Either build one of these, buy one or adapt something from a yard sale by laying a plywood top down to give yourself more area.

Cover sheet: I do a lot of staining up and wood finishing on the layout table so I like to protect it from the stains, oils and polish with a thin sheet of plywood.

I keep work in progress on a shelf underneath, but you could instead build in storage for tools, jigs, devices etc.

Heating and cooling

There is nothing better than working in a warm workshop on a cold Winter's day, especially with rain lashing against the windows. Unless of course, it's a warm Summer's day and I have the doors open to keep the place cool. Either way, the temperature of your workplace makes a big difference to the way you work. With cold hands, I find myself quite distracted and unable to focus on fine details.

I had a very small shop once that my children helped me insulate, and a few shovelfuls of shavings in my wood burner brought the temperature up nicely.

My current shop is well insulated, and heated with a multi-fuel stove. It'll burn shavings, sawdust, offcuts and pretty much anything else I care to feed it with. As I'm mad keen on energy conservation, I also fitted a long heat exchanger to the flue pipe, feeding cold air in at the top, and then allowing warm air to circulate out of the vents by the stove. A little fan circulates the air in my shop, through this unit, all day long.

How you heat (or cool) your workshop is not a big deal, but I will say that it's worth arranging things so that you can work in a relaxed fashion. In order to keep the heat in, you may need to consider some form of air recirculation, which I cover on pages 25 and 26.

Regardless of where on the face of the planet your workshop is located, insulation is going to help to stabilise the heat gain during the day and the heat loss at night. This has the effect of helping to stabilise the humidity to some extent, and preventing the development of rust on tools.

Humidity control can be very difficult to manage, and we'll look at this next.

This is a 20Kw burner, and the heat exchanger gets every last bit of heat I can out of the flue gas.

This machine weighs over a ton, is about 110 yrs old, and makes short work of this sycamore!

My son Matt, who thankfully is qualified for this sort of thing!

Humidity control

Over the winter months, I run a dehumidifier to get the relative humidity down to around 60% at 64°F (18°C). It's important to understand the relationship between relative humidity (RH) and temperature. As the air gets warmer, it can hold more water than when it's cold, so if you warm up any room, regardless of the moisture content of the air, the RH will drop.

In the tropics the humidity can be very high as well as the temperature, and quite frankly, there's not much you can do about it. If it's reasonably constant, inside and outside, it's not a problem

I've worked in Central Africa with dry and rainy seasons. Hot and dry turned to warm and wet, suddenly in a single day. There was an answer, and it was not controlling the environment!

The wood shop was stacked with mahogany boards, grown about 2 miles away and seasoned as it stood before being felled and pit sawn into boards. The wood was made into hospital doors, windows and cabinets and then liberally rubbed with a crude drying oil for weeks before fitting. By the time the rains came, the oil was dry and the wood hardly moved at all. Many coats of finishing oil may be the only answer in some circumstances!

After planking a tree, the wood starts to dry out and season. A year or so of air drying outside needs to be followed with several months in the workshop, which needs to be as stable as possible in terms of humidity.

The real issue is not really the relative humidity, but rather it's the difference between the conditions in which the wood is stored and worked, and the final destination, be it a centrally heated house, a log cabin or stone built bothy on a Scottish island. The aim is to keep the differences in humidity, all year round, to a minimum. If you can't, you may just have to apply many coats of finish, or put up with a little movement in your furniture.

Don't try to save on lighting, detailed work requires a very good level of background light and a lamp for close up work.

Lighting

As a general rule, more light is better than less for detailed hand work. I am a big fan of fluorescent lighting in workshops as you don't get the sharp, harsh shadows of a single bulb. I usually have fluorescent lights above my bench and a small angle poise lamp right by my vise.

Any machines you use should also be well lit, just like your bench. This is a safety issue as well as allowing you to see lines and marks easily. LED lights are dropping in price, and can provide excellent lighting for machines, allowing precise setting of blades, fences, stops, etc.

Your entire shop should have a decent level of lighting, particularly if you live in the north, where winter days are short. In North Wales in December, the sun rises around 8.30 am and by 3.30 pm it's starting to get dim. On a cloudy wet day, the street lights barely get a chance to turn themselves off, so good lighting is a big deal for me. Nothing beats daylight, so if you have the opportunity, fit roof lights in abundance, right above your bench!

This is my primary dust filter. Very little ultra fine dust makes it through to the filter box. (Overleaf.)

Dust control

Despite having half of my shop dedicated to hand tool work, I do produce quite a lot of dust just through hand sawing, sanding and planing. Mostly, I get knee deep in shavings, which I just brush into a pile by the wood stove, but under every pile of swept shavings you will also find a small pile of fine dust. Don't even try to get the fines moved or they'll get airborne. Instead, shift the chips and shavings with a brush and shovel, and suck up everything else with a shop vacuum.

Machines can produce a lot of dust but the type of wood you are using also has a bearing on the dust produced. Kiln dried, fine grained hardwood such as mahogany, will produce ultra fine airborne fibers which can cause a nasty reaction in your respiratory system. I am particularly prone to this sort of thing and a 3 minute mistake has cost me ten days work in the past (unbelievably, more than once, which I have to put down to sheer stupidity on my part!).

The worst offenders have to be saws, planers and routers, so if you have these machines, make sure an extraction system is in place to deal with the dust, and the system is used for every cut. I'm a big fan of cyclones prior to filtration of the air, as these will extend the life of fine particle filters many times over. I built the one shown here as I could not find anything suitable for less than $1500. I enjoy a bit of metal work, so for less than $100 I could not resist the challenge!

I like the idea of recirculating filtered air, so I use a bank of HEPA filters to take out all the ultra fines. I've gone for the super cheap option of a plywood box in a room adjacent to my workshop. The box is divided into two compartments with the air passing through about ten HEPA filter bags, arranged in parallel, for maximum airflow and minimum pressure drop. The clean filtered air is then returned through a duct back into my shop. Recirculation is a big energy saver, otherwise I'd be trying to heat up 1500 cubic meters of cold fresh air, every hour in the winter, and that would be a whole heap of sawdust and offcuts!

If fine dust is a real problem for you, take some time to work out where it's coming from and how you are going to deal with it. As a secondary measure, there are ceiling mounted filter fans that constantly circulate and filter the air.

If you can see and smell the dust, it's going to get into your lungs, be in no doubt about this.

Conclusion

After considering some organizational and environmental factors, I hope that you can use the pointers and suggestions I've given here to figure out the best way to use the space you have. Aim for a warm, safe and organized shop. Improvements as previously described are always worth the investment of time and resources - you will never look back and regret the day you decided to sort your shop out properly!

We'll now move on to looking at some tools to add to the basic shaping and joinery sets we covered in . Apart from having the right tools, it's knowing what you can do with them that makes the real difference in a Cabinet Maker's Workshop.

My HEPA filter box. I run 10 bags in parallel...

...to get the airflow I need.

Section 2
New toolsets

It's true that with the basic tool groups we covered in *Working Wood 1&2*, you can make a fairly good range of shelving units, wooden boxes and probably some nice looking tables of various shapes and sizes. However, to get your shop prepared and set up for cabinetwork, I can assure you that the following tools will prove an invaluable addition to your collection as you start to tackle more complex projects such as those in the next of our series, *Working Wood 4 "Cabinet Making Techniques"*.

Part of the process of getting organized for furniture making is making sure you have all the tools you are going to need, and that they are in very good working order. This section gives you a list of the bare essentials you will need at this stage, and perhaps a couple more besides. It's by no means a full list for cabinet making in all it's splendor, and a few more tools will be introduced in the next part of the course, although surprisingly few.

When you buy tools, get the best you can afford. There is an old Romanian saying that is worth remembering:

"Sunt prea sărac să cumpăr lucruri ieftine."

This translates as "I'm too poor to buy cheap things" and this is a very real acknowledgement that often you get what you pay for when you buy tools. The poor man buys the very best he can, as he knows his livelihood depends on his work, and when cheap tools don't work properly or break, the same man knows he will be in trouble, serious trouble!

That said, if you have got the time and energy to fix up old tools before you need to use them, you could do very well through an investment of effort that could save a lot of bucks. Cheap, modern planes are nowhere near the quality of equally cheap old planes. If you are going to buy second hand tools I've included some clear steps on how to get a selection of common old planes into very good working order.

Chapter 2
New setting out and checking tools

As you look to develop your woodworking beyond a foundation level, you will find that your workshop needs to be kitted out to deal with larger furniture making projects, and this is certainly the case for the next part of this course. For this reason, I'm introducing larger versions of the layout tools used in *Working Wood 1&2*, alongside a selection of useful new additions.

Accurate layout gives you confidence.

"If you can measure everything easily, set out accurately and check quickly, you are probably half way there..."

You'll find these new setting out and checking tools invaluable as you progress through making the various jigs and devices in Section 5, page 179.

Cabinet making almost always involves using detailed plans. These may be your own designs and drawings, a third party's, or just occasionally, people may just make it up as they go along.

If you can measure everything easily, set out accurately and check quickly, you are probably half way there.

For many years in cabinet making shops the larger checking tools used to be shared between a group of craftsmen, and the various squares and straight edges would have been shop made from the best quality, fine grained hardwood. Hornbeam is a particularly tough and strong wood, and although being difficult to work, for centuries it was used across a wide range of applications, from wooden gear pegs to tool handles.

The lack of availability of old, good quality, solid wood layout tools means that we need to turn to machined aluminium squares, straight edges and suchlike. In practice, aluminium and steel tools last very well, are very reliable, and are of course much cheaper to mass produce than hand crafted hornbeam equivalents. I'm recommending some modern equipment in this chapter for practical reasons, despite the fact that when it comes to tools, I prefer the look and feel of all things wooden!

Measuring and marking tools

Long steel rule

Quite often, a tape measure will simply not give you the accuracy you need on your projects. The end gets bent over a little too far, so everything reads oversize, the rivets holding the bent steel tab get worn so internal measurements read under size, and so it goes on. A good three foot (one meter) steel rule just stays accurate, pretty much forever, so it's very useful for a bench mark check, particularly if you are working to drawings.

Digital or Vernier gauge

I have owned quite a few of these over the years, and I've gradually bought better quality ones that have lasted longer. I like checking thickness of stock, widths of grooves, mortise chisels, the thickness of inlay cutters, thickness of corresponding inlay and pretty much everything else as well. If you're okay with reading a Vernier scale, the earlier non electronic versions are more reliable in that the battery can't ever run out!

Dividers

Small dividers are very useful in pairs as you can set out all manner of work where offset measurements are required. I'll step out the marks for dovetail edges with one set and then with another set, mark out the other dovetail edges using the first points as references. A large set is handy for stepping out equally spaced measurements of between 2 to 8 inches.

Flush up one end of the steel rule, then mark off with a sharp pencil or knife.

Nothing beats the accuracy of a Vernier gauge for small measurements.

A set of dovetails can be marked out quickly by 'stepping' out the tail or pin positions.

A panel gauge will give you a fine, but very accurate line to work to.

For less important 'easy to see' lines, a pencil gauge is just the job!

Panel gauge

A panel gauge allows you to quickly run a parallel line down at the exact width required of a panel or a board, after glue up. I generally glue up a little wider than required, and after planing one edge straight, I then use a panel gauge to mark the exact width I need. They are available to buy, but if you look at a few different designs, you'll also notice they're quite simple tools. If you are confident with your basic joinery and shaping abilities, there's no reason why you could not make one of these. The design could also include a captive locking wedge, that is fitted in before the long bar is inserted. They are very handy tools, as we'll see in the next part of the course.

Pencil gauges

It's very handy to have a couple of these knocking around your bench. They don't give you an accurate line to work to, but for quick layout work, I use them to indicate the position of rebates, stopped dadoes, etc. These are very easy tools to make, and old, tatty and even well worn marking gauges are easily converted.

Layout and checking tools

Large try square

This tool is an absolute must for cabinet work. From cutting wide shoulder lines to checking for square, this is such a useful everyday tool that I always have it within easy reach. These were often made by cabinet makers, but I would not recommend the old fashioned solid boxwood type, it's just too easy to damage them when running a marking knife along the blade. A wooden stocked, steel blade square will probably set you back about $75.00, which is well worth the investment.

Large engineer's square

This is a tool that I use as a reference for all my other squares and shop made devices. It's very accurate and stays that way, as it spends most days in a cupboard out of the way.

Large 'T' square

I use this for marking out plywood sheets. It's not very accurate compared to my other squares, but it's close enough for working with plywood and very quick to use.

Miter square

This is also a very accurate tool. The profile is cut by a CNC milling machine to a very high tolerance and it's great for setting a sliding bevel or checking miter jigs, etc.

Short straight edge

This one is 2 foot long and precision ground to a high tolerance. It's very easy to spot when surfaces or edges are uneven, and also to check the flatness of a board or panel.

Size does matter. A small square won't tell you what you need to know for larger frames.

Be aware of the possibility that a square may not be accurate. Check your kit periodically.

Large 'T' Squares are great for larger flat boards.

It's important to be able to check everything you make!

You could also use the edge of a No.7 try plane to check for flatness.

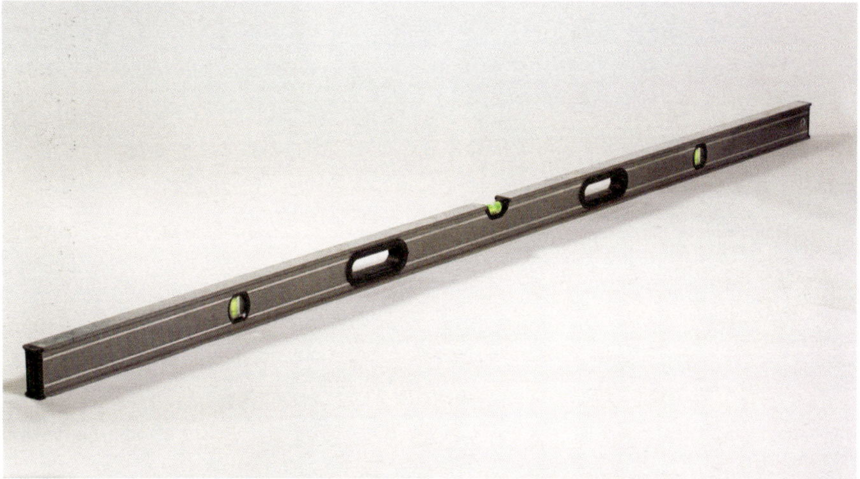

It's not a 'traditional tool', but an aluminium 6ft level is very useful nonetheless.

Make sure your diagonal sticks slide apart easily...

...they are then very easy and quick to use.

Long straight edge

For checking longer edges, I use a six foot, high tolerance spirit level. It's very useful when jointing long boards or checking for curvature in your stock or any other parts. It's not the most conventional of checking tools, but it's light, inexpensive, accurate and readily available in local stores. No wooden straight edge will have anything like the dimensional stability of a machine ground aluminum level.

Diagonal sticks

During glue up, diagonal sticks provide a quick way of checking for square inside a cabinet. In this way, clamps can't get in the way as you make measurements and adjustments, usually against the clock with the glue already starting to set... There are instructions on how to make this checking tool on page 273.

Winding sticks

These gadgets are great for checking your stock for any twist or winding. After placing one at each end of the board, sight down to see if the white lines are parallel. They are very easy to make and I've included instructions on page 293.

Layout and checking tools always need to match the scale and size of your projects. Many moons ago I spent years fitting kitchens, and I had a good collection of very long straight edges and levels, a high accuracy, four foot layout square and numerous string lines. Likewise, the tools outlined in this chapter need to be accurate, dependable and sized according to the cabinets you may want to make.

It's surprising how accurate these simple devices are.

Bold, high contrast inlay makes a visual check much easier.

Chapter 3
Edge tools

The edge tools in this section are a useful selection to add to your existing tools, some of which are available to buy off the shelf, and others you can make yourself. I find edge tools endlessly fascinating as they can frequently be adapted or improved, and can sometimes be used for a totally different purpose than originally intended.

The pattern maker's router.

Tool steel itself is a wonderfully versatile material as it can be softened, shaped, hardened and then sharpened, and for centuries has been used to produce a dazzling array of wood cutting implements. Old files and hacksaw blades are excellent sources of tool steel and I would encourage anybody to create and adapt tools for specific purposes.

The edge tools in this section could all be shop made if you were really keen. Alternatively, you may choose to constrain your tool making efforts to just making the inlay slot cutter and scratch stocks. I have to say that the slot cutter is a very efficient tool for laying out grooves and rebates (see pages 98 and 135), and you simply can't buy this type from a supplier in the configuration shown here.

There is a lot of fun to be had with the scratch stocks shown in this section, and I hope that this collection of edge tools will inspire you with a creative mixture of confidence and curiosity!

Skew chisels

A skew chisel is the most useful tool for getting into awkward dovetailed sockets. I've seen Rob Cosman use a double sided shop made chisel shaped like a fishtail, which obviously works very well for him as he's usually doing a demo against the clock.

When I'm cutting lapped dovetails, I just work my way across the joint systematically, using one skew chisel for one side and the other one for the other side of each dovetail socket.

I have just modified a pair of regular ⅜" chisels to a 6:1 skew angle, and sharpened them up in the usual fashion. I suppose you could use a pair of ¼" chisels but there's not a lot of point in cutting super narrow dovetails as they are just weak. However, if you are cutting fancy little dovetails for show, you could always clean out the corners with a standard ⅛" chisel.

Skew chisels are essential to get into corners...

...on lapped dovetail sockets, for example.

Pattern maker's router

This is certainly a tool from a bygone era as traditional pattern making is no longer economically viable in most circumstances. It has been replaced by modern computer aided manufacture systems which can take 3D models from the screen to real life very quickly. However, aside from pattern making, this variation of a hand router is worth considering for the hand tool woodworker, as it has a unique function.

The National Slate Museum of Wales is right on my doorstep and it's a fascinating place. All the castings for the rail systems, slate cutting machines, water pipes and all the ancillaries were made in house.

The pattern making workshops produced the wooden replicas of the finished castings and these patterns were then sent to the foundry. Cast iron was melted in the furnace and poured into the sand molds, every day until the whole quarry finally shut down in 1969.

The pattern maker's router is a tool I want to draw your attention to!

The Dinorwig quarry, looking towards Snowdon. It's one of my favorite places.

Some beautiful patterns from the pattern shop.

The pattern maker's router will measure and cut reference levels and faces very accurately.

A sharp cutter peels off shavings to the exact depth, over a large area.

The Pattern maker's shop was a busy place, with skilled craftsmen using a wide range of woodworking tools. Some wooden patterns had the most awkward of curves and places to reach, as the craftsman pared, split and shaved away, sometimes in a fashion more like wood carving than joinery work. One of the tools of particular importance in this shop was the pattern maker's router.

This tool provided a way of reaching down into patterns and establishing very accurate levels and shoulders, referencing the top face of the pattern. The extra long sole and deep reach of the cutter could shape, shave and flatten areas with a speed and accuracy unmatched by any other means.

It is this unique ability to be able to reference one face from another that I find most useful. A 'No.71' style router has a fairly short base and quite a short cutter, which is fine for dadoes. However, a pattern maker's router has a very wide base and an extra long cutting leg, enabling a lower face to be accurately referenced from the top face over a reasonably large area. It's very easy to make the smallest of adjustments. Simply slip a piece of paper under the sole as a spacer and reset the cutter height. You then shave off the exact thickness of the spacer, no matter how thin it is. If you are cutting a housing, you'll need to slip paper under the sole each side of the housing.

This is a tool for speed and convenience. I don't make patterns for a living but when I'm cutting a lot of tenons, this is the tool for the job! The most important advantage with this design of router is that tenon cheeks may be cut absolutely parallel with the work piece. After setting the cutter to the exact depth required, you then transfer the line to the end of the tenon.

With the shoulders sawn and the waste split out of the way, you can then quite literally cut perfect tenon cheeks with your eyes closed.

TOP TIP: *Always orientate the cutting edge towards the work piece, as this will reduce the risk of splitting out the edge. Just rotate the cutting leg to change the presentation of the cutter.*

These are not easy tools to find, so you may just need to make your own, which should be fun!

Cutting gauges

A cutting gauge achieves more than a marking gauge, in the same way that a knife will do more than a pencil. When working across the grain, the blade severs the fibers, making a good start on the knife wall or shoulder cut with great precision. When going with the grain, the blade does not really cut the fibers, but instead it separates them. These gauges are used to mark and prepare the surface for subsequent cutting processes.

It's important to be aware of how the blade is sharpened with any cutting gauge you are using. One side will always be vertical and the other side will be ground and polished at 25-35 degrees from the vertical. The angled side of the knife blade must always be oriented towards the waste side. On a magnified scale, the angled side of the blade can be seen to crush and crumple the fibers in order to create the fine trench it leaves behind, regardless of grain orientation.

Turn and lock the cutter so as to cut into the work, otherwise you could splinter the edge.

A matched pair of cutting gauges is essential.

A clean, sharp slice across the grain.

Only one side of the line gets bruised.

The flat side of the cutter faces either towards or away from the stock for each type.

The pins of a marking gauge leave clear lines, but they don't cleanly slice or separate the fibers.

A matched pair of cutters

I would recommend that you acquire a matched pair of cutting gauges, which I'll refer to as internal and external. The internal gauge has the angled side of the cutter closest to the stock and the external gauge the reverse.

A matched pair of cutters allows a groove to be well defined, prior to using a plow plane. It's good practice to always reference any measurements from the same face, in this case both sides of the groove to be cut. This is important because every now and again you may just happen to have stock that has a very slight taper on it, in which case you would get divergent cut lines, i.e. not parallel.

"It's good practice to always reference measurements from the same face..."

If we compare the action of a mortise gauge, which really is just for marking rather than cutting, the fine scratches left by the twin pins of the mortise gauge do nothing to form any sort of shoulder line, they are mere positional indicators.

The cutting gauge is used much like a marking knife, in that the first pass needs to be very light, the second a little heavier and the third, heavier still.

An inlay slot cutter

What we have here is simply a variation on a cutting gauge. Rather than scoring a knife line, the cutter is filed to form a chisel-like edge tool to carve out a narrow trench into which the inlay is fitted (see page 294). Also, as you'll see on pages 98 and 135, it's also a very handy tool for starting off a rebate, or a cove molding.

This works very well with the grain, but a different cutting knife design is required to cut a narrow slot across the grain. In this case, half of the cutter is filed to form a sharp edge on one side, and the other half of the cutter is filed to form a sharp edge on the opposite side. This will be covered in the next part of the course.

The slot cutter shown here is an easy tool to make and great fun to use. Square off the cutter in the vise with a flat file. Take a small round file and cut a curved profile in the end of the cutter, making a slight hook.

Give the sides a good rubbing on a fine diamond stone - this is really important!

Set the cutter in place so that it's aligned parallel to the stock of the cutting gauge. Make sure it's secure and off you go. It works best in fine grained hardwoods, but it will do just fine in oak and ash. You'll use this tool to make a pair of winding sticks, see page 293.

The cutter is shaped and sharpened with a smooth flat file, and a small round file.

Keep the cutter low in the jaws to prevent vibration. A chainsaw file just happened to work nicely!

Honing up the edges is very important. It makes the difference between a clean cut or a ragged cut.

A float could easily be mistaken for a file...

...but the teeth are not fine diamond points, they act like extra wide saw teeth.

A sharp cutting blade will shave the exact negative profile of the shape you have filed in the steel.

A cabinet maker's float

A float is similar to a file in appearance but the cutting action is very different. The teeth are much larger and are single cut (like a mill file), but not hardened to the same extent as on a file, as it's not for use on metal. The teeth will need to be kept sharp by occasional filing with a saw file. A float is perhaps more of a luxury than an essential tool but it can be quite a time saver. With a float, you can take fine shavings off a large area to flatten off rough chisel cuts or adjust a tenon to a perfect fit quickly.

Variations of this tool are essential items for wooden plane makers. They produce a fine smooth surface even in awkward places, such as the throat of a wooden plane. At the time of writing this, floats are still not easy to come by, either new or secondhand, however some specialist plane making floats are available from Lie-Nielsen.

Scratch stocks

Scratch stocks come in all manner of shapes and sizes, and the ones shown in this section are just two designs out of several dozen you could choose from. Don't ever expect to remove a lot of wood quickly with this tool, but it will produce a lovely smooth finish, even with highly complex profiles. These are shop made tools and we'll look at how they can be made in the next section. These tools are not as primitive as the name suggests and work very effectively.

"A float is similar to a file in appearance but the cutting action is very different."

The mechanics of a scratch stock

These tools have historical significance in woodworking because they were used to create decorative moldings even before the evolution and widespread use of more modern molding planes in the 16th century.

Ornate and fancy moldings may be worked to a very high standard using these simple tools. That said, the cutting action does lend itself best to hard, fine grained woods, especially mahogany. A lot more care must be taken on coarser grained woods such as oak and ash, otherwise the smooth cutting action turns into a skipping, juddering and grain tearing disaster that will make you reach for the electric router!

I should point out that although you may come across many different designs the length of the fence is critical, especially if the cutter is some distance from the fence. The ratio between the fence length and the distance from the fence to the cutter should be greater than 1:1. Any less than this, and the risks of snagging and skating off line increase significantly. This is why the type 2 scratch stock on page 47 is such a stable and predictable device.

There is now nothing like the same demand for ornate and 'showy' furniture as there was in the days of Thomas Chippendale. People's tastes and budgets have generally undergone a huge shift, but even today the addition of molded details can still give furniture a more elegant or 'classy' look. As well as cutting straight grooves, a scratch stock will also cut on a curve, following either the internal or external radius. The stock for radius work is modified to create two points of contact, making the cutting action predictable and controllable. Working across the grain will give a good finish, but against the grain can be unpredictable depending on the grain structure and texture.

The wide stock gives this tool stability

Two spacer blocks screwed to the stock will allow the scratch stock to follow curves.

This really is a most interesting tool. Its name suggests the sort of thing that will tear and shred it's way through the bewildered wood fibers, leaving a trail of devastation. But this really is not the case! You'll remember how we looked in detail at the cutting action of a cabinet scraper in the first part of the course, with the finely refined cutting edge. A scratch stock has the same sort of cutting action, but while the scraper was burnished, the cutter of a scratch stock is simply filed perpendicular to the required profile with a smooth file.

You'll deduce then that at a microscopic level, the wood fibers are actually shaved off by the steel edge, which is as sharp as a freshly cut saw tooth. It will leave a glassy smooth finish and will deal with reasonably difficult grain, such as found in highly figured woods.

Note that softwood fibers do not respond well to this sort of cutting action. The intense pressure at the cutting edge causes the wood to compress and give a little, leaving the fibers either uncut, or torn and ragged. What a scratch stock will not do is remove a lot of material quickly. It is really a finishing tool and that's the way to use it. It's important that you carefully remove as much waste as possible, by other means, before using a scratch stock on a heavy, or deep profile.

A scratch stock will even deal with hard, figured wood.

Type 1 - A multipurpose cutting tool

The type 1 scratch stock is a 2 part device. The main body is similar to a marking gauge only heavier, and the cutters are shop made to the required profile and are completely interchangeable. This tool is versatile and reliable if sharp and well set.

You can adapt the cutters to carry out operations that no other tool in your armory could even contemplate. A fine example is fixing the sole of a warped molding plane (see page 146). It can be used for creating simple or complex profiles, depending on the shape of the cutter. With a little modification you can apply an ornate molding to a curved edge, just like a router only with more versatility. Imagine trying to apply a reed profile to the top surface of a curved work piece with a router. After 20 years of using an electric router, I know I would need templates, a fancy cutter and I'd probably prefer an industrial overhead router! Using a scratch stock is just a load more satisfying, enjoyable and fun. Maybe it's even quicker.

These are a few of the cutters I use.

Fitted to the stock are two guides. These allow the scratch stock to follow curves.

Ideally, choose a fixed radius curve or the decorative profile will not follow the edge of your work.

A rough and ready type 2 scratch stock.

Type 2 - The fixed scratch stock

Fixed scratch stocks will generally cut only a single profile. If the same profile is used repeatedly it's often better to make a dedicated tool just for that one job than to constantly re-set a cutter in your type 1 scratch stock. These devices come in all shapes and sizes and give very fast, guaranteed results in the right wood. It's fun to add an elegant detail, using such a simple, shop made tool. See how to make this one on page 58.

A simple sharpened screw in a block of wood...

...can produce a quick decorative feature.

Making the scratch stocks

Type 1

Define the shape

The stock needs to be around 5" in length and around 1¼" thick. The bar (right in photo), is 1¼" square by around 7" long.

The first job is to define the shape for the stock and then transfer it to your work ready to cut out your chosen profile. Mark up both sides so that you can follow a pencil line when you cut the edges neatly with a chisel, as shown on page 52.

Save for a few screws, this is all you need. Choose fine, even grained hardwood.

I'm not specifying a particular pattern to use here, as it's not really that important. Anything like this will do.

Mark up one side, flip the pattern over and mark up the second identical side. This will give you more accuracy than defining the whole shape in paper.

I'm marking up the deep housing, centrally to my stock blank.

Use your fingers as a guide, running a pencil line along the gauge line.

Cut the housing

Mark the center and then the width of the bar on your stock blank.

It's really up to you if you want to cut the shaped profile first, or cut the dado housing. I find it easier to hold square stock in a vise than curved work, so I always do as much cutting, rebating and jointing as I can before I change the outer profile of any work piece. This should all be straightforward for you by now. It's the usual process of:

- Cut your shoulder line.
- Make a knifewall.
- Gauge on the depth. I've gone around ⅝" deep with the housing.

TOP TIP: *Gauge lines are fast, accurate and repeatable. However, I sometime struggle to see my lines, particularly if I'm sawing down to a line as my sawing stance normally means I'm a good distance from the work. The easy fix for this is to take a sharp pencil and run it down the gauge lines. It does not make the line less accurate, the precise center of the line is still obvious, but at least you can now see the line easily.*

As with any housing, start with the first knife cut.

Peel the waste away, right up to the knife line to form the knifewall.

When you saw down to the gauge line, arrange the work in the vise so your thumb is on the same side of the saw as your knifewall. This helps steady the saw, as shown in the photo on the right, if you are right handed.

Using a wide chisel, peel out some waste so that you can get the bar against the knifewall.

Then, with the bar really tight against the first knife wall, make a light knife cut, form the second knifewall, and saw down to your gauge lines.

TECHNICAL POINTER:
When you chisel the waste out, work down to your gauge lines from both sides, alternating the orientation in the vise. If you go all the way from one side, you're probably going to splinter out way below the gauge line on the opposite face, which I'm sure you realize means that you need to cut the whole housing a little deeper, or just start again.

Steady as you go! The knifewall will stop the wood splintering, but you still need to saw carefully!

Create the first shoulder.

Use the bar for a direct measurement.

Work from one side, and then the other. This way you won't split below the gauge line.

A sharp cutter will peel away the shavings to a very precise depth.

TOP TIP: *With every chisel cut apart from the last few, incline your chisel upwards very slightly leaving a slight hump in the middle. This is an easy way to avoid breaking out the other edge, and it's a good habit to get into.*

If you choose to finish the bottom of the housing with a hand router (I do this on every housing as nothing beats a router for accuracy), use the same principle and work from both sides. These simple precautions will guarantee good results.

The bar should be a reasonably stiff fit. This looks good so the stock can now be shaped.

Cut the profile

There is "more than one way to skin a cat" as Mark Twain wrote in 1889, and how you go about cutting this profile is up to you. If it works for you, it can't be wrong. Here's one way of doing it:

Keeping outside your profile lines, saw the bulk of the waste off quickly with a heavy tenon saw (keep away from the lines with your tenon saw). Then cut the curves out with a coping saw.

Now this is where you are going to struggle if you sharpen your chisels with a dead flat bevel. I always put a convex bevel on my chisels and this is just one of several good reasons to do this. Make controlled scooping cuts with a sharp, wide chisel, bevel down, slowly approaching the pencil lines.

TOP TIP: *When you are cutting a convex (hump) profile, turn the chisel over and use it bevel up where you can, as this gives you more control.*

As you approach the shape you want take a smaller chisel and carefully define the shape at both edges. I'm using a $\frac{3}{8}$" chisel here. Take the middle out with a wide chisel, right down to match the profile at the edges.

I'm just marking out what I can take off with a tenon saw. You could just reach for the coping saw.

You could go straight to the chisel after the tenon saw, but I'll just take some more waste out first.

Roll the chisel over the curve, slicing the end grain fibers.

Take a small chisel and carefully define the edges.

This unusual use of a scraper will give you a very controllable and even finish.

TOP TIP: *We all know how to sharpen a scraper by now, but here is a variation that you may find very useful. Get your edges sharp, flat and smooth in the usual fashion, and then rather than turning the edge over with a burnisher, stop right there. Okay, now use the scraper differently, pushing it forwards and away from you, down the curves. You'll find it starts to even out the surface, taking fine shavings in a very controllable way. You can't use this in the conventional way, unless you burnish the edge over and 'raise the burr' in the normal fashion. Try it out, it really works!*

Hold the scraper steady, and just push it down the curve.

The blade holding bar

Set your pencil gauge to the center of the bar and mark along the length on all *four* sides. Make sure you mark the top, as in theory, this is the best fit orientation when you press it into the stock.

On the side, measure off ½" from the opposite end to the stock, and square your first line across. Set your dividers to 1¼" and step off a further 3 marks.

These marks show where to drill the holes that will be used to clamp the blade in place. Drill the holes to match the threaded brass rod. I've used M6 rod which is close enough to ¼" in US measurements. Countersink the holes carefully on both sides.

Give the ends of the bar a pleasant looking round over, or a chamfer. Keep it even and consistent.

Note the orientation of the holes marked out in the next photo, to the 'TOP' shown here.

Step off the holes positions at 1¼" centers.

The countersink detail prevents breakout as the brass rod goes through.

The roundover makes the scratch stock more comfortable to handle.

I checked in some scrap and this scraper blade fits the hacksaw kerf very nicely.

Changing the orientation of the hacksaw blade allows you to cut deeper than normal...

...just like this!. Only some hacksaw frames have this facility, so check before you buy one.

Now, as we are going to use a piece of cabinet scraper as the cutting iron, it makes sense to cut the holding slot with a saw that is very close to the thickness of a cabinet scraper. If it's too wide the blade won't be held firmly enough and will chatter like a wagon load of monkeys. If the gap is too narrow, you'll struggle to get the blade in place. I'd recommend you try out a few different saws in some scrap first to see which kerf width best suits the scraper you are about to saw up. I found that my hacksaw was about right, and not too tight!

I had to change the orientation of the blade to allow me to cut to the right depth without fouling on the frame.

TECHNICAL POINTER: *As you saw down, follow your line and keep on swapping over the side you saw from. Don't just blindly saw down hoping it will be all be alright! It probably won't be unless you deliberately saw with care from both sides, alternating as you go down.*

"Don't just blindly saw down hoping it will be alright! It probably won't be..."

Assembly and finishing

To hold the bar to the stock, use the usual fixing method for brass screws: Pilot drill through both, clearance drill through the top part, countersink for the head, and wind the screws in carefully. I've put two brass screws in for good measure.

Make sure you give all the edges a good 'softening' with a round file, flat file, sandpaper, etc. All shop made tools and jigs should be comfortable to use and handle.

A coat of sanding sealer brings out the grain and stabilizes the wood, controlling the ebb and flow of seasonal moisture.

Scratch stocks were used by pattern makers, for all sorts of intricate profiles. Quite often, a pattern was very unique and so a cutting blade would be shaped for a single, special purpose job. The skill in shaping a cutter for a particular purpose is mostly a matter of care and attention to detail. One method of shaping a cutter is described on page 147. Overleaf, you can see a method of preparing the blanks, later to be shaped into cutters, with a hacksaw and files.

Brass screws are nowhere near as hard as steel screws so drill clearance and pilot holes to suit.

Don't leave any sharp edges. They will just get knocked and splinter off over time.

You could use shellac or hard wax oil, but sanding sealer provides lasting, quick drying protection.

Choose the width of cutter you are going to make and mark this on the steel with a square.

Keep the steel really tight in against the vise jaws as this reduces vibration. A steep angle helps too.

Make the cutting blade blank

Before you decide on the final profile you are going to cut, just make a few blanks to have in stock, ready for use.

Square off an inch of scraper blade, marking it with a sharp tipped black pen.

With the scraper held in the vise jaw protectors (page 188), cut down your pen line holding the saw at a steep angle, which really helps when cutting thin material.

In the bottom left photo, look at the width of steel in the cut that the teeth are acting against. Holding the saw steeply reduces vibration and gives you a much better chance of cutting straight!

Cut some brass rod to size and fit the blade. If you ever need to use the scratch stock to cut further away from the stock, you are going to need a second brass rod and wing nut set to clamp it securely in place.

TOP TIP: *On any surfaces that are designed to slide against a tool or work piece (such as the stock of this device), a quick wipe and a rub with some wax polish is going to make the operation much smoother.*

A steep angle allows you to steer the saw blade accurately down the cut.

Apart from shaping the cutting iron, your scratch stock is ready for use!

Making a type 2 - single purpose scratch stock

This should only take around 5 minutes to make.

It's a very simple little quirk cutter, nothing more than just a wood screw and a block of wood.

The trick is to get the wood screw into the wood nice and tight and then file down the front face of the screw to sharpen the 'cutter'. Now that it's sharp, file the inside of the countersink, to shape the 'cutter'. I used a chainsaw file as it just happened to be the right diameter. With this tool together with some sand paper, it's easy to add a decorative beaded edge to your work.

The best advice I can give you is very simple: Have a go!

Make sure the screw is in good and tight, before you take a file to it.

File a round profile on the inside edge of the countersink

Regardless of the wood type, you need to work with the grain.

Soft woods are difficult to work with any scratch stock, but...

...using fine grained hard wood will give excellent results

STANLEY

Chapter 4
Planes for cabinet making

General purpose planes

In the previous series, *Working Wood 1&2*, the teaching focused on two very widely used planes, one in the No.4 range (4 or 4½) and one in the No.5 range (5 or 5½). In addition to perhaps a chamfer here and there, or some rounding over, these planes are designed to get your work flat and smooth. Despite their immense versatility the limitations for more complex work are obvious, and as we'll now see, other planes are an absolute necessity to move forwards in our woodworking. We'll look at a selection of general purpose planes first and then move on to some specialist planes designed to create grooves, rebates and moldings associated with more advanced work.

Molding planes are great fun to use!

A range of planes is essential for cabinet work.

The No.7 try plane

A long jointing plane is perfect for dealing with wider, longer boards and trueing up edges for jointing. This is the best surfacing tool you could hope for. When razor sharp and finely set, a metal try plane will make short work of producing a lovely flat shelf or table top with a nice smooth finish. All the previous restoration, tuning and sharpening of metal planes covered in *Working Wood 1&2* applies to the No.7, as the design and function is almost identical to the Stanley No.'s 4, 4½, 5 and 5½. Due to the extra length, it's important to be aware of where you are applying pressure to the plane, either towards the toe, the middle or the heel. Using a long plane is no guarantee you will plane a board, or an edge straight and true. Check your work with a straight edge, a square and a pair of winding sticks. For edge planing, the No.7 works particularly well with the shooting stick (page 283), and with a long straight edge for checking (page 35).

The No.7 is particularly heavy, and for that reason it will not be to everyone's taste, however there are some highly reputable woodworkers who will use it for most of their general planing work.

If you need to joint two edges ready for gluing up, the long bench clamp (page 263) and the No.7 are a great combination. The long distance from heel to toe makes it a lot easier to get the joint flat. The long sole rides over the bumps and hollows as the iron skims off the high points, leveling the work nicely. A small No.4 for instance could go up and down like a roller coaster; it's short sole fitting neatly into long hollows, which you won't even notice are there.

Surfacing a table top with a No.7.

Accurate edge preparation is essential before glue up.

One of my large wooden try planes. Made of beech, it's a heavy plane to use.

This old beauty will take the thickest shavings of any plane in my shop, apart from my scrub plane.

A scrub plane is not essential unless you are going flatten and thickness your own stock.

"You'll need to make sure the sole is completely flat, smooth and well waxed for top performance."

Wooden try plane

In common with many wooden planes, a heavy wooden try plane can be set to take very heavy shavings (see page 67 for the mechanics of thick shavings). A wooden try plane will put a 1" wide chamfer on a hardwood corner in just a few passes.

However, if you were to try to take the same depth of cut with a full width shaving, your human engine would soon run out of steam. You need to match your own chosen output effort with the right combination of both the depth and width of shavings. Maybe some hulk of a wrestler could push a wooden try plane over a board, taking full width, thick shavings without a problem, but I haven't met anyone yet who makes this claim! So generally you should set the iron not only according to purpose, but also according to your physical strength.

The mouth of the plane is usually fairly wide compared to a metal plane and this accommodates thicker shavings easily. If you want to take a much finer cut, you could try the trick of packing out the underside of the iron, as this has the effect of closing the mouth a little. By doing this, it's possible to get very fine shavings on difficult wood, particularly if you skew the plane to an angle from the direction of travel. It's worth having at least one of these old beauties in your woodworking arsenal. If you've never used one before, you will be surprised at how well they perform.

Make sure the sole is completely flat, smooth and well waxed for top performance. I have a few of these larger wooden planes, each set up for a different function. One has the iron sharpened with a significant camber each side of the center. I use this as a 'Scrub' plane for working a board quickly down, close to the final thickness. The action is similar to using a wide gouge, and you can just about see the curved iron in the photo. It's not for the faint hearted, and I've injured myself in the past by overdoing it with a scrub plane, so take it easy and look after yourself!

Block plane

This plane is a low angled 'bevel up' plane and tackles small areas of end grain with remarkable ease. For small chamfers and all manner of detailed work, this is the plane I reach for.

Having such a low angle makes it a little more tricky to sharpen than a standard iron, and you may choose to use a sharpening guide rather than hand holding it. I want to stress that this iron takes a great deal of looking after. The lower angle of the iron, combined with the fact that it's frequently used on end grain, means that edge retention is an issue.

I have a replacement blade in mine made of D2 steel, which takes time to sharpen, but does retain it's edge much longer than ordinary O1 steel. I will also mention that the Veritas team has produced a steel known as PMV-11 which has excellent edge retention, even when used on low angle block planes.

Oddly enough, softwood end grain can be more difficult to work than hard wood, as the fibers have more of a tendency to fold and crumple. However, a low angle block plane will tackle this with ease.

You will find one of these a very useful addition to your set of planes.

A low angle block plane will take clean end grain shavings, even on soft wood!

My pair of badger planes. They are a matched pair, with irons skewed left and right respectively.

Shooting a thick slab of Ash for a table top, with a left handed Badger.

A fenced badger plane in action. No other plane will cut a rebate any quicker.

"If at all possible I recommend trying to acquire a left-handed Badger."

Heavy wooden badgers

A badger plane is a large wooden rebate plane. These planes differ from the wooden try plane mentioned above in that the irons are skewed, and reach the very edge of one side of the sole. The skewed iron cuts well, even across the grain. The most common badgers are designed for right handed users, but if at all possible I recommend trying to acquire a left handed badger as well. Having rebate planes in left and right matched pairs allows you to overcome problems with grain direction. A left handed badger will also double up as a good shooting plane, as the skewed blade is ideal for cutting end grain.

I sometimes fix a fence to the underside of my badger planes, which effectively converts them into moving fillister planes. It makes the planes very versatile and quick to set up and use.

You will come across a huge range of planes in the woodworking world: Some simple old designs, some complex and extremely well engineered, some single purpose and many multipurpose, but it's way beyond the scope of this book to look at the entire range. If hand planes are of particular interest to you I can thoroughly recommend *"The Hand Plane Book"* by Garret Hack. However, for the purposes of this course, the planes listed as 'general purpose planes' are well worth acquiring as they are excellent 'all rounders'.

The wooden planes are not past relics and have not been superseded by well engineered metal variants. On the contrary, I believe no cabinet making shop is complete without at least a modest selection. Call me old fashioned if you like, but remember this - I only really like them because they really work!

An introduction to wooden planes

As I'm encouraging the use of wooden planes from both the general purpose and specialist ranges, we will look at them in detail. They are very tactile tools to use, and sometimes the older ones are the better ones, unless you buy your new wooden planes from a reputable contemporary maker.

For centuries, the use of wooden planes dominated many aspects of furniture making, carpentry and joinery. Their manufacture and use then declined quickly as the industrial revolution became the springboard for the mass production of all manner of tools, including metal planes. However, for a few years now, we have seen something of a renaissance in the appreciation, use and manufacture of wooden planes. Contemporary plane makers such as Phil Edwards, are supplying new planes to meet a growing demand for these beautiful and functional tools. Each plane is made to order to a very high standard, with the maker's mark stamped in the heel. Following in the tradition of Matheison, Mosley, Marples and others, these wooden planes are built to work hard and withstand the rigors of every day use.

"For centuries, the use of wooden planes dominated many aspects of furniture making, carpentry and joinery."

Phil Edwards uses wooden planes to make wooden planes, which I think is neat!

Phil at work with a wooden rebate plane, making a similar rebate plane.

The 'maker's stamp' in quartersawn beech.

The mechanics of thick shavings

The mechanics of a wooden plane are very interesting. The wedge holds the iron in very tightly, and the wedge and iron are in intimate contact with the body. The sheer solid mass of the whole tight unit prevents the iron from vibrating. Now, in terms of the physics, a large solid mass has a much lower resonant frequency than an iron in a metal plane, held in by sprung steel and fancy adjustment systems. So the fact that a wooden plane iron can't vibrate as much as an iron in a metal plane, allows the wooden plane to take thick shavings without juddering. This is why some wooden planes can take a lot of stock off quickly, compared to their steel counterparts. Some are for this purpose, but others are definitely not!

An overview to handling wooden planes

The finer details and intricacies of wooden planes are such a subject that they are worthy of quite a few books in their own right. Within the remit of this book however, I'd like to address the basics so that you are comfortable with the dismantling, assembling and adjusting of wooden planes. Once you have learnt the basics, the same approach can be applied to almost any wooden plane, regardless of complexity or function. There is one common element to all wooden hand planes: The iron is held in place with a tight wooden wedge, and *that* is the crux of the matter. We'll now look at some typical wooden planes, and what to look out for when buying them second hand.

A typical wooden molding plane.

Terminology and construction of wooden planes

The following description best applies to wooden rebate and molding planes. Other wooden planes are similar in constructional terms, but differ greatly in size, shape, design and function.

BODY Usually made of beech, quarter sawn for stability in service. The edges are chamfered, including the rounded corners, to make the plane more ergonomic and comfortable to use. Check for cracks and splits in older planes.

WEDGE Also made of beech and planed down by the maker to fit snugly into the throat, trapping the Iron in place. The pointy end of the wedge is shaped so as to not to hinder the upwards movement of shavings and must be tight against the iron with no gaps to trap shavings. It's interesting that you can tell a great deal about the previous owners by the condition of the wedge. A careful user will have looked after the wedge and not beaten it into oblivion with a blunt instrument. If the wedge is damaged and unusable you can always use it as a pattern to make a new one from a nice piece of beech.

IRON The cutting edge is shaped according to the profile of the plane and the long narrow part (the tang) protrudes out of the throat, gripped by the wedge. Normally soft steel is used for the tang, with much better quality hard tool steel for the cutting face. The iron is usually tapered, being thicker at the cutting end and thinner up the tang. This taper has the effect of tightening the iron against the wedge if any slight movement occurs in use. If the cutting part of the iron is badly pitted, be aware that you'll have to take a lot of metal off to get back to a gleaming polish. Sometimes deep pitting can be a sign of poor quality steel. A lack of homogeneity between the carbon and iron can lead to rapid corrosion and deep visible pitting. Check the iron if you can as it may well affect the value.

Check the body for warps, splits and cracks.

This wedge is in good condition, so the rest of the plane has probably been looked after.

The cutting iron from a typical hollow plane.

"You can tell a lot about the previous owners by the condition of the wedge."

This throat looks clean and tidy. Notice the skew angle. I have to admire plane makers!

Nothing in the escapement should hinder the free flow of shavings or the plane will jam.

This complex plane has been fitted with a boxwood insert. Box is a very hard, dense wood.

THROAT This is the tunnel going from the top, right through the body of the plane to the sole. It forms the housing for the wedge and iron and is one of the most difficult parts of the plane making operation. Specialist layout tools and floats are used to perfect the position and shape of the throat. Check that the wedge when fitted in place with the iron, is an exact fit to the throat at the top. If it's not a good fit, the wedge may be from a different plane, and this will definitely have an effect of the performance as well as the value.

ESCAPEMENT This is where the shavings emerge as the plane is pushed forwards. If they are not able to escape freely the mouth gets clogged and the plane stops working. Rebate planes usually have a conical or circular escapement to take into account the fact that they will generally be taking off heavy shavings that curl out like apple peelings. Most molding planes have side escapements, ejecting the shavings upwards vertically, and then to the side.

SOLE The sole is either a simple continuation of the main body, or it may have some very fine grained hard wood joined to it to reinforce vulnerable edges. The traditional wood for reinforcement is Box, taken from the hedgerows and seasoned carefully, hence the term 'Boxing' meaning the addition of box wood strips in the sole. The boxing can become loose with age and should always be checked for tightness and bond strength.

MOUTH (see overleaf) This is an important part to check carefully. As with metal planes, the gap directly in front of the blade or iron needs to get proportionally wider according to the thickness of shavings produced. Unlike a metal plane with a moving frog, the mouth of a wooden plane is a set distance. A rebate plane will typically have a wider mouth than a molding plane for the aforementioned reason.

Sometimes the mouth of the plane is wider than you want, perhaps through a previous owner having planed the sole in order to flatten it.

TOP TIP: *To tighten the mouth for fine work, a trick that sometimes works is to slip a thin packer down the back of the iron to bring it forwards a little.*

If the mouth is damaged and splintered, the plane won't really work as well as it should. Replacing the mouth of a plane is possible, as is replacing the sole, but in either case, consider other alternatives first. If as a last resort you do re work the mouth, work carefully and patiently to achieve good results.

TOE The toe will have some form of identification on it. It could be the name of the plane maker, the name of the owner, the number designating the iron radius or usually all three. Cabinet makers used to work in close proximity to one another, so knowing whose tools belonged to whom was very important. These days, very few cabinetmakers are in danger of mistaking their tools for someone else's and so the owners' name stamp rarely corresponds to the owner and user of today. The plane maker's stamp on the toe is the first indication of the rarity and hence value of the plane. The planes produced by very early and highly acclaimed makers are often worth a great deal more than you might imagine.

HEEL The heel often bears the marks of previous users who have beaten their sorry planes into submission with a metal hammer. It's not unusual to find planes with so many hammer marks in the heel that the wood is almost split. Such treatment is never necessary and the plane should instead be spared such punishment by the using a wooden or plastic mallet. (See page 72 - 'To retract the iron'.)

This mouth is a little wide, but undamaged.

The 'toe' of a No.10 round plane

This is an example of the sort of unnecessary punishment I'm talking about.

A sharp tap on the bench can loosen the iron.

Grip the sides of the iron and slide it out of the sole.

Reassemble everything loosely before placing the plane on the bench the right way up.

Dismantling a wooden plane

To remove the iron

Without going into the physics of friction, shock loading and momentum, suffice to say that the wooden wedge can be loosened with a sharp tap to the plane body whilst gripping the iron and wedge. Most people will strike the heel end of the plane with a mallet. Others may suggest tapping the fore part of the body upside down on the bench whilst holding the iron and wedge.

I use a panel beater's mallet, as the plastic head won't damage the wood. Gripping the wedge and iron in my left hand, and holding the plane body against myself, a sharp tap to the heel end of the plane loosens the wedge enough for the iron to be pushed out through the sole. This is a similar procedure to retracting the iron, described overleaf.

TOP TIP: *Only take the wedge out for cleaning and restoration, otherwise just leave it in and withdraw the iron through the sole as you press the tang of the iron down the throat.*

To assemble the plane

Replace the iron through the underside of the plane, and put the wedge back in loosely from the top. Turn the plane the right way up, allowing the iron to touch the bench top. Give the wedge a little tap to tighten it, then tap the tang ever so gently. Tapping the tang will advance the iron out of the mouth, allowing it to take a shaving. Tap the wedge again, this time a little harder and this will lock the iron in position.

Adjusting a wooden plane

See also 'Aligning the iron' on page 74, and bear this in mind as you are adjusting the depth of cut.

To advance the iron

To take a thicker shaving a gentle tap or two on the tang will move it incrementally further out. Alternatively, a gentle tap on the toe of the plane will also advance the iron. After each tap to the tang or toe a further tap to the wedge is required due to the iron being tapered. As the iron moves down, a very slight gap opens between the wedge and the iron (indiscernible, it's more like a slight loosening), so a gentle tap to the wedge tightens the iron, making the plane ready for work.

To retract the iron

To retract the iron in order to take a thinner shaving, there are two methods and each have strong advocates:

1. Hold the iron and wedge, and tap the rear of the plane upside down on the bench top. Every time you tap the rear part of the plane you must follow this with a tap to the wedge in order to make sure the iron locks in position. Tapping the rear part of the plane not only retracts the iron slightly, but also loosens the wedge a little at the same time. (Tapping the front of the plane will move the iron forwards for a deeper cut.)
2. Hold the iron and wedge as if to dismantle the plane, then strike the heel with a mallet. This retracts both iron and wedge. A gentle tap to the wedge then secures the iron back in place.

A gentle tap to the top of the tang will advance the iron.

Tighten the wedge after every adjustment.

Tapping the heel on the bench.

Grip the iron and the wedge and give the heel a sharp tap with a plastic mallet.

4 Planes for cabinet making

With most wooden planes it's possible to make both alignment and positional adjustments, and these will be made at the same time as adjusting the depth of cut.

Adjusting the position: This is moving the iron from side to side in the throat of the plane. This will allow you to line up the iron with, say, a profiled sole, or allow you to align the corner of a rebate iron with the side of the plane. This is carried out by pressing the iron sideways and moving the tang from side to side gently. This will 'walk' the iron one way or the other as required. A gentle tap to the side of the iron as shown here is a quick way of lining up the corner of a rebate plane.

Adjusting the alignment: This is tilting the angle of the iron to make it parallel with the sole of the plane, much like the lateral adjustment lever does on a metal No.4 for example. In this case, the tang itself is the lateral adjustment lever.

TECHNICAL POINTER:

Do not try to make adjustments if the wedge is too tight. The tang will easily bend as the steel is much softer than the heat-treated cutting edge.

So these are the three adjustments:

1. Depth of cut - Determines how thick or thin the shaving is.
2. Position - This is the 'side to side' position.
3. Lateral alignment - Is it aligned parallel to the sole of the plane?

Adjustment is not as complex as you may think, and with a little practice you will not only enjoy the satisfaction of using these old tools, but you'll also appreciate their versatility in your shop. And don't forget - when these tools are really sharp, they really work!

Sight down the sole, tapping the iron until it's flush with one edge.

It's important to get the iron aligned parallel to the sole, as well as flush to one edge.

If the wedge is jammed

If the iron and wedge in an old plane are stuck in super tight, place the plane on the bench the right way up on some scrap wood. Then take a block of wood and a steel hammer, and holding the wedge and iron, give the end of the plane a severe bash, making sure the block of wood is in square contact with the back of the plane before you hit it. Do NOT wallop the plane itself as this will leave ugly hammer marks or cause real damage, and I have strong views about people doing this sort of thing to planes!

Alternatively, put the wedge top in the bench vise with the plane upside down Hold the plane with your left hand and gently apply upward pressure. Then tap the rear of the plane with the mallet. The wedge will release, even on severely over tightened planes.

If the iron and wedge are jammed, use a block of wood and a steel hammer, or invert the plane and grip the wedge in a vise.

STANLEY

Section 3
Specialist planes

What I really like about owning a good range of specialist planes is that I always have options. Whether I'm making a molded cornice, cutting a groove or planing out a rebate, I know I can get pretty much any job done with a few planes.

Right at the start of this chapter, there is one point I want to make very clear: These tools do not take the place of machines, so don't ever expect to churn out lots of shaped stock quickly. If it's just down to speed, use something with a motor, every time. If it's about taking your time to learn new methods, and enjoying the challenge of mastering hand tool techniques, you'll find this section will give you the confidence to start cutting easy rebates, accurate grooves, and beautiful moldings.

The following planes are included here as they each perform a very specific and unique function. When these planes are sharp, set up well, and in good order, there's a lot of useful and productive enjoyment to be had with them. However, one word of caution that applies to all the planes in this chapter - choose your wood wisely and work with the grain. I make no apologies for a steady stream of reminders of exactly this principle, throughout the entire chapter.

A selection of specialist planes gives you options.

"...having at least two rebate planes to hand leads to a much smoother workflow."

Chapter 5
An introduction to rebate planes

You might argue that a circular saw will generally cut a rebate with more accuracy and speed than any skilled craftsman using any design of rebate plane. I am not going to argue on that one. I've cut more rebates with a circular saw than I have with any hand plane, but despite this, I firmly believe that a modest selection of rebate planes does have a valid place in any cabinet maker's workshop. I don't want to rely on a table saw for all my rebating work, but furthermore, something interesting happens when hand planes are tuned up and razor sharp - you actually want to use them. If a job warrants the set up in terms of sheer volume of work, I'll use a saw or table router without hesitation. However, for a lot of every day bench work, having some reliable rebate planes to hand is just invaluable.

There are many different styles of rebate plane.

Rather than examining the history of rebate planes or the diversity of makes, styles and purposes, we're going to focus on getting a few different types of plane restored, tuned up and razor sharp. We'll also look at several rebating methods (pages 94 and 114) and I'd suggest you experiment and choose whatever suits your style of work best.

The ability to cut rebates is an essential skill, and once you have got the basics, your competence will increase in proportion to the amount of practice you get.

New planes, or newly restored planes?

I'll mention here that if you buy a new rebate plane, you will generally get top quality for top dollar, which is fine if your budget allows. Actually, it's better than just fine, as top dollar rebate planes will pretty much work beautifully, straight out of the box. New metal and wooden rebate planes are both available these days.

With older rebate planes, it's likely that you are going to need to spend a while getting everything working as it should. The wooden planes are in some ways easier to get into good shape than their metal counterparts, being less complex, but metal planes have the advantage of being easily adjustable even in relatively unskilled hands. I used a wooden bodied, German made Ulmia rebate plane for over a decade before my father gave me his old Stanley No.78. The Ulmia range of planes and tools are made to a high standard and are still available by mail order from Dieter Schmid in Germany (www.Fine-Tools.com). Wooden planes often have some character that you need to contend with, for example, the Ulmia I just mentioned needs the wedge tapping in much tighter than other wooden rebate planes I use. Even after tightening the wedge, I know I can still adjust the iron fairly easily from side to side, even though it never moves during use. It's just a quirk of the plane.

"The wooden planes are in some ways easier to get into good shape than their metal counterparts."

My German 'Ulmia' rebate plane is a reliable workhorse.

These are my four most used wooden rebate planes.

The round escapement allows plenty of room for thick shavings to 'escape'.

Straight vs. skewed iron. Both work well, but I prefer skewed.

"...having at least two rebate planes to hand leads to a much smoother workflow."

Wooden rebate planes

I own quite a few of these in different widths and they are a joy to use. The absence of fence and depth stops means that for a series of identical rebates, using a guide is by far the easiest option with these planes. For setting up and adjustment see pages 71 to 74, as the basic mechanics of adjustment are the same for most wooden planes. I will mention that it's very important to adjust for square. You do this by tapping the top of the iron to the left or right a fraction, and then checking shavings on both sides for thickness. Just like a metal rebate plane the cutting iron usually needs to be flush with either the left or right edge of the sole.

A typical wooden rebate plane is designed to take off a lot of material, quickly and quietly. For that reason, the escapement (where the shavings come out) is usually conical or circular, allowing plenty of room for thicker shavings to curl out and fall to the side as you progress down the work piece.

The iron may be straight or skewed over at an angle. My German made rebate plane has a straight iron and works a treat, with shavings flying out like home made tagliatelle pasta when I get into the swing of it.

I have a much older rebate plane with a skewed iron. It's about ⅞" wide and if you can pick up one of these, you'll find it very useful. The skewed iron actually pushes the cutter towards the shoulder you are forming, thus helping the plane stay tight in against the work piece.

As a bare minimum, a wooden rebate plane ¾" or ⅞", preferably skewed, is a plane you probably need to get hold of. Straight rebate planes (as opposed to skewed) can be easier to 'steer' when you are first starting off, and are much more commonplace.

TOP TIP: *The wooden badger planes on page 65 are also rebate planes, and for taking off a lot of material quickly, no metal rebate plane will ever come close in terms of speed and performance.*

Two are better than one

In my experience, having at least two rebate planes to hand leads to a much smoother workflow. I keep one adjusted perfectly for right hand corners, and the other adjusted likewise for left hand corners. However, if I'm working on moldings I actually keep a second pair of rebate planes to hand but set up slightly differently. I find it useful to set the iron slightly back from the corner on the second pair, as this allows me to quickly remove stock for a round ovolo profile without any risk of nicking the adjacent fillets etc.

The moving fillister plane

This is a plane I will mention here, but not because it's a necessity, but because it does have a very important place in woodworking history.

I actually prefer using wooden planes to metal ones. Perhaps for others of you who enjoy the simple pleasures of using wooden planes, a moving fillister may well be part of your everyday tool set and not just a historical artifact!

The wooden moving fillister plane was once the workhorse of every cabinet shop on pretty much every continent. The development came about through an obvious need to introduce some degree of control to the standard wooden rebate plane.

Some wooden rebate planes were made with a wide sole, and fitted with a moving fence, usually adjusted with some heavy brass or steel screws. It's a pattern used by plane maker, Phil Edwards. Moving the fence is just the job for a large 'London pattern' screwdriver. Another feature of a moving fillister plane is the depth stop. This allows the user to quickly get down to the bottom of the rebate without being concerned about going too deep.

A modern, beautifully made moving fillister plane.

Rebate width is adjusted with a large screwdriver...

...and the depth is controlled by a brass depth stop.

A modern 'panel raising plane'. The skewed iron is a necessity.

The razor sharp 'nicker' allows for cross grain rebating.

Another feature of most moving fillister planes is the 'nicker' which cuts the fibers ahead of the iron for cross grain work.

Of course, keeping the plane level as you work is of paramount importance. Even the depth stop won't help you if you accidentally lean the plane over, producing a rebate that slopes towards the edge of your work. So, the moving fence and the depth stop are the characteristics of a moving fillister plane.

Some types of moving fillister are designed to produce a sloping rebate and these are used for producing raised panels. We'll look in detail at raised panels in the next part of the course, but these planes are worth a mention here, as they are a development of a moving fillister plane. Shown above left, is a beautiful modern panel raising plane with a fixed fence. Nice one Phil!

There is another variant of the moving fillister, called the 'sash fillister'. The moving fence is fixed to a pair of arms, allowing the plane to take it's reference from the opposite side of the work piece.

All of the planes we've looked at are still available today, either second hand or new. There are also good resources to be found on making your own wooden planes, if you've a keen interest in that.

As metal planes became more common in the workshop, almost every type of wooden plane (except for molding planes, see page 119) was gradually replaced by a metal counterpart. The metal planes were hardy, reliable and easy to adjust, and the Stanley No.78 which appeared in 1885, was one such plane. It became very popular, very quickly, and the Stanley Rule and Level Company ramped up production and churned them out in their tens of thousands.

In some ways, the Stanley No.78 is not only a rebate plane, but also a type of moving fillister, and this is the plane we are going to look at next.

This is the Stanley No.78 rebate plane, shown without the fence.

The Stanley No.78 rebate plane

I own several rebate planes, and this Stanley No.78 certainly gets a lot of use. They've been manufactured for over 100 years now, with very little design change, and are so popular that you can even buy a new one today for around $100. The cutting iron can go right up against a shoulder, and the width of cut is the full width of the sole. The No.78 is easy to adjust and comfortable to use, but I could not manage without my old wooden rebate planes. I enjoy the simplicity of having each one set for a different purpose, reducing the need to make major adjustments to any plane as I work.

I enjoy using my Stanley No.78, and it works well, but there are metal rebate planes on the market that are far superior, and I'd always advise anyone to buy the best they can afford when it comes to tools. The No.78 is ubiquitous, new and used, and many different planes are similar in style and proportions. The following tune up procedure will sort out any plane of this ilk.

The same principles apply to any plane really, it's just that the expensive ones usually don't need anything like the same amount of fettling. They just work!

A quick look over an old plane will tell you if it's worth restoring.

Clean up

As with any old steel plane, it's worth giving it a good going over before getting it sharp and well tuned.

Check the casting for cracks and chips etc.

Inspect and check that all the parts are present and correct. (Some spares are available at www.stanleytoolparts.com.)

Clean up any rust with a fine emery abrasive sponge, or some wire wool, and use a paintbrush to get the dust out of all the corners.

Take off all the casting burrs from around the edges using a smooth file.

Take the whole plane apart so you can clean it up properly.

Brush the dust out of the corners...

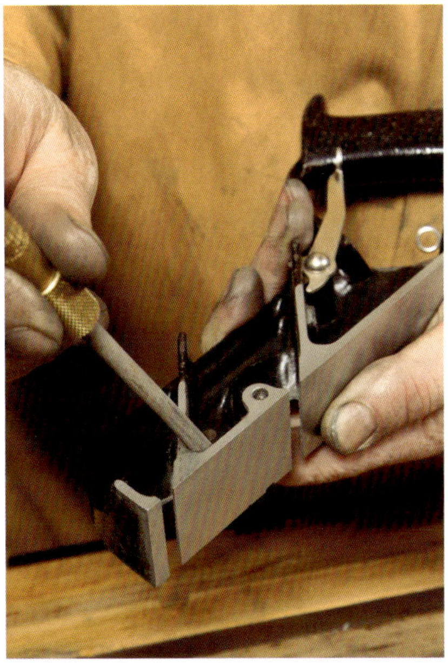

...file down the sharp edges...

...including the edges of the sole.

Flatten and polish the sole

Just as you flattened your bench planes, apply the same procedure to the No.78 and you'll get the same results.

The sole will initially look uneven, so you will need to grind it flat on a series of increasingly finer grades of emery ('wet and dry') paper.

Work with the coarsest grit first and keep going until the sole is flat and looks uniform. Shown bottom left is a photo of a very uniform, if somewhat coarsely abraded, surface texture.

Progressing through the grades of abrasive will eventually give you a smooth, polished sole.

There's a good chance that the cast iron sole is going to have a slightly granular texture, so even when it's polished up nicely, it's still going to look a little dappled if you examine it closely.

It's unlikely that the sole of the plane is very flat or very smooth.

A glass plate, a few sheets of emery paper, and a whole lot of patience will transform your plane.

Starting with a good coarse flattening, right through to...

...a gleaming polish!

The edges of the plane may snag up the emery paper, so use the diamond stones instead.

It's unlikely that you've abraded the plane so much that it's out of square, but it's worth a check.

Any metal part that moves against the work piece needs a good polish up.

Flatten and polish the side face

Apply the same treatment to the side face. Due to the shape of some parts of the casting, you may find that the side face has a tendency to snag and rip the abrasive paper. The best solution to this is to use the diamond stones as a lapping surface.

Check for square as you work on the side face. A perfect 90 degree angle is very important, but thankfully this is unlikely to need correcting as the cast body of a Stanley No.78 will have been machined very accurately by the manufacturers.

Check the depth stop and fence

Flatten and polish the fence. As supplied from new, the fences are quite rough, and giving the fence a good polish will help the plane glide along the wood.

You can see here that I've given the fence a good polish up. Any metal surface that moves against wood needs to be silky smooth.

Polish the sole of the depth stop, giving the leading edge a little round over so it can't snag the wood.

Sharpen up the cutting spur (nicker)

This nicker normally lives tucked up against the side of the plane body with no protruding cutter. The cutting spur only comes out when you need to plane across the grain, which is why there are only three spurs on the rotatable nicker. To get the nicker set up properly, it's imperative to get it really sharp. It's only purpose is to sever end grain fibers, prior to being lifted out by the plane iron, so if the nicker is not sharp enough, you'll be left with a ragged cross grain cut, which is definitely not what you want!

> **TECHNICAL POINTER:** *You will need to check the alignment of the nicker, as shown on page 92, so don't get the flat face polished beautifully unless you are sure that the alignment is perfect. Get it looking good by all means, but bear in mind that the final finish may only be possible with the spur installed in the body of the plane.*

There are two faces to grind, hone and polish, as with any edge tool. There is a chance that the nicker has never been sharpened, or at best sharpened badly. Polish the flat face first (the outside face as you look at the side of the plane), going down the grades on your diamond plates.

The nicker is normally stowed so it does not protrude, hence there are only three cutters, not four.

This needs work on both faces, just like a chisel.

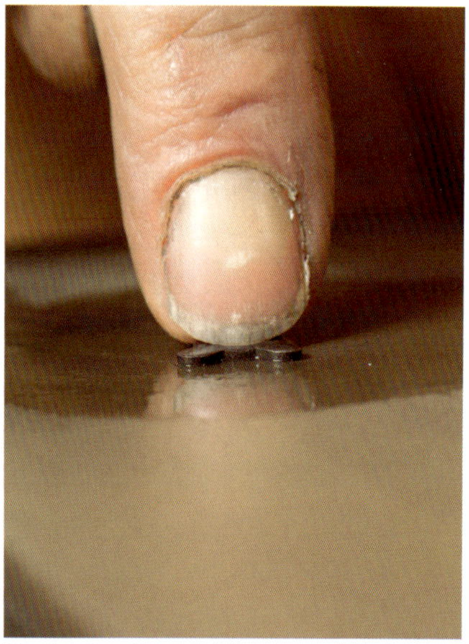

The flat face (outward facing) is polished...

...by working down the grades of diamond stones or emery, until it's smooth and shiny.

The other side is then sharpened up either using diamond stones...

...or by filing and honing in the vise.

Either way, it's going to need a good stropping on the leather to get it...

...polished up and ready for work!

TOP TIP: *Sharpen up two of the nicker blades. Use one at full size for softwood, and sharpen the other to protrude much less, about $\frac{1}{32}$", for hardwood.*

Holding the nicker in a pair of locking pliers, work on the back edge, giving it a good rounding at about 30 degrees, moving from coarse to fine stones.

Alternatively, hold it with locking pliers in the vice (shown on facing page) and use a flat diamond file followed by a ceramic slip stone. Either way, finish it off on your leather strop so it will cut cleanly. (See photo on left.)

Use a smooth, fine diamond file to make sure the bedding plane is flat and true.

File out the throat

With the cutting iron removed, check the throat and bedding plane for flatness. If it's not perfectly flat take a flat, fine file (or a small diamond plate), and gently even out any high spots and protrusions. The casting may have been indented at the edges, through neglect and rough handling by previous owners, or rusting and age may have left the throat in need of some attention.

Rust proofing

There are a few recipes used to prevent rusting of the polished surfaces, or any other surfaces where the black paint has been knocked off. Some folks suggest a wipe with camellia oil, and others use beeswax. Both work well, and I use both. I actually use both at the same time!

I just keep an old jam jar with a good shot of camellia oil, a few table spoons of soft wax and some solvent all mixed together. The camellia oil has a very low surface tension and so will spread into and cling to, every pit, bump and undulation in every surface. The wax just helps the plane to glide over the work piece. You don't need to use a lot. A little and often is far better than drowning your plane once, and then forgetting all about rust proofing and lubrication. This is good practice for all metal planes, plane irons, steel straight edges, cast iron machine tables, etc.

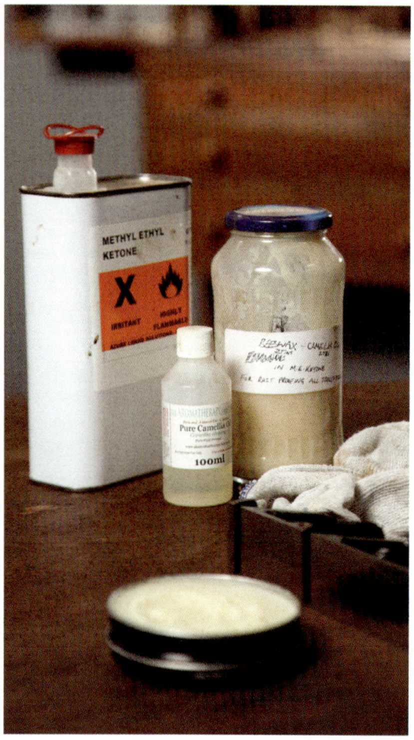

The oil/wax mixture is fine for all metal parts.

Work on the flat face before the bevel. This iron is going to take some work!

The performance of a polished iron is well worth the effort on any edge tool.

Set up and tune up

Sharpen up the cutting iron

Again, polish up the flat face first to a reasonable level of reflectivity. When it comes to the bevel a common mistake is to sharpen up dead square, but this can cause the side of the iron to scrape on the side of the rebate, making it look a little ragged. Instead, when you initially regrind and hone the bevel, deliberately go a little out of square. Also, just relieve the side of the iron slightly, as this also stops it from dragging.

The bevel is sharpened up on the stones and stropped on leather as you would for any plane iron. How to get a mirror finish in 2 minutes is described in detail on pages 208 to 211 of *Working Wood 1&2*.

The angle I'm measuring here needs to be a little less than 90 degrees.

Just take a couple of degrees off the edge as shown here.

Alignment of the cutting spur

Carefully check the alignment of the spur with the corner of the sole. I hold a metal ruler up to it with a good light. Sometimes, as is the case here, the recessed pocket is too deep and the spur does not reach the outside face. This is a guaranteed source of problems when you plane across the grain and needs to be rectified.

If this is the case, unscrew the nicker retaining screw and shim it out with some ordinary copier/printer paper. Shim it further out than the side face, but only by a tenth of a whisker (impossible to eyeball, but you get the idea) and then lap it flush on some 1200 grit emery on a glass plate. The outer edge will now be aligned perfectly with the side face of the plane and will cut better than you can imagine!

In this photo, you can see that the nicker doesn't quite line up with the edge of the sole.

It's an easy fix. Just remove the retaining screw...

...fit a small triangle of paper in (to act as a packer), then...

...replace the nicker and the screw, and to finish off...

...give the nicker a good rubbing on a sheet of 1200 grit emery.

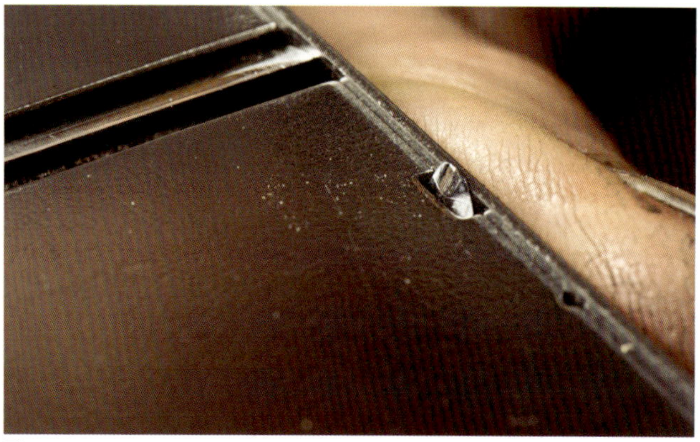

This process aligns the nicker very accurately.

Just a gentle tap is all it takes to adjust the iron parallel to the sole. Don't forget to re-tighten the cap iron with the thumbscrew when you're done!

Setting the plane iron correctly

There are three factors in setting the iron correctly, and the first two described below must be carried out simultaneously.

1. Position of iron: The very corner of the iron needs to line up with the edge of the sole. With the lever cap slackened off, tap the iron across and check it with a steel rule.

2. At the same time as you are checking the position you also need to adjust the parallel alignment of the iron, by giving the top of the iron a little tap as shown in the photo above. I use the corner edge of a pine batten to run down the sole on the left and right sides of the cutting iron. The thickness of the shaving tells me if I've got the iron parallel.

3. The depth of cut is adjusted using the lever after you have slackened off the lever cap screw, but don't forget to re-tighten the lever cap after adjustment. Don't ever set the iron to take a hefty shaving. Leave the heavy work for a wooden plane. Thin to medium shavings are what this plane was designed for.

Install the fence and depth stop and make sure the lever cap is tight. Set the fence for say, a ½" rebate. Set the nicker so that all three spurs are inboard, you won't need a nicker for planing with the grain as you check the set up.

Place a piece of straight grained wood in the vice. Starting at the far end, take a short pass to create a short, shallow rebate. Holding the plane steady, repeat a few passes, each time extending the length of the stroke. I will mention that this is just a check to see how your plane performs, as personally I would not rely on the fence for clean, accurate rebates, and I'll explain why in the next section. I use a cutting gauge to slice the top surface before cutting a rebate - see pages 94 to 99.

There is a list of common rebating problems, and how to fix them on pages 102 and 103. Make sure the plane is level and the fence is pressed firmly against the work. All being well, you may now be able to progress the rebate down to your depth stop, along the entire length of the test piece. The following rebating methods will give you a choice of techniques for clean, accurate rebates.

Rebating methods

There are numerous methods for creating rebates, and some folks are strong advocates of a particular method that just happens to suit them. However, I would encourage you to develop your own preferences regardless of who says what. The following list of methods should be helpful as you put the specialist planes previously listed to good use.

In all rebating processes I'd suggest you run a cutting gauge along your work to define the rebate, and take it down to a good depth. Doing this first will give you a much cleaner cut line at the top surface of your work than you would get by just launching straight in with any type of rebate or grooving plane.

Knots and wild grain

I am going to stress here that any kind of uneven, wild and wiry grain, including knots and areas around knots, is best avoided in the early days of learning to create grooves and rebates. Not that such wood can't be worked - with sharp irons and care, it is possible, but it will add unnecessary difficulty, which could frustrate you. With both softwood and hardwood, select clean, clear sections for all the areas you are going to groove, rebate, mortise, mold, etc.

Rebating with the Stanley No.78

Planing with the grain

When rebating it's possible to work with the grain and get a lovely clean finish straight from the plane. However, it's more likely that using a cutting gauge to define the edge of the rebate before you start, is going to give you a sharp, clean shoulder. Remember, you can often cut a rebate from either side of a work piece! You could lay your work piece flat on the bench or hold it in some device, such as the long bench clamp or a sticking board.

"Remember, you can often cut a rebate from either side of a work piece!"

Holding your work in a vise gives you more control.

Use the correct cutting gauge, so the waste fibers are compressed.

Hold a thick guide batten in place. It will give you a large area to press the side of the plane against.

This is a great method for repeatability.

Use the depth stop as you approach your line.

The fence on the No.78 is not ideal, but works fine if the shoulder is well defined beforehand.

A reliable method is to hold a batten down on top of your work and use this as a guide for the side of your rebate plane. Once you've got a straight shoulder you can dispense with the guide and deepen the rebate, setting the fence and depth stop on the No.78.

Alternatively, if you are working a series of identical rebates, you could also make up a guide for using in the long bench clamp (see page 263). The guide shown in the photo, middle left, is for quickly cutting a ½" wide rebate on the edge 1⅛" stock. All you have to do is press the plane firmly against the guide, and then when you are nearly down to depth, remove the guide from the clamp and set the depth gauge on the plane.

Using just the fence

The fence on a No.78 lets it down somewhat, which is a polite way of saying it's pretty useless! The single arm that the fence is fixed to invariably has a little too much play, allowing the fence to wiggle about a bit - not ideal for accurate results! By all means persevere with it if you're mad keen, but quite frankly, you are better off using a wooden fixed fence, as previously described. The one use for the fence, which is very handy, is when you have cut a groove with the Record No.44 (see page 113). Simply set the fence so the edge of the iron lies in the groove, set the depth stop, and plane away to your hearts content, knowing you already have an accurate shoulder, thanks to the No.44!

> *"The fence on a No.78 lets it down somewhat, which is a polite way of saying it's pretty useless!"*

Planing across the grain

One way of starting is to mark out the rebate, gauging out the dimensions all round, then set a guide in place, holding it down firmly.

> **TECHNICAL POINTER:**
> *Take a fine dovetail saw, and working on the farthest edge from the start of the rebate, saw down to your gauge line. This will prevent the fibers splintering out on the end of each pass with the plane.*

Set the nicker to correspond with either a hardwood (1⁄32") or softwood (1⁄16"). You may want to run a marking knife along the guide to start the cut, or some folks prefer to carefully draw the plane backwards, holding it firmly against the guide as the nicker cuts the top fibers ahead of the plane iron.

Keeping the plane body against the guide, take successive passes down to your gauge line, checking for a level cut every few passes.

It's obvious that a guide made from thicker stock will make it easier to keep the plane vertical, but as you get more confident, you can use a thinner guide.

A saw cut is essential at the edge of the board.

A sharp nicker and a rock solid guide make the job quite straight forward.

Using a thinner guide makes it more important to concentrate on keeping the plane horizontal.

The bevel of the cutting knife must be on the waste side of the line.

Starting off free hand is an advanced technique that will need perseverance to master.

Using a wooden rebate plane

A moving fillister (page 82) is the most accurate version of any wooden rebate plane, but should you choose to use an unfenced, standard wooden rebate plane I would strongly recommend starting off with two planes. Set one with the iron flush with the right hand edge, and the other set flush to the left. This will allow you to work on any part of the rebate, and correct any errors without fiddling with your planes. (That is of course if your irons are set parallel to the soles and flush to the edges!)

Having got your iron sharpened and set as described on pages 91 to 93, measure and mark out your rebate using a gauge. Notice that I'm using the internal cutting gauge, bruising the wood on the waste side of the line.

- Incline the plane over and cut a shallow 'V' shaped groove, using your fingers as a guide.
- Deepen the groove with a few passes and then level up the plane, working a level rebate up to the side of the first groove.

This method is very quick and simple but could take a while to master. In inexperienced hands the plane iron can drift very easily, unless it is 'steered' carefully and accurately.

> *"A moving fillister is the most accurate version of any wooden rebate plane..."*

Starting with an inlay slot cutter

A fast and accurate method of setting out and starting is to use the inlay cutting tool (page 42) to define the sidewall of the rebate. You may just find that the corner of the plane iron sits in the little slot and follows the tiny groove a lot easier than the knife line left by the cutting gauge. You then simply level up the plane, and using your fingers under the fore-part of the plane as a guide, continue to deepen the rebate down to the required depth. In this photo on the far right, I've just reached the depth of the slot made by the inlay cutter.

Use a guide

Alternatively you could use a guide in conjunction with the long bench clamp (page 263). This method is particularly useful if you have to produce a whole load of standard sized rebates, in the same sized stock.

Use a steel rule to check your work as you progress down to the correct depth.

> **TOP TIP:** *As you have no depth stop, use a strip of wood that your plane iron will catch on when you reach the required depth. This will slide along under the plane as you take the last pass. The strip I'm using has an arrow on it to show the direction of movement as soon as the depth is reached.*

The slot cutter gives you a head start...

...making starting off freehand much easier.

There is no easier way than using a fixed guide. It's fast, accurate and repeatable.

Check your rebate - this looks square enough!

As the cutting iron snags the sliding batten, you simply can't cut too deep.

This wooden fillister plane is ideal for cross grain planing, thanks to the skewed iron and nicker.

Forming a knife wall (as for a housing dado) prior to planing across the grain works very well.

Cross grain planing

Some wooden rebate planes have a nicker fitted directly in front of the plane iron. This is designed to cut the cross grain fibers before being cut and lifted by the plane iron. A skewed iron will perform very well across the grain, as it has more of a sideways slicing action, peeling off the fibers from one end first, ad then curling them out as the blade advances. A straight iron is more likely to slice and lift out entire fiber bundles, which can lead to a slight judder even with a very sharp iron.

If no plane with a nicker is on hand, another way is to form a knife wall down to the required depth before you start the rebate. This method is essential when you are using a rebate plane without a nicker. If you are unsure about planing across the grain, this is sometimes a good way to start even if it takes a while longer, as it will guarantee a clean and accurate shoulder.

The finished cross grain rebate. With some judicious chisel work, there's often not a lot of planing to do to tidy up and finish the rebate.

Cutting a stopped rebate

Regardless of which plane you choose to create your rebate, a stopped rebate always involves cutting a recess equal in length to the distance between the cutting iron and the toe of the plane you are using. The Stanley No.78 has a forward position for the cutting iron, which is ideal for this purpose. With the iron in the forward position, the adjustment is a little more fiddly, as there is no depth adjustment lever at the front. The lever-cap retaining screw needs moving to the forward position before assembling the iron.

The recess will form part of the rebate and so it's marked out to the same depth and width as the rest of the rebate.

Start by creating a knife wall on each face, defining the limit of the rebate.

Mark on the distance between the end of the rebate and the cutting iron on your plane, adding around ¾" for good measure. Square this mark down to the bottom of the rebate. This 'limit line' defines the minimum space required for the front of the plane, as measured along the bottom of the rebate. Use a cutting gauge to neatly slice the edges of the rebate on both faces.

In the same way as you would cut a mortise, make a series of vertical chisel cuts, getting deeper as you approach the line you have marked.

Mark up your stopped rebate. I've used a black pen to make the lines clearer to see in the photo.

Define the end of the rebate with knifewalls on the adjacent faces.

With the cutting iron in the forward position, mark out for chiselling.

Remove the waste just as you would when cutting a mortise.

Chop out the waste and clean up the pocket.

I've set up a guide and a stop block to reduce the chances of making a mistake.

Chop and pare out the waste, leaving a clean and well trimmed pocket. There is no need for an awkward vertical cut on the right hand side (in this case), just pare down at an angle to meet the 'limit line'.

Now it's time to plane the rebate. I usually use two rebate planes, as starting the cut with the iron in the forward position of the No.78 is not easy! I am using a batten as a guide, clamped to the top of the work piece, and also notice the 'stop block', in the middle photo, clamped at the far end of the rebate. This is necessary to prevent you from over shooting with your plane. If you try this without a stop block, you will damage your work.

The finished 'stopped rebate' is shown below.

"If you try this without a stop block, you will damage your work."

With the clamps removed, you can see the finished rebate stops right on that initial knife line.

Common rebating problems

1. If the rebate gets narrower as you get deeper:

(a) You need to check the alignment of the blade in relation to the side face. If it is set back from the side face, the cut will get narrower so adjust it out a bit accordingly. Check it with a straight edge.

(b) You are perhaps not holding the fence firmly against the work. Try again!

2. If the rebate looks uneven and tatty:

(a) The blade could be blunt - check it and sharpen it if required.

(b) You could be rushing and wobbling the plane around as you cut. Work steadily with control of the firm forward pressure, and keep the plane level.

(c) Check the grain direction. Planing with the grain makes all the difference.

3. If you plane deeper than you intended:

(a) The depth stop is incorrectly set
or
(b) The depth stop screw is not fully tightened

4. The plane judders badly:

(a) The blade is set too far out. i.e. you are trying to take too much off in one go.

(b) The blade could be blunt

(c) You could be going against the grain.

(d) The cap iron may not be locked down tight.

(e) You could be faced with any combination of the above! Go through and check everything systematically.

5. Your rebate gets wider towards the end of the cut. This is a problem normally associated with unfenced wooden planes:

(a) If the cutting iron is protruding too far out of the side, this will cause the plane to 'eat' into the side-wall of the rebate you are cutting. Check the iron with a straight edge.

(b) You could be steering the plane sideways into your groove. You need to apply pressure to the side of the plane behind the cutting iron, otherwise you will increase the chances of cutting into the shoulder.

In the above case, using a solid fence, set parallel, will solve this problem. (See 'Moving fillister', page 82). Cutting the side walls of the rebate using a grooving plane will also give you more accuracy and eliminate any sideways 'drift'. See page 113.

I set the cutting iron a little in from the edge to demonstrate the effect when cutting a rebate.

Working against the grain is to be avoided - always!

If you don't hold the plane upright, this is the result.

6. You plane a low angle chamfer:

(a) This is a common problem. Planing a rebate dead flat by hand can be a struggle. Check the blade alignment to see if it's set right - adjust accordingly.

(b) If your iron is set right (parallel to the sole), you may need to resort to using a parallel guide as shown on page 98.

(c) You may just need more practice. Concentrate on taking a steady shaving without leaning the plane or wobbling about as you progress. If you are still struggling, see 6(b).

7. You plane a rebate sloping inwards towards the shoulder:

(a) This is most likely the setting of the iron. Check that the iron is parallel to the sole. If I was a betting man, I'd put money on your iron protruding further out by the shoulder, taking a heavier shaving on this side compared to the other side of the iron. Check it and fix it. (Page 73).

Carelessness can result in a slope in the other direction as well.

Chapter 6
An introduction to grooving/plow planes

This is a unique category of planes and for the hand tool woodworker there is simply no practical alternative to them for cutting accurate grooves. Of course, the electric router is an efficient and accurate alternative and it is certainly the right choice for larger production volumes.

My screw stem plow plane is very old, but very reliable.

Historically, these planes have always been some of the most expensive tools in the cabinet maker's shop, apart from a brace and full set of bits. Their relative complexity (in plane making terms) has always been reflected in the price, but much more so in wooden planes than the modern metal versions. Modern metal plow planes, made in the US or Canada, are superbly engineered and require no tuning and only occasional sharpening.

The basic design principles that made a plow plane so useful in centuries past have remained unchanged to this day:

- A cutter, selected for it's particular width, is held securely in the plane body.
- A side fence accurately positions the cutter in relation to the work piece.
- An adjustable depth stop gives an accurate and repeatable groove depth.

With both wooden and metal varieties, these three principles have been incorporated into every grooving plane ever built, with varying levels of simplicity, ingenuity or sophistication. The performance of the plane however, is not just a function of the build quality, but rather it comes down to how well the plane is set up.

Wooden plow planes

It's possible to get hold of wooden plows that, although being slower to set up and adjust, perform equally as well as any engineered metal plane.

The range of plow planes available on the second hand market encompasses a startling range of both quality and value. Starting at only a few notches above general firewood, they can reach the dizzy heights of closer to $25,000 worth of solid ebony No.112 (Ohio Tool Company), and they are all just plow planes! With such a range of planes on the market, you could pay either bargain basement, or top dollar prices, but without a sharp iron and a often a good tune up, you could get equally disastrous results, regardless of the relative dent in your wallet.

The difference, if you ignore rarity/collectability and value, is of course in functionality. I have used old wooden plow planes with wobbly arms and wedges that don't tighten up well enough, and they were nothing close to precision tools. Sure, you can make them work, but it can be very fiddly and time consuming. A good wooden plow should come with a full set of irons and may cost between $100 to $500. When you pay more than $500, you are in the realms of a serious collector (or perhaps an equally serious user), as there are scores of planes under the $200 mark that will work equally as well when sorted out and sharpened up. Whether you find one that's fixed with wedges or has a higher quality fence held by threaded wooden arms (known as a 'screw stem plow plane'), is a matter of choice, but you will generally get what you pay for.

However, if you are looking at getting a new wooden plow plane, around the $500+ is to be expected and you'll be getting a quality tool that will last a lifetime.

TOP TIP: *The real advantage with a wooden plow plane is the extra depth of the groove you can cut. It's unusual to need a groove deeper than ¾", but if you are cutting moldings in deep stock (page 128), cutting a groove to over 1" is not uncommon. Most metal planes won't cut a slot this deep.*

This type of plow plane is set for width using wedges to secure the arms.

I keep the set of irons rolled up in a piece of felt tied up with string.

The work is held securely on my 'sticking board', from page 261.

Metal plow planes

These are relatively inexpensive compared to their quality wooden counterparts, and I have to say they are a much more practical alternative, in most circumstances. You can switch irons in a jiffy, reset the fence in seconds and change the depth of cut with equal alacrity.

I would recommend a metal plow plane over a wooden one, in terms of sheer pragmatism. If you can stretch your finances to buying a modern metal plow plane then get one without hesitation, as it will save quite a bit of restoration work. This is of course providing that it's either a new one by the likes of Veritas or Lie-Nielsen. Alternatively, get yourself a second hand plow in good condition, perhaps by Record or Stanley.

As the Record No.44 was manufactured literally by the truckload, there are still plenty to be found in good condition, so it makes sense to look at how to get the best out of a secondhand one, which is what we'll do next.

Record No.44 plow plane

I'm going to recommend the Record No.44 plow plane. I've used a No. 44 for years and it works a treat. They are easy to fix up even if they are not in good condition.

My first encounter with the No.44 was in the making of a ledged and braced gate for my then soon to be mother in law in my attic workshop about 25 years ago. Thankfully, the plow plane performed admirably, the gate was delivered on time, and the future mother-in-law was suitably impressed!

The No.44 is not complex in terms of design, but the cutter is easily adjustable, as is the depth stop and fence. If the grain is favorable (chosen well), it's easy to plow a deep groove quickly in hard or softwood, leaving a neat and smooth finish all the way down.

On older and more worn examples, the nickel plating is usually starting to peel, so ideally you would get hold of a fairly shiny looking plane. If your budget is really tight, a good clean up and some wax will get the plane into a serviceable condition, even it looks fairly rusty and pitted. I'm assuming that your No.44 is going to need a bit of TLC and encouragement to work properly, so overleaf we'll go through a check list to get your plane in good order.

Restoration

Strip down and clean up

Take a large flat-head screwdriver, and undo all the machine screws that hold the parts together. You'll need a finer screwdriver for the blade retaining screw. Clean everything thoroughly.

Check the depth stop

If the depth stop on your plane has a wobbly foot, it's an easy fix. To correct it, turn the stop over and look at the point where the post is riveted to the foot. The riveting has come loose so hold the post (or leg) in a pair of locking pliers, support the pliers with a block of wood and grip a piece of heavy steel in the vise as shown in the photo, bottom right.

Check you've got all the parts to your plane and dismantle it on a clean surface.

The cutting depth adjustment screw. The stepped collar holds the iron.

The blade retaining screw, or cutter clamping screw, releases the blade.

The foot is loose due to a small gap just here.

This is the set up I used for punching the center of the riveted foot.

The indentation I made has tightened the foot.

Flatten the underside afterwards.

Give the skate a gentle smoothing...

...and take off any little burrs.

A quick tap with a punch will spread the metal a little and tighten up the foot which will then just need a rub down to get it flush and smooth again.

Polish the skate

Go easy with some fine (600 grit) silicon carbide paper with a little water as a lubricant, as shown in the middle left photo. The idea is just to get the underside of the skate silky smooth. Don't worry about taking a little of the plating off, it's all going to get rust proofed in a while.

A gentle filing

This is all that's required to take off any burrs left over from the previous step. While you're at it, check for any other sharp edges you could snag yourself on.

In particular, check the front leading corner of the skate. You want a little round over on this so your plane lands and travels smoothly at the start of every pass, bottom photo.

Check the threads

Every machine screw should be clean and turn easily. You can clean grot out of the threads with a fine wire brush, holding the screw in a pair of locking pliers.

The leading edge of the skate benefits from a little rounding over, so as not to snag the work.

Rust protection

I use a mixture of camellia oil and beeswax (dissolved in a little methyl ethyl ketone -MEK), which leaves a light coating over every surface. I put it on with a small brush and then give the whole thing a rub down with a cloth to take of any excess. This goes a long way towards rust prevention and is a lot more practical than any kind of lacquer, which would just gum everything up.

The side fence is an essential piece of kit to ensure accurate results.

The side fence

If your No.44 (or similar) has not got a good shop made side fence, now is the time to make and fit one.

You'll need the existing fence, a couple of small screws and some fine grained hard wood. Sapele, utile or maple are just fine. I've used some iroko here, which I don't recommend (as it is liable to bend when you cut it), but I just happened to have a nice flat piece. I chose a piece about 3/8" x 8" x 2½".

Mark and cut the recess for the cutting iron.

Brush on a coat of sanding sealer.

Plane it very smooth and give it a good round over on 3 sides of one of the faces. With the fence assembled temporarily, mark out a recess in the fence to match the little pocket in the casting. You'll need to saw this out, and sand the edges as you can then use the No.44 for rebating, as shown bottom right.

I'm using sanding sealer to finish the job as it's tough stuff, and when lightly sanded and waxed it's as slippery as a bucket of fresh mackerel, which is just what you want!

Fit the wooden fence to the metal frame...

...and nip the screws up tight. You are then ready to give it a try!

The recess in the fence allows you to cut rebates with the No.44.

These two cutters are going to take a lot of work to restore properly. All the deep pitting has to go!

Work on two small irons at the same time as it will be easier.

With the flat face polished, the bevel does not take long to sharpen, just as you would for a chisel.

The cutting irons

By now, you'll know that the flat faces of all the irons need a good polish first.

> **TOP TIP:** *It's a lot easier to flatten and polish the faces of the smaller irons if you do them two at a time and hold them with a stack of rare earth magnets.*

The bevel of each iron can be sharpened in the usual fashion by going down the grades on the diamond stones. Strop them on leather as you would for a chisel.

> **TOP TIP:** *It may be easier to hold the smaller cutters in a pair of locking pliers. It will help you to not grind a skewed bevel by mistake.*

Rebuild and adjust

Put the plane back together again and install an iron for a 'try out'.

Set the iron in place, and using the adjusting screw at the top, advance the iron so it just peeks out past the skate. Nip up the blade clamping screw, and lock down the little cast cap iron.

> **TECHNICAL POINTER:**
> *The screws that hold the fence to the arms can sometimes allow the fence to move, as can the depth stop if not tightened fully. Even a screwdriver may not apply enough force to grip the arms, in which case you'll need to use a pair of locking pliers to nip them up tight. I'm sure this is on the verge of heresy, but having been caught out by this problem myself, I just can't take the risk again!*

Anyway, with everything fitted and tightened, choose a test piece of wood (watch that grain!) and starting at the far end of the groove; take a short stroke or two to see how it cuts. If the shaving is thin and wispy you may want to adjust the iron for a thicker shaving.

Slacken the cap iron.

Back off the blade clamping screw.

Advance the Iron with the depth adjustment screw.

Re-tighten in reverse order.

TECHNICAL POINTER:
The cap iron needs to be centered on the top of the iron. To achieve this it can be moved sideways, either away from, or towards the main body.

Set the iron to take a fairly thick shaving. This is what the plane was designed for! You can take fine wisps, as shown on the left of the photo below, or hefty thick shavings as shown on the right. I would aim for something like the middle shavings, perhaps even a bit thicker. Thin shavings are a complete waste of time, you will just expend a lot of time and effort creating a groove that should have taken you a fraction of the time.

Depth adjustment: The cap iron is released first, then..

...the cutter clamping screw. The cutter depth is then adjusted and the assembly re-tightened.

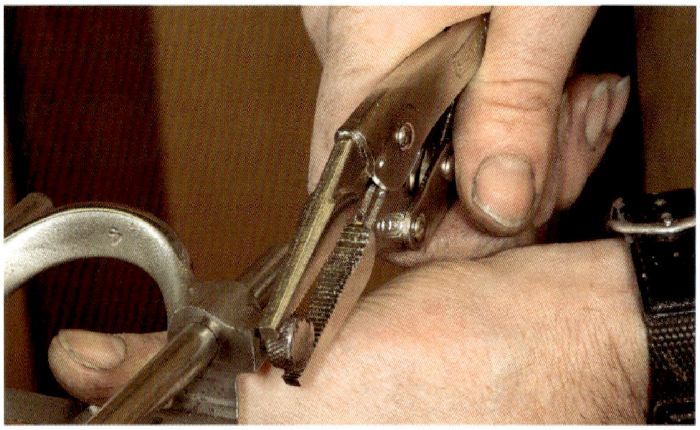
If the fence moves, you could ruin your work. Tighten those arm screws!

Get the cap iron positioned centrally on the cutting iron.

A selection of shavings removed using three different cutting depths. Thin shavings from a plow plane may look lovely, but are a complete waste of time!

Make sure you know exactly where all the grooves are to be cut.

A little nick off the end of the board will indicate precisely...

...where you need to set the cutting gauges.

Methods and techniques with the No.44

Work holding

This is the first thing to sort out no matter what operation you are planning to carry out. The sticking board described on page 261 can always be modified, adapted or indeed scrapped at any time. If you figure out a better way to hold your work, just do it. My sticking board gets dismantled, re-made, it has new bits tacked on, old screws removed, stops and fences fixed to it - all of this on a regular basis. Don't be shy about chopping it up, changing it around or screwing extra bits on. Just make it work for you and your chosen work methods. There is also the long bench clamp described on page 263, which may be useful. Any shorter pieces can be held in the vise, providing that they are wide enough for the fence not to snag on the vise jaws.

Grooving procedure with the No.44

Mark out the groove with a pencil gauge. I use a soft pencil and squiggle a few lines just to remind myself. The reason for marking the grooves so clearly is that if I'm working at my bench or layout table I'm forever picking up pieces of marked up wood and turning them round to check the layout. I need to easily see the positions of every joint, rebate groove, housing, every chamfer, every molding, etc. Unlike standard joinery work, get into the habit of laying out with a soft pencil, up to the stage of actually defining the groove or rebate, then switch to a cutting gauge or marking knife.

Set your plow to the right position and tighten the fence so it can't move. Hold your fence firmly against the work and nick the corner slightly. This shows you clearly where the cutting iron is going to form the groove.

Use a matched pair of cutting gauges and, referencing the same edge, cut a pair of tram lines to match the cutter position. For each gauge line set the cutting knife to the precise edge of the nick you made with the grooving iron. These cut lines will prevent the top fibers from splintering out as the plane iron glides forward. There are alternative methods, more suited to batch production that we'll look at in the next part of the course.

TECHNICAL POINTER: *The grain direction is a big deal - get this the wrong way round and you'll regret not choosing the wood more carefully. You'll split out the top surface and judder your way down into a ragged trench. Try it, but only once, and you'll learn all you need to know about grain direction in about 5 seconds.*

After setting your depth stop start at the farthest end of the cut and take a few short shavings. Take a few more and gradually work back towards the start of the groove.

TECHNICAL POINTER:
Keep the fence held firmly against the work piece. Just push the plane forward. It will take the exact thickness of shaving you have set it for. Your main concern is moving down the work piece at a steady pace and with precision, not pushing the plane downwards to try to make it work!

You'll notice I'm holding the work between a pair of screws on a sticking board. This is an easy work holding method and works really well. Any marks in the end grain left by the screws would normally disappear as the convention is to groove the stock before cutting to the exact length.

Rebating with the No.44

The No.44 can also be used as a quick and easy rebate plane. The wide cutter does not have to be used in a groove, but can instead be set to cut only the edge of the work piece, thus forming a rebate.

For narrow rebates use an appropriate cutting iron and set the fence to cut a rebate, not a groove. Use a cutting gauge to mark the width and depths on each face respectively.

For wider rebates, choose a narrow cutter (say 3⁄16"), and as before, mark the rebate on the stock with a cutting gauge. This time, set the cutter to the first gauge line by adjusting the fence, and the depth stop so the cutting depth corresponds to the other gauge line.

With the first groove cut re-set your fence and depth gauge to correspond with the first groove, but this time work from the adjacent face.

Take long, steady, and even strokes.

The little overhang shown here is crucial.

For narrow rebates, this is one method.

For larger rebates, cut two narrow slots that meet. Align the iron precisely to the mark shown here.

With the depth stop set, simply cut the second slot to form the rebate.

With the groove in place, a coarse set wooden plane will do most of the work in no time.

The depth stop is set correctly, and the No.78 finishes the job in a few passes.

TOP TIP: *Don't forget to pinch up those adjusting screws. Also, notice that I've switched to the long arms to reach across the work. This is because the grain direction was such that I could not work in the other direction.*

With your fence and depth gauge set, plow the second groove until your rebate is finished.

TECHNICAL POINTER:
The work must not be able to move, and it needs to overhang the edge of the bench slightly so that nothing gets in the way of the fence. Put a couple of extra screws in the sticking board to make sure the work can't get dislodged, otherwise you'll go off track very quickly, which of course would probably mean starting again from scratch.

Alternative methods

You may choose to plow the first groove to create an accurate shoulder line, then with your coarse set wooden rebate plane (note: a badger plane will cut the quickest rebate), quickly plane down to near your line. Then just take the last few shavings with a finely set No.78 or whatever plane you prefer for finer, accurate work.

This is a very quick method that you may want to adopt as you grow in confidence. The plow and solid fence guarantee an accurate groove, the wooden plane will hog off huge amounts of stock quickly, leaving very little for the No.78 to remove.

This is an example of using a series of planes, each dedicated to a single purpose. This is usually much more efficient if you are cutting a series of identical rebates.

Larger rebates

Every now and again, it's useful to be able to cut a wide rebate. There are a few different methods for this, using a combination of different planes.

For example, a standard rebate plane with no depth stop will allow you to keep going down until you snag your fingers on the work piece. In this case, the work would be held vertically. However, it's not likely that you will get a very accurate rebate.

A better method is to tackle the rebate in a different orientation. In this photo, you can see I have the work piece flat on the bench, but raised up on the sticking board to allow the fence of the No.44 to reference the side face easily.

The groove you cut with the plow plane obviously defines the shoulder of the rebate in depth and width.

You could miss the next step out if you like, and go straight for the badger, but I'd recommend that you reset your plow and put a small rebate along the front edge. This gives you a very accurate reference line to work to, as you remove the waste from the middle.

The first groove you cut is very useful when you set up to use your badger plane. Set a wooden batten as a guide, holding it tight onto the work piece, and arrange it such that the very corner of the plane iron just about falls within the groove. Make sure that it has no chance of touching the sidewall and ruining the smooth finish.

TECHNICAL POINTER:
As you are now taking off a fair width of material, don't forget to back off your Badger iron to take thinner shavings. Thick shavings taken over a considerable width require energy and force that will most likely dislodge the whole set up, or even move your whole bench across the floor!

You can't beat the accuracy of a well placed groove for any size of rebate!

Using the same depth setting, a narrow rebate on the front provides an excellent visual reference.

With no fence fitted this badger plane needs a guide, held in place with hold downs.

The finished rebate. It's neat, tidy and after a light sanding, can be given a protective coating of varnish, hard wax oil or some other wood finish.

The result of this method of work should be a very accurately cut rebate. In the photo above, I've removed the guide batten and moved the shavings so you can see the work holding more clearly. The reason for using two screws at this end of the work piece is to resist the considerable forward force exerted on it during the rebating process.

"...the days of being daunted by rebating and grooving will be gone."

Conclusion

The rebate planes (wooden and metal) work well as a team, and for guaranteed accuracy the plow plane is unbeatable for rebates. The plow plane is a very versatile grooving tool and works best when cutting grooves that exactly match the width of any of the cutting irons. Have a go using all of the methods outlined above and perhaps start out using softwoods, not because the planes work better or easier on softwood, it just seems better as we practice, to turn pine into firewood rather than a nice piece of hardwood!

Grooving and rebating are absolutely essential processes to be able to carry out with speed and precision. Once you get used to setting up the tools, and keeping everything super sharp, the days of being daunted by rebating and grooving will be gone. Enjoy learning, enjoy practicing and most of all, enjoy putting your creativity to good use as you work wood with a smile on your face.

Chapter 7
An introduction to molding planes

Workshop shelves were once crammed full of the most incredible range of molding planes, often catering for the individual preferences of wealthy customers, as well as being used for everyday production pieces. They are great fun to use, and once set up and sharp, it does not take long to convert plain and uninspiring stock into an eye catching decorative molding.

These planes are seen by many woodworkers as being fiddly to adjust, difficult to sharpen and even more difficult to use reliably. This is absolutely correct, unless you have the right sharpening tools, the knowledge of how to use these tools, and a modest amount of skill and understanding in terms of the practical use of the planes.

The aim of this section is to bust the myths surrounding these tools and to enable all those who have an interest, to get to grips with molding plane basics.

"They are great fun to use and once set up and sharp, it does not take long to convert plain and uninspiring stock into an eye catching decorative molding."

Once you start using molding planes, a whole new range of options suddenly becomes available.

Why use a molding plane?

In terms of function, molding planes are generally stacked up against the wonderfully versatile electric router. Electric routers are truly versatile - you fit the shaped cutter, and you create a molded section to the exact profile you've chosen with very little effort.

The carbide cutters will merrily machine hundreds of meters of stock, and providing you take all the measures to control the dust, noise and vibration, you could not ask for a more time and labor saving machine. Multiple passes with different cutters allow more complex profiles to be created and so on and so forth. In fact, the limitations of the router only become apparent when:

1. You want to reproduce a small molding that you can't get a cutter for or...
2. You need to produce a molding that's so large that you need a $8000 spindle molder, a power feed unit and multiple sets of special cutters and limiters. In the middle photo, I'm holding an average sized router cutter alongside a molding that did not take me long to produce by hand methods. If you appreciate the difference in scale, you'll see why molding planes could be a very appropriate alternative!
3. Younger folks, teenagers and even kids want to get involved with some fun, hand cut molding profiles. There is no way I'd let younger family members near an electric router.
4. Older folks who just want to enjoy the simple pleasures in life, without the noise, dangers and fiddly adjustments of electric routers; who just want to enjoy the satisfaction of producing something simple yet beautiful. If my father were interested in making moldings (Jesse James, 83 years and going strong), he'd be in doing it by hand. As it happens, he's too busy running a bunkhouse, mountain biking and hill walking, to get involved with detailed woodwork!
5. Then there's also folks like me, who just love the challenge, the simplicity and sheer versatility of molding planes, who don't need to churn out hundreds of meters of molded stock for a living and who genuinely enjoy taking pride in hand made furniture. Folks who, when it's time for the machine don't hesitate, but when it's time for molding with a hand plane, enjoy every last bit of it (written with a smile on my face!).

At this point, you may well be thinking that none of the above will ever apply to you. Your electric router is your best friend and you've invested so much in fancy carbide cutters that you don't want to even contemplate any other way of molding wood. If that's you, skip this chapter - unless you are just plain curious!

This is very simple with an electric router. However...

...would this molding be quite a headache to reproduce with a router?

The legendary Jesse James... " I've never needed an electric router!"

The 'valuable' old tools and the sharpening tools - they've usually parted company decades ago, never to meet again!

"A Cabinet Maker's Workshop revolves around the sharpening system."

Sharpening philosophy

I've noticed that many folks selling old tools invariably sell cutting tools as 'stand alone' items. The often intricate yet simple sharpening tools, are not right there alongside the saws, molding planes, etc. They have become separated, probably never to meet again. Perhaps you know folks who, through inheritance or happenstance, have come by splendid collections of woodworking tools? All too often, without realizing the value of the old, scruffy (and probably well worn) sharpening tools, they focus on the larger metal and wooden artifacts (planes, chisels and saws), totally neglecting small files and slip stones.

In this way, families of tools drift apart, as does the knowledge that goes with them.

This is the very reason that I'm keen on presenting sharpening tools in matched sets (page 151) that all stay together on standby, whether for some serious restoration or just a quick touch up. This is an observation on human nature here: If we make sharpening systems as easy as possible for ourselves, it's going to happen more frequently. This means having a simple, quick and efficient process, and knowing where to find everything we need at a moments notice. Get a marker pen and put a large asterisk by this in the margin: A Cabinet Maker's Workshop revolves around the sharpening system.

Lastly, molding planes are usually in need of some restoration and fixing up, quite apart from sharpening. See page 143 for a short section on bringing old molding planes back to life.

Your first molding planes

Molding planes are both fun to use and very functional. However, it's very important to understand that there are two very distinctly different categories of molding plane. These are:

A. Hollow and round planes

B. Everything else!

Joking apart, the difference with hollow and round planes is that they are incredibly versatile. Almost any molding can be created with a set of hollow and round planes.

The 'everything else' category is really indicative of the fact that every other sort of plane is fairly specialized, to one degree or another, and dedicated to a single profile. For example, a ⅝" reverse ogee plane will only cut that profile, likewise with a ⅜" ovolo plane. This photo shows a complex plane that cuts a cove and an ovolo, and obviously is not easily used for anything else!

There are a few other types of plane such as a 'snipes bill' or a 'side round' that are more multi-purpose, but they are less frequently used than a set of hollows and rounds. The speed and accuracy of a dedicated plane is often very useful, but as you read the following recommendations, be aware of the importance of the undeniable versatility of hollow and round planes.

This is a very effective, but very specialized plane.

A matched pair of No.10 hollow and round planes.

A bench plane would do this easily...

...but certainly not this!

A round plane will cut a cove profile.

I've listed four starter planes, two below, and two overleaf. These are a pair of matched hollow and round planes, and two small sizes of dedicated ovolo cutters. I have to stress here that this is just a suggestion. Please get yourself any molding planes you happen to like,
but just bear in mind the following:

1. Starter planes should be simple: Hollow and rounds are the most basic and most useful. Don't set your sights on a wildly complex profile unless you're confident about learning the intricacies of getting the iron restored and keeping it sharp.
2. Starter planes should be useful: Aside from hollows and rounds, chose a profile, or profiles, that you would like to use frequently
3. You don't need to acquire full sets to start with. Just buy a few individual ones and see how you get on with them.

The four recommended molding planes:

Matched pair of hollow and round planes

(1) Hollow No.10: Hollow planes will simply round over a corner as shown here (middle left photo). However you could obviously produce the same result with an ordinary bench plane. A hollow plane will also do this, (middle right photo) called an 'ovolo' molding. (Technically, it's an ovolo and two fillets - but this is often shortened to just 'ovolo' in plane terms.) There is no way a bench plane can be used to do this, which is why these wonderful wooden planes have proved their worth over centuries!

(2) Round No.10: Round planes will cut a cove molding, which is a concave profile. Just imagine what you could do with a few different sizes of hollows and rounds?

Small ovolo planes

(3) Ovolo plane ¼", shown in front.

(4) Ovolo plane ⅜", shown behind.

The respective moldings produced are on the left hand side of the photo.

These two planes are good starters as they'll allow you to put a molding on cabinet doors and more substantial frame and panel work. They allow fast reproduction of identical moldings, leaving very little to chance when used correctly, even in inexperienced hands (see page 140 on how to use them). In the next part of the course, *Working Wood 4*, you'll see how these planes work together with the grooving and rebate planes as you make some lovely hand cut cabinet doors.

These are a great pair of ovolo planes to start you off.

This pair of planes can be used to produce a decorative cornice, like the one on the facing page.

Hollows and rounds - A potted history

Hollow and round planes have very simple curved sole profiles, and when set up right they are a joy to use. These planes have been put to good use by craftsmen for centuries, possibly from before early Tudor times right through to the late Victorian era. Their decline during the Edwardian period was largely due to the introduction of mechanization into all aspects of furniture making. Rotary molding machines were introduced, producing a huge variety of standardized moldings, and most furniture makers came to rely on industry for the bulk of all molded work. The pace of industrialization meant that the skill and knowledge associated with molding planes became less commonplace, to the point of almost vanishing in a single generation. The emergence of the electric router in the 1940's allowed small shops and individuals the flexibility of shaping wood, importantly without specialist hand planes. Routers and every other machine were embraced in all industrialized countries as makers sought to increase production speed and raise their standard of living.

This is a planer/molder. It replaced a full set of hollows and rounds, but it's not quite as portable!

This molding is built from two molded parts, glued together and then mitered.

Some folks have the view that using a set of wooden planes to create a molding is a time wasting distraction (time is money, isn't it?). Others may have regularly used molding planes all their woodworking lives (not just for nostalgia), and indeed many other folks want to learn to master hand tools (every hand tool maybe?) and will probably enjoy every last bit of it!

Hollows and rounds are traditional hand tools and are great fun to use. If you only stick to an electric router, and never give these planes a try, you're missing out on a whole new spectrum of creativity.

I just happen to like hollows and rounds, as well as hand tools in general, as I find them very versatile, and the process of creating something of beauty with hand tools is priceless. These planes used to be the basis for all molded details in every wood shop from Kilmarnock to Kentucky, and everywhere else in between.

The numbering system

Hollow and round planes are available in graduated sets of $\frac{1}{16}$" increments. A half set comprises all the even numbers up to 18. The numbering is not strictly according to a proportional $\frac{1}{16}$" increment all the way through.

From No's 1 to 12, the incremental steps are in 16ths so a No.12 would be $\frac{12}{16}$" or $\frac{3}{4}$". Above a No.12, the increments are in $\frac{1}{8}$" so a No.14 equates to 1", a No.16 - 1$\frac{1}{4}$" and a No.18 - 1$\frac{1}{2}$".

The reason for the change in increment is for the common sense argument that larger radii need larger changes to look different. To the eye a curve cut to a radius of 1$\frac{1}{4}$" looks very much like a 1$\frac{3}{8}$" radius. However, between a $\frac{1}{4}$" molding and a $\frac{3}{8}$" molding the difference is very noticeable.

What are you cutting?

It's worth mentioning that the sole of a hollow or round plane represents about 60 degrees of the arc of a given circle. This means that you can't hold the plane at a fixed angle and get a nice 90 degree round over or cove. You will need to take several passes, varying the angle that you hold the plane at, but only by around 15 degrees steeper or shallower. This naturally means that it's often necessary to blend in successive parallel cuts, along the length of a molding, in order to get the shape you want.

The skill in blending in these cuts can be developed with time, but there is also a very important sharpening technique (see page 163) that makes this much easier.

Eighteen planes make up a half set of hollows and rounds.

The 60 degree angle is the maximum you can cut in one pass with a hollow or round plane.

Methods of molding

To start with, I'd like to recommend a book by M. S. Bickford, *"Mouldings in Practice"* (Lost Art Press) which is possibly the most comprehensive instructional guide on molding design and layout in existence. The emphasis is really on good planning, and the need for accurate referencing.

From an introductory point of view there is little point looking at a wide range of different molding profiles when the two most important issues are:

- Understanding what you can and can't do with a molding plane and
- Understanding the methods that guarantee success.

Once these are established, no molding will ever be too difficult or too complex to make. It will just come down to the obvious maxim: Small, simple moldings are quick and easy, whereas larger complex moldings, take a lot longer to make. Best of all, you can choose which molding you want to make, and then enjoy the challenge of working to a high standard.

From a teaching point of view, the following information on molding methods is really just the tip of the iceberg, but it will get you started along the way. Once you've started, practice and experience will improve the final finish and reduce the time taken to produce beautiful molded profiles.

Beyond a simple ¼" ovolo there is a limitless range of moldings, varying in design and complexity.

Myth busting hollows and rounds.

To start off with I'll just bust a few myths surrounding these planes. Molding planes are versatile and will produce crisp corners and graceful curves, but they are not for removing a lot of waste. Furthermore, having a sharp well set molding plane does not guarantee good results. There is no point just attacking your work with a molding plane hoping to get a nice, even and professional looking finish. It's not going to work. There is a very well established method of work, and if you stick to the following principles and practices, getting good results is far more likely.

It would be sheer madness to whittle away at your work with a finely set molding plane without first removing as much waste as possible.

So, the first principle to put into practice is to remove as much waste as possible from the right places, using other means.

Timing is not just the secret of good comedy, knowing when to reach for a molding plane is going to make the difference between success and frustration for all your molding work.

The second principle has got nothing to do with the molding planes themselves, and it's this: Always remove the waste by the most efficient means possible, whilst still working accurately.

So let's just forget about fancy molding planes for a while, as there are other considerations of far greater importance before you reach for a hollow or round.

Every molding starts with a design, so let's look at how we produce this one.

I've marked out my plan for removing waste. There are many different ways to approach this.

It's important to cut the rebates accurately.

"It's much quicker to sharpen the straight cutter of a rebate plane than the curved profile of a molding plane."

Remove the waste to a plan

Every molding profile you could ever create with planes, will only consist of curves, transitions between curves and steps (or fillets). The real difference is just the amount of waste you need to remove, and the relative complexity of getting it out.

We have looked so far at rebate planes and grooving planes and it stands to reason that the cutting edges of these fairly simple tools are far easier to sharpen and maintain than a curved cutting iron. We must therefore rely very heavily on using these planes to full advantage as we remove the waste.

I would also suggest that you don't limit yourself to just planes. For a wide molding, you may be able to saw off a large amount of waste. (A circular saw could very well be the ideal tool for the job, as could a panel saw). Even more radical, perhaps ask yourself 'Can I split it off safely with an axe?' Follow the axe with a heavy wooden try plane and most of the waste could be gone in minutes! Would a very sharp gouge with successive heavy chops, scallop out most of the waste for a wide cove before you start? These are simple shaping techniques that we looked at in *Working Wood 1&2*. Heavy, coarse tools should do 95% of the work, and providing you work accurately, the last 5% can be removed with relative ease.

With the accurate rebates and grooves in place, sawing, chopping, splitting and paring are the most practical methods of getting rid of the waste quickly and efficiently. There is very little point in cutting any more grooves than is strictly necessary, when the wood in between will split out quickly.

Be very aware of the molding profile, but work on the waste for as long as possible. The closer you are to your finished profile, the better your molding planes will cut.

So there you have it, the real crux of the matter is invariably overlooked. From a purely practical perspective, cutting the waste out efficiently and accurately is the big deal, not the last few passes with some fancy molding plane!

Directional control

So, we have covered the area of waste removal, and you'll now understand my previous reference to timing. However, the next important aspect is more to do with setting up the work ready for a molding plane.

A hollow or round plane can be likened to a bobsleigh. If you have a pre-made track to go along, it's all good, and conversely without one you are in for an unpredictable ride.

Without some sort of track or groove, these planes have a mind of their own and will shoot off towards one side or another without the slightest provocation. So, after getting rid of the waste, directional control is the next big issue.

The answer is to deliberately form a 'pre-made track' exactly as per Cresta Run, as this will guarantee directional control of your plane. A bobsleigh has runners in pairs, and that is exactly what is required here.

TECHNICAL POINTER: *If by now, I have mentioned checking the grain direction so many times in so many Technical Pointers, that you are getting fed up hearing about it - just remember, it matters more than anything else, and most people forget this occasionally.*

"...after getting rid of the waste, directional control is the next big issue."

The narrow slot cut by this gauge (see page 42) helps guide successive passes with a rebate plane.

The bulk of the waste has been removed, but there is still more to go!

Now it's time to reach for the molding planes. A No.10 round, a No.12 hollow, and a No.16 round.

Suddenly, at seemingly the very last minute, the molding is transformed!

A hollow plane needs to run down a pair of edges that fall within the sole profile. This pair of edges will give you absolute control. In practice, a simple chamfer on a corner will do the job nicely for a hollow plane- it's really that simple!

A round plane needs to run down a groove, with the edges of the groove giving the plane the directional stability required. In practice, you can form the groove any way you choose. A plow plane will cut a lovely channel to run down, a rebate plane on edge will form a 'V' shaped groove which works fine, and basically any tool can be used that gives you an accurate slot or groove, referenced from the face or edge of the work.

So, working to your plan, you need to make sure that as the waste is removed, every curve is set up with a track for your hollow or round to run down. I've used a plow and a pair of rebate planes here to define the tracks. Top photo - It may look like enough waste has been removed here, but it's still not the right time to reach for the molding planes!

Finally, I've taken out about as much as I need to make the molding work quick and easy. A finely set rebate plane will allow you to further define the profiles, deepen the tracks, widen the grooves, etc.

In the bottom photo you can see the finished molding looking just like my initial sketch from page 128. The pile of shavings produced by the molding planes was a good few handfuls. However, the plow and rebate planes I had previously used produced a few good bucketfuls!

TOP TIP: *Just like the scrapers used for spoon carving, you can shape cabinet scrapers to suit the curves of a molding, which is sometimes very useful, depending on the grain.*

Here are some practice exercises using hollows and rounds, where the initial stock removal is limited so you can just get on with trying out a few molding planes.

We'll look now at how you prepare the stock for a simple round over, a simple cove or hollow cut, and then how the ovolo planes are best used.

Practice exercise 1: Using a hollow plane

I am making the assumption here that you have got your planes and irons into very good working order, sharpened and shaped as described on pages 155 to 170.

Take a piece of favorably grained wood and start your rounded profile with a chamfer on the corner. Make sure the chamfer is above the line of your finished round profile. With the chamfer in place, it's time for your No.10 hollow plane.

Some may advocate starting at the far end and taking a series of cuts, getting longer each time until a full-length shaving is taken. You can do this, or just start from one end and plane steadily and carefully right down to the far end in one go. Either way, plane off shavings until you get really close to your finished profile.

Listen carefully to the cutting sound. With the iron set to a reasonably fine cut you should hear an even 'hiss' out of the plane as you take a shaving, feeling no vibration at all in your hands.

If you hear lower notes you could well be taking too thick a shaving so back off the iron a little. (See pages 72 to 73 for cutting iron adjustments.)

By holding the body too upright or too low you could over cut the mark, or your plane could dig out a channel one side or the other depending how you have set up the iron. If you go too far, even with a simple round plane, you are going to need to plane the surrounding area down to recover from the mistake, or start again with new wood. Great care is required as you get nearer to completing the finished shape.

TOP TIP: *Hollow and round planes have no stops, fences or depth gauges. If you go too far with a hollow or a round, you are going to have to take action to recover, perhaps even starting again from scratch. Sometimes you can simply plane down the surrounding area, allowing you a second chance - a good trick to remember!*

"Listen carefully to the cutting sound."

After 7 passes with a wooden plane, I had removed enough of the corner to form a track for the hollow plane, without touching the arc I was aiming for.

If you plane a chamfer almost down to the top of the arc, you will see a pair of shavings emerge from the escapement with every pass of your molding plane. If you judge it right you'll only take one full width, whole shaving off your work right down the middle. To finish the molding you will then need to incline your plane by 15 degrees and take some off the top, and then do likewise with the lower section, carefully blending the passes so as not to get obvious steps.

This rounding process should be simple and straightforward, but it's still worth getting some practice in before trying it out on a project.

To cut a 90 degree round over, you will need to blend in successive passes at the angle shown above...

...through to the angle shown here. The difference in plane angle is around 30 degrees between the photos.

Practice exercise 2: Using a round plane

A round plane is going to create a cove, the opposite of a round, so mark this out first with a pencil gauge. I ran two lines down my stock with my pencil gauge set to around ¾".

If you reference the pencil gauge from the face and the face edge, you'll end up marking out a 45 degree cove. This is a good method to start with as cutting a regular cove is easier than canting it over at some arbitrary angle. There will be plenty of opportunities to experiment once you have a sound grasp of the basics!

Bearing in mind what we know about waste removal, there is a section on the corner (shown hatched) which can easily be removed with a bench plane.

Hold the work on a sticking board with a 45 degree timber screwed to the regular fence. This makes the whole job much easier. I'm using an angled support batten to lift the work up to the right height.

Tap the work so that the screw 'bites' into the wood, and then wind in another screw (at a slight angle towards the work) at the other end, just nipping it up tight.

Mark up both faces.

This is the waste I can take out with a plane.

Tap the stock hard up against a screw, so it bites in and grips the work.

The other screw needs winding in at a slight angle. This pulls the work piece in tight.

Take the waste off the corner, down to the gauge lines.

The slot cutting gauge is a very accurate means of giving the rebate planes directional control.

The corner of the rebate plane will follow the slot, getting deeper with each pass.

As this is a simple cove with no fillets (steps), it's best to remove most of the waste with a heavy chamfer. I'm using a heavy wooden try plane to hog off a lot of wood quickly.

Make sure the chamfer is even all the way down. Next, you could either set up the No.44 to plow an inclined groove almost down to your line, or you could mark a central slot with the inlay slot cutter from page 42.

I'll show you the slot cutter method, as it's wonderfully quick and the grooving method with a plow is self explanatory.

> **TOP TIP:** *If you use two rebate planes for this, you can alternate between left and right hand cuts, making it very easy to 'steer' the groove as you go down.*

Set your cutter to the rough center of the chamfer, it's not important to be really precise.

Now take a rebate plane with the iron just peeking out of the right hand corner, and run this carefully down the slot you've just cut, leaning it over at 45 degrees to the chamfer. Go nice and easy, not rushing, just make sure you follow the slot.

Take a second and a third pass, each time going deeper with more confidence. Keep your eye on the shape of the 'V' groove you are cutting. It needs to be even all the way along.

Keep a close eye on the final cove you have marked, switching to your second plane in order to remove the waste required to keep your groove roughly central in the cove.

Using the method of alternating between planes will allow you to widen and deepen the groove until you are almost touching the deepest part of the cove.

Finally, guide the round plane down the 'tram lines', again producing a pair of shavings, and then go really carefully down to the point of taking one complete full width shaving from each side. The cove is wider than the sole, as is often the case, so blend the cuts in so as to get a smooth and seamless transition with no steps or scoops.

TOP TIP: *When you are getting really close to your finished profile, retract the iron slightly with a couple of taps to the heel of the plane. Don't forget to re-tighten the wedge! The difference now is that the job is slower, but much more controllable.*

A Recap on the basics

Now that we have covered the basic operation and methods of using hollows and rounds, what we know is this:

1. Every molding must be planned, as this will dictate the position of the initial grooves and rebates.
2. Molding planes are for the last few shavings (5%), not for heavy stock removal (95%).
3. Each pass with a plane needs to blend in with the previous when a profile wider than the sole width is being created.
4. Hollows and round need a track to run down to give directional control.
5. The shape of the iron is very important to avoid 'dig ins'.

Switch between right hand and left hand set rebate planes...

...working almost down to the arc you are aiming for.

With a track defined, use the round plane and remove the very last few shavings, down to the line.

Preparing the edge for a reasonably large ovolo. As much waste as possible is removed first.

Blend in each pass with a finely set iron. This will give you a lovely, even curve.

"Adding fillets to a molding is when the fun really starts."

Practice exercise 3: Adding fillets

Adding fillets to a molding is when the fun really starts. It's not very far removed from what you've just done. A fillet is just a step somewhere in the molding. A classic ovolo profile is simply a rounded section with a fillet on each side. Fillets can be created as transitions between round and hollow profiles, and are used effectively as eye-catching features in many moldings.

We are now going to look at creating an ovolo with two fillets, using a bench plane, a rebate or plow plane, and the No.10 hollow plane. Have a go at this ovolo molding:

On a piece of 1" thick stock, mark out a pair of lines ¾" from face/edge corner.

1. Cut two rebates evenly on both sides, 3⁄16" deep.
2. With a bench plane reduce the middle of the round over down almost to full depth. This has created the all important 'track' to run your hollow plane down.
3. Take your No.10 hollow plane and form a rounded profile right down to the fillets. Go easy as you approach full depth, carefully blending in each pass.

Once you have formed a good looking ovolo molding to go alongside your previous cove, there is not a lot more to learn about hollow and round planes that can't be gained by experience. We'll now look at dedicated molding planes, which will only cut one profile.

Spring lines

Molding planes dedicated to a particular profile are said to be 'sprung' if they are designed to be used at an angle to the work piece. The spring lines are usually marked on the end of the plane as a guide for the user. Continental style planes are not sprung, so are used with the plane held vertically.

The plane iron is set at a bedding angle and the mouth of the plane is always going to be tightest at the lowest part of the sole. The higher up the plane you go the wider the mouth becomes. The 'spring' of a plane evens out the differences between the lowest and highest parts of the plane's profile, giving a more uniform mouth opening.

The advantage here is that the performance of a sharp plane is vastly improved by having a fairly tight and uniform gap in front of the iron, regardless of the complexity of the profile.

Another advantage with sprung planes is that if you can reduce the variation in profile of a plane sole, you also reduce the susceptibility to breakage and general wear. By this I mean that an obviously sharp and angular part of the plane sole is going to be more difficult to make, and it's also going to be more susceptible to damage from everyday use. A snipes' bill plane needs a lot of looking after for this very reason.

I prefer sprung planes as the irons are easier to sharpen, even when they are skewed. Skewed irons are a firm favorite in hollow and round planes, and many other wooden planes for that matter. A skewed iron will tackle the end grain far easier than a straight iron, but a word of caution, be prepared to sharpen up with monotonous regularity when you're working on end grain!

The cabinet work in the next part of the course will be based on the assumption that you have acquired a suitable pair of starter ovolo planes, new or second hand, and that you have also developed the skill to use them and the sharpening kit (pages 152, 169) to keep the planes in good order.

The 'spring lines' marked on the end of the plane, show the horizontal and vertical lines in use.

" A skewed iron will tackle the end grain far easier than a straight iron..."

On most cabinet doors, there's only enough space for a small ovolo - and that's why these sizes are important for cabinet work.

Ovolo planes

The purpose of combining different profiles into one cutter is to guarantee a quick and efficient route to a uniform profile. In doing so, the plane maker effectively dictates the exact profile that can be cut by a particular plane, almost to the exclusion of all others, thus creating a specifically dedicated tool. Uniformity in moldings is very important when it comes to getting corners to match, either internal or external, and planes dedicated to a single profile make this task a lot easier.

"Uniformity in moldings is very important when it comes to getting corners to match..."

These ovolo planes are just one example from the incredible range of different profiles that molding planes have been designed for. A typical cabinet maker's shop would have perhaps have a hundred or so molding planes, often in graduated sets for adding detail and elegance to their furniture.

The importance of acquiring ovolo cutters in these smaller sizes becomes very apparent when you consider the thickness of a cabinet door frame (shown above).

With an average of an inch in thickness and, say a variance of ⅜" up or down (i.e. ⅝" to 1⅜"), there is not much space to fit a molding with a radius of much more than ⅜". For this reason, a good set of starter ovolo planes could perhaps have irons selected in the range of ¼", 5⁄16" or ⅜" radius round cutters.

If you are interested in making larger framed doors, radii of ½" to ⅝" would not be out of place, and this may suit the front door of a house very nicely.

Practice exercise 4: Ovolo planes

These specialty planes are designed to form the same sort of profile that you created in the last exercise. They have a depth stop and also a side fence, and therefore it's far easier to get a good result without the risk of going too far.

For the sake of uniformity (which is definitely what we want), I'm going to recommend that you measure, mark and cut the rebates as the first operation, rather than just diving in with your ovolo plane with no preparation.

It's true that an ovolo plane will cut a good profile with no such preparation, save perhaps a chamfer, but get some solid molding success behind you before trying this, as it is quite easy to lean one way or another and make quite a mess of your wood quite quickly.

Measure your ovolo plane to get the dimensions of the rebates and transfer these to your stock.

Just as before, cut the rebates in the usual fashion, and chamfer the center as required. This needs to be quite a small chamfer as seen in the photo.

TECHNICAL POINTER:
Depending on grain direction, you may need to use the plow plane with long extension arms to cut the rebate on the face side of the work. Grain direction always dictates the method of work.

Now take the ovolo plane and using the fence and depth stop as guides, work the rounded part down to the required depth, being aware of the spring lines and the angle you hold the plane. You should get a nice even profile with no sweat or stress. That's the beauty of a dedicated molding plane - guaranteed results.

A small chamfer is just enough to guide the hollow part of the sole.

The ovolo plane will very quickly round over the central section, giving a very uniform result.

With no rebates, the cutter will need sharpening more regularly, but it's a quick method!

Practice exercise 5: Advanced ovolo cutting

Have a go at cutting an ovolo starting with just a quick chamfer on the corner of your work. The most important element for success is keeping the plane held steady at the correct angle to the work, according to the spring lines marked on the plane.

Conclusion

Well, if I was in a position to insist here, I'd be encouraging all of you to invest in a complete half set of hollows and rounds, not just the two I've mentioned in the previous texts on the subject. Making moldings is a wagon load of fun, and it's more like art than woodwork. Dedicated planes are enjoyable to use as well, so pick up a few nice decorative molding planes, if you get the chance, and get stuck in to sorting them out and restoring them to their former glory.

The most important thing to remember is that you need to plan the order of play for making the molding and then direct the majority of your effort and concentration into removing the waste - the right amount of waste, from the right places, in the most sensible and ergonomic fashion possible. This is far more important than the easy finishing touches with a molding plane!

However, the care and diligence with which you maintain and use your molding planes will always be evident in the finished molding. In the next part of the course, we'll be looking at how we combine moldings with joints and the structural elements of cabinet making. So between now and then I hope you take up the challenge of producing your own hand cut moldings, and better still, I hope you enjoy every minute of it.

"Grain direction always dictates the method of work."

Just for fun!

Quite often in older furniture, moldings and grooves were combined with some other decorative features, one of which is called 'dentil work', not to be confused with 'dental work', although the word has the same root (pun intended!).

Dentil work was carefully measured and marked and then either chiseled out or made using an alternating pattern of saw cuts to give a castellated effect.

Here's a quick and easy procedure that adds a nice bit of detail alongside a simple molding.

I've plowed a groove about 1/16" deep alongside a 45 degree cove, made using a No.10 round plane. A leather worker's stitch marking wheel is used to produce a series of pin marks evenly spaced along the length of the channel.

You then simply make a series of chisel cuts, at 45 degrees, using every other pin mark as a reference point. I've plowed a 1/4" groove and I'm using a full width 1/4" chisel. Make the cuts so that the very end of the chisel reaches a whisker over half way towards the next pin mark.

Reversing the direction of the chisel, you then chop down again at 45 degrees, so the cut releases a little wedge of wood, leaving a 'V' shaped pocket in between the untouched raised sections forming a nice set of 'teeth'. In the middle photo, I have made the forward and reverse cuts and I'm now carefully prizing out the waste.

A quick rub with some wood stain (I'm using a hard wax oil in the photo) and the contrasting teeth really start to stand out. You can include this detail as part of a cornice molding on the side pieces of a shelf unit, or anywhere else you like. The scale needs to be in proportion to the thickness of the timber used. Have fun!

The stitch marking wheel is a fast and accurate layout tool.

Use a chisel to match the groove size, and go in at 45 degrees. Keep the depth constant.

After the reverse cuts, pop the waste out carefully, cleaning up the 'V' shaped notches as you go.

Accurate layout is the key to this sort of work.

Molding plane restoration

Dismantling and cleaning

These instructions are aimed at fixing up molding planes, but a lot of the same principles can be applied to most wooden planes.

To get an old plane into serviceable condition, the first job is to get it cleaned up with everything fitting together as it should. See pages 67 to 74 on how to dismantle and rebuild a wooden plane. With the plane dismantled, use some methylated spirits or cellulose thinners to get the dark, ingrained grot off all the surfaces, including the wedge and iron. I use medium or fine wire wool as an abrasive, going fairly carefully so as not to wear away the wood. Wear gloves for this. The solvents are very fast drying, and once cleaned up and dry you can then give the plane a quick wipe over with some shellac. You can use a 2lb cut of button polish or garnet, depending on the color tone you are aiming for. Either way, work quickly and get an even coat over every outside wooden surface. Take care not to get shellac down the throat, but on the wedge is okay.

Wire wool is softer and much less aggressive than sandpaper. It also won't clog up and scrape the surface like sandpaper.

Check the wedge for a good fit in the throat. If it seems too tight you could make up a sanding stick as shown below, the same sort of shape as the wedge, with some 120 grit sand paper glued to it. Use this to relieve the tight spots in the throat. The wedge should slide in smoothly with hand pressure only. If it still jams then take it out and relieve the throat a little more with your sanding stick.

If the body of the plane does not look straight (sight down the sole too), you'd better go straight to the section on the facing page, 'How to straighten out a molding plane'. If all is well and it looks good and straight, carry on with the next steps.

Buff up the first coat of shellac with a piece of clean wire wool and then apply a second coat. Let it dry and then give this a light buffing, again with wire wool.

Once again using wire wool, remove any rust from the iron, and if the tang is crooked then straighten it out. Clear shellac acts as a good rustproofer for the iron. It's going to need more work to get it sharp, but a light coat of shellac is still a good idea at this stage.

Next, give the plane body a light coat of beeswax all over the outer surface, including the sole, and buff it up.

When the wedge and iron are in place you can apply a light coat of wax to the wedge, but only in it's assembled condition. You don't want to introduce wax in between the wedge, iron and throat, as the wedge may then have a tendency to work loose. To get the iron super sharp see chapter 8, page 151 for an introduction to sharpening molding plane irons.

Not as good as a plane maker's float, but a sanding stick is quick and easy to make.

There is a clear bend in this plane - Ideal for a demonstration!

How to straighten out a molding plane

Before you launch into any restoration of an old molding plane, it's always worth checking that the plane is not rare and valuable. A valuable plane is often only valuable in it's original condition. Once you have done your restoration work it may then work beautifully as a tool, but it's value may have been reduced one hundredfold. So please check before you start.

Most second hand molding planes are old and will often have worm holes, cracks and perhaps some twist or wind. A molding plane that is curved is not uncommon, and left uncorrected, it will never perform as it was supposed to. The good news is that fixing up a bent molding plane is not a big deal. You'll just need your shop made scratch stock (type 1, page 48), a good selection of files (see pages 152 to 153), a bench plane, perhaps a rebate plane, plus an hour or two of careful attention.

I found one with a significant bend, which is ideal to demonstrate how to fix this problem.

> **TOP TIP:** *Re-working a bent old plane is your only option if you want to get it into good working order, but remember to work with the grain. You will probably need to use a bench plane and a rebate plane, so get these sharpened up and set the irons for a fine cut before you start.*

The first step is to flatten the main body. Work on both sides, and check your work with a straight edge.

The No.4 plane may leave a few little undulations, so give it a polish up with a very finely set block plane if you need to. Check again and use a scraper for the final finish.

With the body flat and straight, restoring the sole is the next task.

Fixing the sole

The sole of the molding plane in this case is made up of some flat sections (side fence and depth stop), and a concave central section. Before setting to with a rebate plane or anything else, the first job is to make a cutting blade for the scratch stock that exactly matches the sole. This does require some care and attention and the procedure is described on the next page.

A 12" rule is straight enough to check the flatness.

A block plane will smooth out any plane marks or...

..alternatively, use a finely set cabinet scraper.

The body is now flat, but the sole is still curved.

Black in the steel blade with a pen.

Trace the profile onto the steel.

This process involves tracing the profile of the sole onto a piece of steel scraper blade, and then filing it to the same shape.

- Use a marker pen to blacken the end of the steel. (This is the same as dabbing on some 'engineers blue'.)
- Use a scriber to trace the profile onto the steel.
- The profile should be clearly visible.
- Use a combination of coarse and smooth files to get the profile close to what you want.
- Check the profile against the sole of the plane.
- Pay particular attention to the sharp corners.

TECHNICAL POINTER:
As you approach the correct profile, the last few strokes with the file need a lot of care and attention. You have to keep the file flat (horizontal) across the end of the steel when it's in the vise. A 90 degree corner will act like a scraper in two directions. Conversely, if the edge is out of square the scratch stock will only cut efficiently in one direction - which could be useless if that one direction happens to be against the grain!

This is a close up of the tracing. I'll file down to the dotted lines shown on each side

File down to the lines you traced, and then...

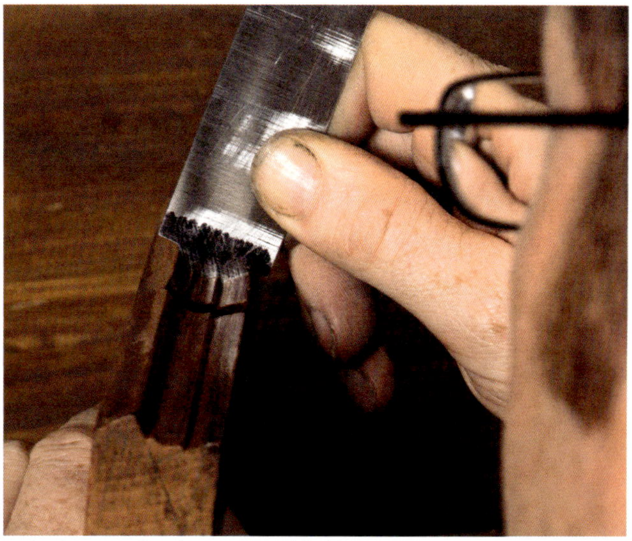
...check to see if you've got a good fit. If not, more careful filing is needed.

The ovolo profile of this plane has a built in fence which touches the side of the work piece, and a depth gauge that touches the top surface of the work piece. In this case the body is now straight, but the fence is still curved. The arrows in the photo below show where it needs a little planing to straighten out the fence. Get the fence straight with a rebate plane and then work on the depth stop, which may also need a little attention with a rebate plane.

The scratch stock now needs setting up to achieve the right match for the sole profile. This is where you set the scratch stock blade in the correct position in the holder. A quick look down the sole will tell you which areas need working down, and which area is much closer to the correct profile, which in this case is the middle. This means that towards the middle of the sole you will be taking off the least amount of material. For this reason, set the scratch stock blade to line up perfectly with the profile around the middle of the sole.

To check it slide it along and it should start to drag and scrape at the parts of the sole that need to be removed. Reset if necessary, and check again. When you are sure that you will be working on the right areas, only then start to slowly work away at the areas that need reducing down.

The old hard beech of the wooden plane body should produce fine shavings, so don't expect this to be a quick and easy operation. The scratch stock will take the sole down to the right profile, but be careful around the mouth of the plane. You don't want to snag the grain or the blade will skip. Work slowly and carefully, raising the scratch stock up a little if you need to. Do not try to take off too much in one go.

TOP TIP: *It will really help to apply a little wax to the sole as you work. The blade will take most of it off on the next pass, but it will make a much smoother job of it.*

The red tape shows the high spots on the fence.

With the fence straight, I'm now working on the depth stop.

This is where you find out if you have filed the cutter correctly. Go easy and don't force the cutter, you are scratching the surface, not excavating wood!

It's taken some work, but the plane should now be totally straight...

...and ready for use! Hurrah!

Once the sole is scraped down to the right profile, put a thick coat of wax on the sole and work it into the grain well. The same abrasive green cloth can then be used to remove the excess wax and buff the sole. Two coats of wax will do the job nicely. Some people recommend sealing the grain with shellac first, and you can do this if you like, but frankly, I don't think it really matters. The sole should now look straight.

Finishing the plane

There is a good chance that the body of the plane, where it has been planed to flatten it, will be a lot lighter in color than the rest of the body. This is not something to worry about, as you've just rescued the plane from the kindling stack. Even so, you can use some garnet shellac (page 399) on the pale wood to introduce a good color tone to the bare patches. A light coat of beeswax will give the plane a nice sheen when it's buffed up.

Conclusion

If you've run into difficulties with any of this, it's likely going to be down to the shaping, filing and setting of the cutter in the scratch stock. You can re-set the cutter and take off a few more shavings. It's worth persevering for the sake of the plane. This is definitely not a slap dash job. It takes care, patience and a lot of attention to detail. The only real way to learn is to have a go, and always take off less rather than more. It's easy to take off a few further shavings, and doing this is certainly a lot easier than putting a few shavings back on.

Restoring molding planes is well within the abilities of nearly every wood worker. It's a challenge, it's fun, and you get a lovely plane at the end of the job!

Section 4
Chapter 8 Sharpening curved plane irons

Amongst all the tools and machinery at any woodworking show, it's always guaranteed that there will be booths from several businesses selling sharpening equipment. Of course each manufacturer is selling the 'best' equipment -electric grinders, Japanese water stones, oilstones, diamond 'stones', the list goes on.

A sharp iron leaves a lovely finish.

But I have noticed that very often an issue that is not well addressed is the provision of tools for sharpening curved plane irons. This is probably not always going to be the case, as the resurgence of interest in molding planes is bound to catch the attention of the tool makers sooner or later. It's true that a range of slip stones has always been available, but what are the best methods and practices for sharpening curved irons?

There are several DV.Ds available describing different approaches to sharpening molding planes, but the processes described do have a level of laborious complexity that could put you right off the whole concept. It's not that the methods shown don't work - they really do, and are demonstrated by excellent craftsmen for whom I have a lot of respect. If you casually delve into the many books on old hand tools, the whole subject area is often conspicuous by it's absence, which is curious.

I'm going to introduce some very general sharpening tools and methods that make sharpening molding planes a very straightforward business. Perhaps of greater interest to some, I'll also show how some special purpose equipment can be easily made, and used to great advantage, bypassing the need for anything other that a few bits of wood, some emery paper and some nice, soft leather.

If you thought sharpening a curved iron was never quick and easy...think again!

General sharpening tools

For any serious joiner, cabinetmaker or general woodworker getting tools sharp and keeping them sharp is always going to be high on the list of everyday priorities. This means that every woodworker must have a reliable methodology and system of sharpening, for every kind of cutting tool that they use. The set described here is an addition to the previous set of sharpening tools covered in ***Working Wood 1&2***, which were primarily for sharpening straight edges. This further set deals with sharpening curves, and also specifically the curved irons found in wooden molding planes. The list of equipment is not exhaustive, but will get you started on shaping and sharpening the profile cutters covered in this book. The method for using this equipment is given on pages 161 to 170. The shop made specialist sharpening gear introduced on page 169 should be seen as a further addition to your sharpening set, and not any kind of replacement.

Older plane irons were often made of two different pieces of steel. A very hard piece of tool steel was forge welded to a much softer backing piece. The softer part of the back of the iron extended right up to form the tang. In the top photo, approximately the top third is defined by a faint joint line, above which is very hard tool steel. This is an important factor to consider as we look at sharpening curved plane irons.

Steel files

These steel files will cut the shapes in the scraper blades, modified to match a given molding profile, for use in the scratch stock.

Depending on the hardness of the steel, you may be able to reshape molding plane irons with these fine cut files. As with most tools, cheap files will perform badly so buy from a trusted manufacturer with a good reputation, and you will be able to shape even fairly hard steels.

About 1/3rd of the way down the thickness, the faint line shows the laminated hard steel face.

Buy the best files you can - the hardness makes them cut well and last longer.

"...getting tools sharp and keeping them sharp is always going to be high on the list of every day priorities."

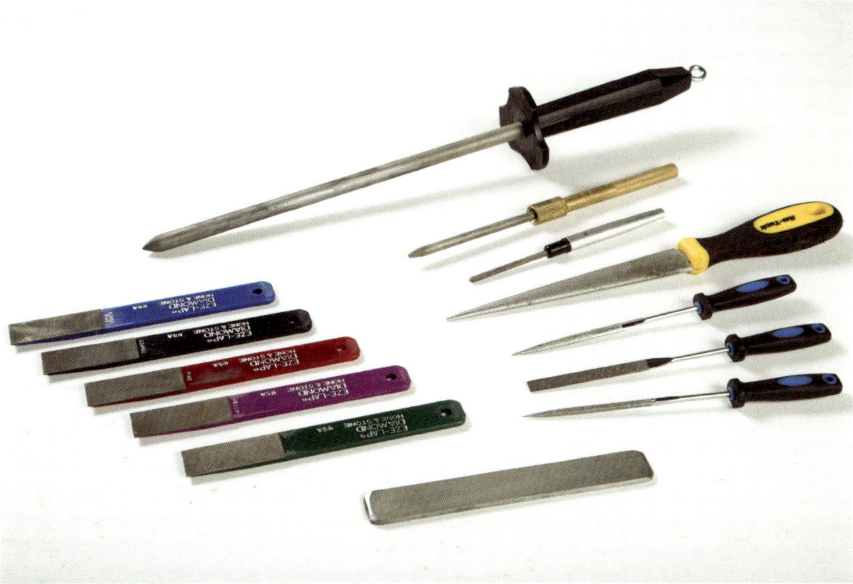

This is a selection of the diamond files that I use.

This is a small, round diamond file made by Eze-Lap. It cuts slowly but leaves a very fine finish!

Diamond files

These files are my 'go to' collection whenever I need to cut really hard steel. The performance is far superior to an emery slip stone, and they'll happily put a keen edge on a 'glass hard' piece of hacksaw blade, or any other steel cutting tool. Diamond files will leave a surface that requires a good honing with ceramic slip stones.

Emery slip stones

The shapes and sizes of emery slip stones can vary considerably. The 'standard' cross sectional profile is usually that of a 'tear drop'. With some stones, the cross sectional profile decreases towards one end, allowing a large range of curved cutters to be ground. However, this is not a tool to be used vigorously in long sweeps, or you will invariably remove too much metal from the center of the iron. Instead, careful strokes should be used to refine the cutting edge evenly across the whole width. Always lift up on the return stroke or the sharp edge will damage the slip stone. Several different grades are available, but a stone of around 600 grit will probably be the most useful if you are not going to invest in a few diamond files.

I use these with a little soapy water to lift off the fine cuttings.

This is a coarse round stone. It cuts fast but wears down quickly.

Ceramic slip stones

These little fellas are very brittle. Go easy with them. Don't clink them together or drop them. These slip stones are not for shaping steel, however, they are super hard and will leave an exceptionally fine and smooth surface. Use these with a gentle pressure in long even strokes. The white stones here are around 1500 grit, which actually gives a high polish even before stropping.

A set of super fine ceramic stones will take even hard steels to a high polish.

Marker pen

When marking up steel for reshaping, a permanent marker can conveniently take the place of a little bottle of 'engineers blue' marking fluid. Generally speaking, I'm usually working on small areas so a bit of judicious scribbling gives me a steel surface that easily shows up scriber marks.

A cheap permanent marker pen takes the place of 'engineers blue' marking fluid.

Scribers

Hard steel scribers are ideal for marking out steel cutter profiles. Depending on the purpose, I'll use a standard scriber similar to a sharp steel pencil, or a purpose made scriber for carefully following an existing profile. I put old hacksaw blades or files into a hot fire, and leave them there until the fire goes out. It makes the steel soft enough to cut with a hacksaw before shaping and sharpening. Heating once more and quenching in water then produces a glass hard steel, which certainly benefits from a gentle tempering.

A conventional scriber, a shop made scriber, and some samples of the tool steel I use for cutters.

Profiled strops

Regardless of the sharpening method, curved irons are best finished off on curved strops. This set here will do fine for the molding planes I've recommended you start with, but if you acquire more planes, you will need more strops. (See page 174 on how to make these.)

These are the strops for the planes I have recommended.

Some ingenuity is required to get a good hold of the iron whilst working on the flat face...

...and I find a stack of rare earth magnets is ideal.

Initial restoration of curved irons

There are three initial steps to take with any curved iron before you consider starting on the sharpening stage proper (covered on page 167). These are:

1. Polish the flat face.
2. Match the shape and check the bevel angle.
3. File a relief angle.

After this has been carried out, we'll then look at two different methods of sharpening, first using the general set of sharpening tools, and then a very fast and easy method, using shop made tools.

I'll demonstrate the steps on a larger ovolo cutting iron, but bear in mind you use the same process on any curved iron.

(1) Polish the flat face

Polish the flat face, just as you would do with any bench plane iron or chisel. This means working your way down to successively finer grits, from 220 grit to 1200 grit, using 'wet and dry' silicon carbide paper.

The problem with small irons is that they are difficult to hold, and even more difficult to keep absolutely flat against the abrasive paper. You definitely don't want the narrow irons to rock from side to side, which can be quite a challenge.

Placing a piece of flat glass on a piece of ⅛" steel plate will allow you to hold the plane iron with a few rare earth magnets, and at the same time the magnets pull the iron down onto the abrasive paper thanks to the steel plate under the glass.

I keep a tray of water alongside where I'm working as this washes the emery papers and keeps them wet, ready for use as I work down the grades.

TOP TIP: *If your iron has been attacked by a previous owner in a rather unsympathetic manner, the flat face may not be flat in the slightest. It may have been rounded over towards the cutting edge. If this proves to be the case (you'll know very quickly by looking at where is being abraded), place a thin wedge to the side of your emery paper. Rest the tang on the wedge and as you move the iron in a circular motion, allow the tang to move up the wedge, as you go around in circles. As the tang moves up and down the wedge, this tilts the face of the iron, in a sort of rocking motion. This allows you to get a high polish on a slightly curved 'flat' face.*

The wooden wedge lifts the tang a little, which is sometimes exactly what is needed.

TOP TIP: *The old 'stack of magnets' trick works really well when sharpening on diamond 'stones', as they are made of nickel plated steel.*

The magnets apply quite a lot of downward pressure, as well as being a useful holder.

This is a small, ¼" ovolo plane iron before restoration.

...and then after a good polish up.

This is a larger ½" ovolo iron.

After working through the grades of abrasive paper, Polish up the 'flat' face on a leather strop, and you'll be ready to work on the bevel.

These three photos illustrate what you'll probably start with, and what you're aiming to achieve.

(2) Match the shape

Before we even look at how to sharpen the iron, the very first job is to check the shape of the cutting iron. To do this, insert the iron into the body and set it so it best fits the profile, as you sight down the sole.

TECHNICAL POINTER:
Hollow and round planes are slightly different, as the profile needs to be 'feathered out' at the edges. See pages 163 to 165 for details about this.

In the case of the iron in the middle photo, the very best fit I can get is still just not good enough. You can see it's uneven, protruding out too far on the right compared to the left.

Use the black marker pen to put some ink down by the cutting edge on the flat face you've just polished up nicely.

The matt black ink of the permanent marker allows the sole profile to be traced on to the iron using a shop made scribing tool. Using a standard scriber will not allow you to scratch a line that truly represents the sole profile, as you would only be able to trace the pattern around the mouth. Add to this of course, the fact that you would need to hold the scriber at some arbitrary angle, and it's obvious that a different solution is required.

Adjust the iron for the best match possible...

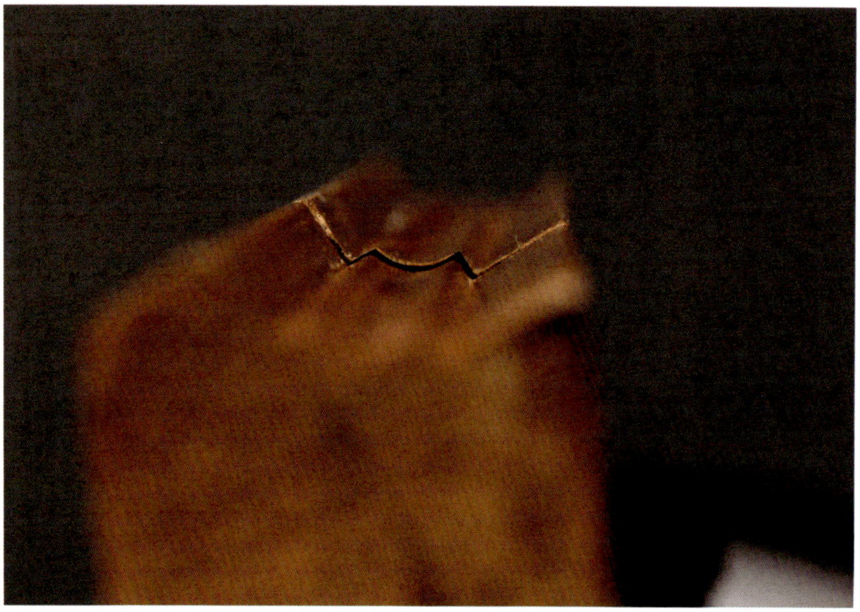

...then check if you need to match the shape of the iron to the sole.

This iron needs a little attention.

Use a marker pen to 'black in' the end.

With the cutter in place, scribe the sole profile on...

...so it's clearly visible when you retract it.

The tool for the job is easily made from a piece of old hacksaw blade. I used quite a large blade, (thrown out by a local steel fabrication company) so I have plenty to hold on to whilst marking. You could easily use a piece of cabinet scraper sawn down to size and filed to the right shape.

Fit the iron in and set it up protruding a little, and go for the best match you can with the sole, as in the previous photo.

Now take your shop made scriber, and carefully follow the profile of the sole, transferring the profile onto the iron by scratching the black ink on the iron, using the sharp end of the scriber.

With the profile clearly marked, the next step is to file the iron down to the lines you have just traced.

TECHNICAL POINTER: *The shape of the end of the scriber is very important. It should have a 'V' shaped underside all the way to the point where it meets the slope at an angle of about 30 degrees. The 'V' shaped underside ensures it will get into the sharp corners.*

Take the edges right down to the lines.

Use fine diamond files for all the work on the edges.

Diamond files

With better quality irons, the process of hardening and tempering will have been very controlled, producing a cutting edge that lasts well. The only drawback for us is that there is a good chance that even the best quality steel files will skate over the super hard cutting edge to no avail. If this is the case, I strongly recommend you do not soften the iron by heating it up with a gas torch. It's just not necessary.

These days, a wide range of diamond files is available that may be used to tackle even the hardest of tool steels. The diamond files are great for getting the iron into shape, but they are often too coarse for any kind of sharpening.

Keep the file as flat as possible, at all times!

File a flat edge

Working carefully, file off the steel right down to the scriber line, keeping the file dead flat across.

This will result in a very blunt end to the plane iron, however the shape will match the sole perfectly!

Again, take your marker pen and just dab some ink on the flat blunt edge. This will give you a very clear reference to work to as you create a relief angle on the back of the iron.

You will be left with a dull, steel edge.

> *"I strongly recommend you do not soften the iron by heating it up with a gas torch."*

Black in the edge, all the way across.

A good set of files will cut the bevel back to the right angle, but will probably just skate over the hard cutting edge.

Cut the bevel to the right shape.

All we have done so far is cut the front face of the iron down to the right shape, so it's now time to work on the bevel. You need to ensure that all the surfaces on the bevel, curved or straight, are filed back to an angle of around 25 degrees. I use a single cut mill file, as shown above, to remove the soft steel from the back of the two part laminated iron. A round file will work on the curved part of the bevel. This is really a restorative part of the process, and once shaped correctly, the iron can be sharpened dozens of times before needing to repeat this step. The front third of this particular iron is very hard and so can only be shaped by using diamond files.

(3) File a relief angle

A 'relief angle' is formed when the very edge of the bevel is cut back and shaped using diamond files, removing the very last traces of the marker pen applied to the blunt edge, shown on the facing page, bottom right.

It is this very small section of the iron that is worked on during every day sharpening, and the rest of the bevel, having been cut back to the correct shape, is left well alone.

Diamond files will cut the hardest of steels.

Use a combination of appropriately shaped diamond files held at a little over 25 degrees (there is no point in refining the whole bevel) to follow the exact profile you need, almost removing all of the black pen on the very end of the iron. A traditional corundum slip stone will work too if you've got one and you're keen to use it. Sharpening is the next stage and we cover this on page 166.

TECHNICAL POINTER: *After shaping the iron, filing a relief angle is the first stage of the sharpening process. The slope should always be at a tangent to the edge you are working on. If you are putting a relief angle on an iron with sharp 90 degree corners, make sure the slope direction also changes by 90 degrees.*

I've cut the front edge right down to the last trace of black marker pen. It's ready sharpen now.

"Filing a relief angle is the first stage of the sharpening process."

Compare the sharp corners in this photo to the final profile, bottom far right, overleaf.

The problem is illustrated nicely on the left side of this iron in this photo.

"I don't believe there is ever a need for the edges of a hollow iron to come to sharp points...."

Matching the shape - hollow and rounds

While we are talking about matching the shape, it's worth a quick look at hollows and rounds before we get to the two sharpening methods.

Unlike any other sort of molding plane, hollows and rounds are designed to be used at different angles to the work, as opposed to holding the plane to a fixed 'spring line' or holding it flat against a fence. A simple molding often requires a 90 degree round or cove, but the sole profile will only cut 60 degrees, or less, of this. This obviously means that multiple parallel passes need to 'blend in' very smoothly, with no steps or undulating transitions. I therefore recommend that you feather out the edges of the plane iron. This may well seem unconventional to some, but I find it works incredibly well.

Rather than either a hollow or a round iron coming to an abrupt end at each side of the profile, it's far better to reduce the effective cutting width to perhaps ¾ of the maximum. In practice, this means that the edges of the iron, despite being razor sharp, take off virtually no thickness of shaving at all.

I don't believe there is ever a need for the edges of a hollow iron to come to sharp points, as you are not going to need to get into tight, acute corners. I can guarantee you will find hollows and rounds far more controllable and enjoyable to use when you make the profile adjustments I'm suggesting here.

Shaping round planes:

Step 1 As we did previously, black in the end of the iron with a marker pen and, with the cutting iron in place, sight down the sole, getting the iron aligned, tight, and protruding slightly.

Step 2 Take the purpose made scriber and trace the sole profile onto the iron. You will need good eyesight and a strong light source to see the line.

Step 3 Remove the iron and working carefully on the far left and right edges, file a slight curve, dropping the shape below where it 'should' be on both sides.

Step 4 Replace the iron and check if you have 'feathered out' the edges. If it all looks good, you are ready to sharpen up. If not, repeat the above steps as required.

The shop made scriber is the ideal tool for the job. Black the end of the iron in first.

Work the edges of the iron down further than the scriber line to feather out the cutting surface.

The finished shape - Notice how the iron disappears into the sole at each side, this completely changes the way this type of plane performs.

Shaping hollow planes:

Step 1 My advice here is to get the iron out of the plane, get your diamond stones (or whatever you chose to use) on the bench and get those sharp, pointy corners off! Use a coarse stone first and round them over slightly. Include these feathered edges when you sharpen and polish up the iron.

Step 2 Replace the iron and go through the checking and adjusting procedure until you are sure that there is no way those nasty corners are ever going to dig into your work. You do need to make sure that there is a smooth reduction in protrusion of cutting profile at the edges. Again, 'feather out' the profile to nothing, don't just come to an abrupt stop.

For me, this slight feathering really does make hollows and rounds a joy to use. You are now ready to get the irons sharpened up to a gleaming finish and that's what we'll look at next.

Get those nasty sharp corners off! Use a coarse stone initially.

After some rounding and polishing, this is the profile you are aiming for.

Sharpening follows matching the shape. In the photo, I've set the iron out further than I would for normal use, just so we can see it. This iron is good to go!

Sharpening

Lets get back to the ovolo we started with. You've now got an iron that is matched perfectly for shape but it still needs a good keen edge putting on it to work properly.

Incidentally, you should not expect to need to re-match the profile very often, unless of course you make the mistake of being a little heavy handed and inconsistent with your routine sharpening.

The secret to routine sharpening is to work carefully and attentively, treating the iron with a lot of respect in the sure knowledge that if you over cut the profile at any one point, the whole iron will need taking down to the depth of the mistake you just made. So, please go easy on the irons and they'll give you no trouble!

Every so often you will need to 're-grind' the primary bevel at 25 degrees across the entire width of the plane iron. When the part of the cutter with the relief angle is perhaps more than ⅛" wide, that is the time for a re-grind. You may need to use a combination of steel or diamond files for this, and afterwards, matching the profile as previously described may again be required. To start with I'll go through the common procedure of sharpening up using the general set of sharpening tools.

Step 1: *Diamond files - carefully!*

Step 2: Ceramic stones to polish up the edge.

Here's a photo of the edge after using the ceramic stones. - Nearly there!

Method 1: General sharpening tools

This traditional sharpening method does require a great deal of care. Without a lot attention to detail and patience, it's very easy to unwittingly change the shape of your iron.

Holding the iron in a vise, the curved bevel is worked on with files and then slip stones. The sequence of operations follows the exact same mantra of 'grind, hone and polish', introduced in *Working Wood 1&2*.

Step 1 For this step, I'd say you can't beat using good diamond files. 'Everyday' sharpening means working only on the very small section at the end of the iron defined by the relief angle, removing an equal amount of steel from all of the secondary bevel, following every curve and corner. The trick is to file right down to the cutting edge, then just about touch it, removing steel from the edge with light even strokes. This will form a very slight burr.

TOP TIP: *Take as little metal off the cutting edge as possible. Put your finger on the flat face and draw it back over the cutting edge (very carefully), feeling for the fine wire edge you are aiming for. The wire edge should just about be detectable as a roughness on the edge. The wire edge should be as even as possible.*

Step 2 After the diamond files have been used to get a fine burr, further refinement is needed and ceramic slip stones work very well for this. Good quality ceramic slip stones are both super hard and super fine. There is no need to work on the whole bevel, just the little secondary bevel (the relief angle) so lift the back of the stone here just a whisker so you can simply polish all of the diamond file marks off evenly. This stage is finished when the areas you have worked on look shiny and polished.

Step 3 The final finish is obtained by the use of a shaped leather strop coated in buffing compound (I use 'Grey' which equates to 12000 grit). You can either polish up with the iron held in the vise, or with the leather strop in the vise and the iron held at 30 degrees.

With care and attention almost any curved cutting iron can be sharpened using this method. For more complex irons, the obvious difference will be the time taken to sharpen up, and quite possibly also the range of sizes and shapes of diamond files and slip stones required. Have a go, I can assure you that with the right tools and a good helping of patience, none of this is beyond your capabilities. As with pretty much every other aspect of fine woodworking, get good before getting fast!

A shaped strop can be used like this, or...

...this way could be easier.

With either method, you will get a very well refined cutting edge that will cut very nicely.

This is some of the sharpening set that I use for my molding planes.

It's a simple enough principle: The abrasive surface matches the curve of the iron.

Method 2

This second method of sharpening up curved irons needs to be preceded by the 'once in a blue moon' restorative processes of polishing the flat face, matching the shape and filing a small relief angle on the iron.

I have to say that this is by far the quickest and most efficient method of sharpening I have ever come across. With a little practice, you will find that you can easily keep an exact shape to within very high tolerances using this method.

Is it really this easy?

Comparing Method 2 with Method 1, I have simply replaced the diamond files with 180 grit emery paper and the ceramic slip stones with 600 and 1200 grit emery paper. The real time saver is that the abrasive paper is glued to a channel, or held on a rounded surface that closely matches the curve you are working on.

In practice, there must always be enough clearance for the iron to not touch the entire width of the sharpening media, all the way across, at any one time. This gives you a bit of 'slack in the system', and makes the process more controllable, not less.

For both rounds and hollows the iron can be 'steered' in either a channel or along a dowel allowing you to vary the pressure to the left or right. This creates a lot of flexibility for correcting mistakes and importantly, helps you avoid making them in the first place. You can check at any point by replacing the cutter back in the plane, and eyeing in down the sole.

With experience, you'll get very fast at this.

It's quite likely that your collection of molding planes will grow as you use them more and with new planes, you will also need to add to your collection of bespoke sharpening strops. The correct strop is simply selected according to the profile you need to work on.

A brief demonstration

For hollow planes:
(They cut a rounded profile)

Hollowed profiles need to be sharpened on something circular. It could be dowelling, quadrant molding, or shop made, round nosed profiles. If you make up a 'loop' of abrasive paper, there is no need to actually fix the abrasive paper down. The loop slips over the dowelling (or whatever), and is held in place by something heavy (I use an old steel bolt), suspended in the hanging loop. This set up can be held in the vise, making it very easy to change over the grade of emery paper.

I sometimes use a loop of 120 grit sandpaper for some restoration work, as it cuts the tool steel quickly, even if it leaves a coarse finish.

As one part of the emery loop dulls and gets worn out, just rotate the paper loop so you get a nice, sharp, fresh surface. In this way, the entire surface of the paper can be used for sharpening.

The very last stage of the process is simply to polish the curved iron on the strop, with no emery loop at all.

I have a good range of circular profiles that I use for the final polish of molding planes. Each one consists of a simple wooden holder wrapped in soft leather. These circular leather strops all function as a backing support for the emery loops I use.

Start by selecting a strop which fits the cutter. Adjust the cutter angle to about 30 degrees to check.

Slip the strop into a loop of emery paper and pop a heavy bolt in to give it some tension.

Draw the iron back, lift it off and repeat. Swap the paper over, getting finer each time.

Polish up the cutting edge.

It does not take long to get a good polish.

You can make strops to suit most shapes and sizes of cutter you could ever need.

In summary the steps are:

Step 1 Select the right sized strop for your iron, slip the 180 grit emery paper over, and set up as previously described.

Step 2 Carefully draw the iron back towards you, keeping an even pressure on the strop and aiming for an angle of around 25-30 degrees. The angle I'm holding the iron at in the photos is obviously less than this, but that is simply because I lift up the iron as I draw it back, ending up at around 25 to 30 degrees. It's just a quirk of my particular technique, as I'm so used to doing this with chisels and straight plane irons.

Step 3 Swap to finer grits and repeat. I usually use three grades, depending on the condition of the iron: 180 grit, 600 grit and 1200 grit.

Step 4 Remove the last loop of emery paper, apply some buffing compound, and finish the iron off on the leather strop.

I'll just point out that you don't need to polish up the whole bevel, it's only the very edge that really matters.

TOP TIP: *This method also works for complex molding irons. You just need to select the profiled strop that best matches the curve that you are working on.*

For round planes:
(These cut a hollow profile)

A round plane iron needs to be sharpened in an abrasive channel. Details on making these channels are on page 174. You need to select the curved channel that fits the radius to be sharpened. Secure it in the vise.

Step 1 As before, you start on the coarser grade, removing just enough metal to get a fine wire edge.

Step 2 Move down the channel to the next grades of emery, concentrating on honing up the very edge at an angle of 25 to 30 degrees.

Step 3 Finally, use the concave strop to polish up the edge to a nice silvery gleam.

The materials for making this sharpening kit very cheap and once you've collected together the emery paper, glue, soft leather and some profiled sticking or moldings, it's all quite straightforward and quick to make. You may struggle to believe this, but using profiled strops has reduced my sharpening time for hollows or rounds down to about a minute all in. I'm not sure if there is anything quicker, but out of personal curiosity, please let me know if there is!

Ovolo cutters

Using the procedure outlined in Method 2, I use the round strops to sharpen the curved part of the cutting iron.

For the flat sections, I use my diamond stones.

It is then back to the round strop for the final polish.

One channel with three grades of emery glued down. The matching leather strop is in front.

Hollows and rounds are very quick to sharpen.

Sharpen up one side of the cutter...

...and then the other side.

The channel is sawn out to between 110 and 120 degrees to compensate for the sharpening angle.

A handy strop for ovolo cutters

This is not a necessity, but serves as an example of how easy it is to use a little ingenuity when it comes to sharpening.

I use 120 degree double sided strop to polish up both flats of the ovolo cutter simultaneously. The 120 degree angle will approximate to 90 degrees at the points of contact of the inclined iron.

Moving to the side of the strop, I then use a matched rounded profile for my most commonly used pair of ovolo cutters, which are $\frac{1}{4}$" and $\frac{5}{16}$" for cabinet doors. Each side of the strop has a different radius of curvature to match the aforementioned cutters.

There is no reason why you could not make a similar shaped piece of wood and stick three grades of emery to it. Now that would make sharpening ovolo cutters even easier!

Having understood the principles, I'm sure many of you will develop all manner of curved strops and profiled sharpening tools.

One side of the strop is for $\frac{1}{4}$" radii and the other is matched to $\frac{5}{16}$". This strop replaces...

...both of these.

You need some simple materials to make some special tools.

Making hollow and round sharpening tools

What you'll need

Wood for the round irons

Some knot free, straight grained pine, poplar (tulip wood in the US) or some other wood that is easy to work. For each radius of cutter you will need one piece, about 2ft long, 2" to 3" wide and for the thickness choose something about ¼" thicker than the width of the molding cutter.

Wood for the hollow irons

As I mentioned earlier, choose dowelling or some other product with the right radius of curvature. For each size, a 6" long piece will be required. If you intend to make strops for very small radii, dowelling is too flexible to be any used on it's own. See the facing page, top, for how to get around this. The dowelling needs to be a slightly smaller diameter than the profile that your molding plane cuts. This takes into account the additional thickness of the leather that gets wrapped around it, and the important clearance needed at each side of the iron during sharpening.

Leather

Choose a soft and pliable grade of leather, not more than $\frac{1}{16}$" thick.
If the leather is too thick or inflexible, you won't be able to bend it easily over the curves and hollows. Thin leather also has the advantage of not allowing the cutting edge to 'sink in' very much, which sometimes is the cause of the cutting edge folding over, reducing the angle and the ease of cutting.

Glue

A new tube or tin of contact adhesive is what you'll need. Make sure it's not an old can from the back of the shed, as the solvents will have caused the glue to thicken, and you really don't want lumps when your sticking down some fine leather.

Buffing compound

Grey is fast and cuts the steel back to a high polish.

Three Grades of Emery

Buy in some sheets of 180, 600 and 1200 grit emery. You'll need a craft knife and a straight edge, as you are going to cut the sheets into strips.

This is the sort of profile that works for smaller hollow planes or ovolos.

Just wrap the leather round, stick it down, and identify the size the strop is made for.

For hollow plane irons

These are very simple to make as each one consists of a short piece of dowelling with some soft leather glued around. Choose your dowelling to suit the sole of your plane.

Fix the leather in place with contact adhesive, and trim off any excess leather.

Give any strop you've made a liberal coating of buffing compound and keep them in a drawer or box, out of the way of sawdust and shavings.

For small radius hollows

I should point out that below ⅜", dowelling becomes impractical due to it's flexibility. However, a purpose made block is easy to make. Use a 6" piece of 2" x 1" timber and plane a low angle chamfer on both sides. Round the top over with a finely set plane, finishing it off with a careful sand down. This will provide a good support for the leather, which can now be glued down.

Round plane irons

I would advise you first go through the process of sharpening your molding plane using Method 1 on page 167. Once you have a modestly sharpened iron, you can easily make the shaped abrasive channels shown here.

Each profile of round iron needs to have it's own sharpening tool, and once made, it makes sharpening a round plane very easy and quick.

This is where you will need the 2ft long pieces of wood.

In principle, the first job is to carve out a groove slightly wider than you need in a piece of suitable, knot free wood. The full procedure for this is given overleaf.

This procedure is for using the round plane to create the cove channel.

1. Take the 2ft long batten of, say 2" x 1", and run a slot down the center with the inlay slot cutter.
2. Next, follow this with the corner of a rebate plane to widen the slot, (see page 135, 'Cutting a cove') and lastly, use the required round plane to plane an even, hollow, cove profile all the way down the batten. You will need to plane a groove slightly wider than the iron width so you have a little slack in the system. To do this with your hollow plane, press your plane slightly into each side of the channel, inclined over a little, and you will widen the channel easily.

TOP TIP: *If you think that the cove channel you've just cut would benefit from a good sanding down, as you are making matched pairs of hollow and round strops, the matching round strop used with some sandpaper will work for this.*

3. Depending on the size of the iron relative to the batten, you may need to put a steep chamfer on both sides of the cove with a bench plane.
4. Cut strips of emery. I recommend 180, 600 and 1200 grits. You'll need three strips, one for each grade, at 6" long.
5. Cut off a 6" long piece of your planed wood as this will get covered in soft leather for the strop.
6. Cut your leather to suit with a sharp layout knife.
7. Now apply contact adhesive to the emery, the leather and both long and short bits of wood.
8. When just about tacky, start at the far end of the long batten and glue down the 180, 600 and 1200 grit emery in that order.
9. Stick the leather down to the short batten, making sure it's pushed well into the curved channel.

Start the cove cut with the slot cutter, follow it with a rebate plane and then your No.10 round plane.

With the channel cut, chamfer down the edges, as you can't have a flat surface each side.

Slice up the emery paper on a scrap board.

Cut off the 6" piece for the leather strop.

Glue down the emery and leather strips.

Smooth down the leather, pressing it firmly into the channel using a piece of scrap leather.

This is how the emery channel should look. Note the steep chamfer on each side.

Having an easy method to keep your irons sharp will put a smile on your face!

TOP TIP: *Use an offcut of leather to smooth down the emery into the glued up channel.*

When it's all set, the sharpening tool is ready for use and you can try giving the iron a really good hone and polish. Load up the leather with some buffing compound and you're good to go.

You simply start on the coarse emery, drawing the iron towards you a few times, at about 25 degrees, until you can either see or feel a slight burr.

With the iron lifted up a fraction, move onto the next emery, and so on, finishing up on the leather. You should end up with a very even looking, mirror polished iron. This will now cut beautifully!

Conclusion

I hope that the clear explanation of sharpening curved irons, combined with the simple methods, will inspire you to get a few molding planes and give it a go. There is something very satisfying about planing curved profiles, especially with well adjusted and razor sharp planes.

A full set of matched profiled strops is quite straightforward to make, and I suspect that once you've tried sharpening a profiled cutter using the set, you'll never do it any other way again. Shaped strops and abrasives are simple to make, and with a little imagination they can be suited to all manner of cutter profiles. The whole process of sharpening suddenly becomes very quick and efficient, and quite simply - enjoyable!

In *Working Wood 4 - "Cabinet Making Techniques"*, you will rely heavily on the new sharpening tools as you make an elegant cornice, entirely by hand, fitted to a sturdy traditional wall cupboard.

Section 5: Traditional jigs and devices

We all like to make life easier for ourselves. Designers and makers produce things that are ergonomic and practical, and then as consumers, we surround ourselves with them, arranging everything ergonomically. It's why cups, kettles and tea bags all live in close proximity to each other - you just know it makes sense. In the workshop, we follow the same patterns and steadily acquire the things we believe to be most important to our work. Perhaps a century or so ago, a typical cabinet maker would be in no doubt as to what was needed in the workshop. These days it's all a bit different, as good results can be achieved using a very wide variety of power tools. This section of the course will, I hope, bring back a bit of clarity and serve as a window on the past and a very empowering glimpse into the future. There are so many holders, clamps, gadgets and gizmos, which undoubtedly transform the tricky or mundane aspects of furniture making that to try to get by without a good selection would be thoroughly counter-productive. Jigs and devices can also give hand tool methods a new lease of life, fully complementing a workshop full of machines. They don't replace machines, but they will certainly give you more options!

Shooting a miter is easy with a well made jig.

Lots of time and effort can be saved through machining wood and often this may be the best way to get the job done. I find it a very rewarding process, to be able to make a lot of progress quickly through using mortising machines, band saws, routers etc., but the main purpose of this course is to provide a good grounding in hand tool woodwork. In the specialist realm of cabinet making, a thorough understanding of hand tool methods is very useful (if not essential), as it furnishes us with the knowledge of how to do the job properly with the right procedures and processes, in the right order. Armed with this excellent background knowledge, using machinery takes on a new purpose, which is to facilitate the high standards of craftsmanship, that you already have a confident grasp of. It is these high standards of craftsmanship that the following jigs and devices will help you attain.

Introducing jigs and devices

General work holding

Vice jaw protectors

These are very useful for protecting your wooden vise jaws while you do some light metal work at your bench. See page 188.

Vise jaw protectors.

Saw horses

There are many designs for saw horses, and so long as they are the right size, good and sturdy, the design and construction is of little consequence. The saw stools shown here are screwed and glued as well as having a lot of mechanical interlock. The hardwood gusset plates are just for added strength, taking the 'belt and braces' approach. They do allow a much greater load to be placed on the stools and prevent the splay from widening in both directions as they are loaded up or dragged across a rough concrete floor. See page 193.

A sturdy pair of saw horses.

Clamp bar guides

When you want to clamp up a box or frame of some description, a common problem encountered is where to set up for clamping. Your bench is usually not ideal and the most important thing is to set up on a perfectly level surface. If you don't do this you'll glue and clamp a twist into your project, the consequences of which are usually disastrous. When used in conjunction with saw horses, a pair of clamp bar guides will allow you the convenience of establishing a perfectly flat reference plane upon which your project may be placed with confidence instead of apprehension. The wedge shown here allows you to level up the clamps before you start to use them. See page 211.

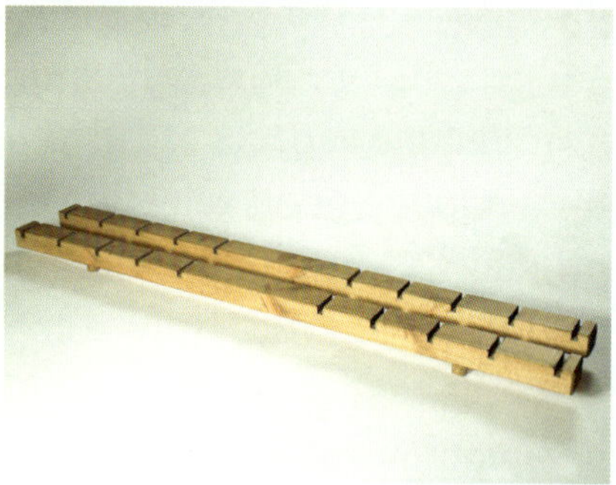

Clamp bar guides, simple but very useful!

Caul clamps

A set of these clamps is a cabinet maker's best friend. Whether you are working with thin stuff or slightly heavier boards, these clamps will hold the ends of the work absolutely flat. This will allow you to mark the joints accurately, then saw and chisel the waste out without excessive vibration. You can also use them when gluing up panels to make wider boards as they will take out all mismatch in edge alignment and bow as the sideways clamping force is applied. These clamps have their origins in the realms of veneer work, and later in the course we'll be using them for this as well. See page 219.

Adjustable caul clamps.

Bench work holding

A shop made, pop up bench dog.

Bench dogs

The bench dogs shown here are very easy to make and live in the bench top, out of the way until needed. You just pop them up with a screwdriver when you need them and then tap them back into the bench when you're done. I don't think it could be any easier. See page 231.

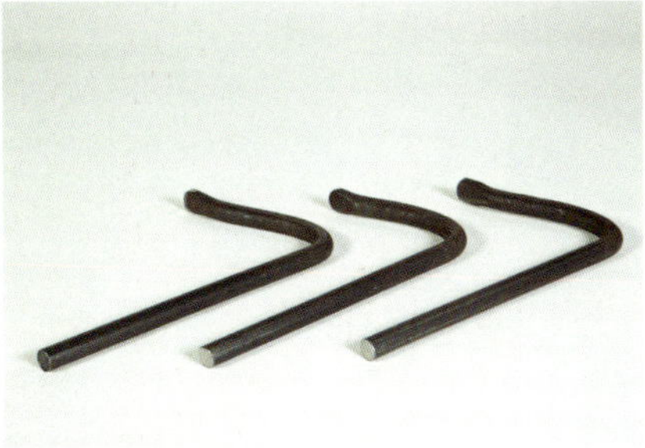
Hold downs are fun to make.

Hold downs

These are an ancient design. There are engravings from medieval times showing the carpenters bench with bent iron hold downs. They are fairly simple to make, for perhaps three bucks, and there is also a good range of very well made hold down clamps at wood working stores. They cost a bit more but you may find them more convenient to use. See page 239.

An extra leg for your bench.

Extra leg

This is something you definitely can't buy in the store. With one end of a wide board or plank held in the vise, it fulfils the purpose of supporting the other end while you plane or otherwise work on the board. It's fully adjustable up, down, left and right. See page 247.

Sticking board

Very few old examples of these devices are around today. To the untrained eye, these simple holding devices would have looked like tatty old scrap wood, full of nail holes, hammer marks and probably not a second thought was given as they were cut up for firewood. However, a sticking board will hold your stock solid and true in a way that no bench vice can. See page 261.

Long bench clamp

There are several different ways of preparing the board edges for gluing together, and so far we've looked at holding them in the vise. However, for larger boxes, chests or cabinets, holding the boards in the vise is not an option. This device will clamp two boards, side by side and allows both edges to be planed at the same time. It's also useful for rebating, grooving and molding work, as it will hold not only the work, but also guides and spacers for working efficiently. For instructions on how to make it, see page 263.

This is my sticking board. I modify it to suit the work in hand.

A long bench clamp has many uses!

Other workshop devices

Shooting stick

This is just a simple device to keep your bench plane perpendicular to the work piece. I have not yet met anyone who can plane the edge of long, thin stuff, keeping the plane at a perfect 90° all the way down the board. This device just clips onto your plane and makes the job easy. See page 283.

Tapered sliding dovetail jigs

This is a pair of jigs that will allow you to cut dovetail housing across the width of a board, and the corresponding dovetail on the end grain of the shelf for example, to be fitted into the housing. I prefer to cut a tapered housing, as it is just as easy to cut as a parallel housing. The added advantage is that it only tightens as it is tapped towards the front of the joint.

They are fully adjustable for any taper you will need to cut. See page 299.

Diagonal sticks

This device will allow you to check for square inside a cabinet, even after all the clamps are in place. I find clamping up a cabinet, box or chest can be a bit of an ordeal if you can't easily check for square. The sticks are extended right into opposite corners for a quick comparative measurement. See page 273.

Winding sticks

These are very handy when you want to test a board for twist, or 'wind' as it's sometimes called. The 'white' lines are created with stringing/inlay, fitted into a narrow groove. You simply place these at the front and farthest ends of the board and sight down to see if the contrasting lines are parallel. See page 293.

This a very handy device to keep your plane level.

I've used utile for these jigs as it stable and takes a good finish.

Diagonal sticks. If you need to work on large cabinets, just make a longer pair.

These are made from oak, fumed with ammonia to darken the wood.

A left handed badger plane works well for shooting end grain.

The 'sanding plane'. It's great for small moldings, no matter how complex.

Shooting boards

This is almost a whole subject area in it's own right. I know of no woodworker who can quickly convert a rough sawn board end into a trued end grain edge without the laborious and iterative process of repeated checks for square. The finest of craftsmen would not waste their time demonstrating their planing prowess just for the sake of it. Thankfully, a well made set of shooting boards will allow a relative novice to true up a cross cut board end, putting either a miter angle, a bevel angle or a perfect 90 degree angle on the board end in no time.
I will quite often use a heavy wooden badger plane (a left hander) with a shooting board, as the width of the cutting iron and extra weight allow 2" thick end grain to be trued up with relative ease.

The function of a shooting board remains the same, regardless of the arrangement of the angles, shoulders and sliding track. In principle, a hand plane is placed on it's side on the sliding track, the wood is held firmly against a stop, and provided that the plane is adjusted correctly (page 244 of *Working Wood 1&2*), the edge can be trued up to the desired angle. The most common angled cuts are 90 degrees, 45 degrees on the miter or 45 degrees on the bevel. If you ever need to make wooden hoppers or beehives, you'll find a shooting board can be easily knocked up to allow you to shoot a compound miter ready for dovetailing. (Note: The compound geometry dictates the need for both a left and a right hand device.)

Although the angles and configuration are dictated by the basic purpose of the shooting board, the scale of the device is really down to the size of the board you need to fit on it. Bear in mind that you always need some 'run in' and 'run out' on top of the maximum width of board, so always incorporate this in the design dimensions. I have a huge shooting board that is a skeleton frame of batten and plywood, allowing me to shoot about 2ft of end grain. I have several smaller shooting boards in daily use, depending on the type of work I'm doing.

TOP TIP: *With every shooting board that follows, it should be noted that you can always use a 'sanding plane' on any work with fragile edges, molded work and the like. The sanding plane will not break out any end grain edges and can be used across the grain, with the grain and against the grain at any angle.*

The challenge in making shooting boards is to have enough patience and perseverance to get them made to a high degree of accuracy. A shooting board that is reasonably close to 90° is quite useless, as you will build the inaccuracy into every cabinet you make. Doors won't shut properly and things just won't line up as they should. Be very aware of this before you start, and be fully prepared to adjust or remake any critical part as many times as you have to, to get the angles spot on.

Sliding fences - every time!

My justification for sliding fences is simple. If you know that you are going to break edges out at the back of the cut with every swipe of the plane, this limits the way you can use the work piece. You never want broken out edges on show. The alternative is to use a piece of sacrificial batten every time you shoot end grain. Either way, it's an issue you have to address. See page 324.

Large shooting board

When you need to shoot the end of a wider board or small table top, you need to apply more effort and travel further with your plane than you do with smaller work pieces. This large shooting board allows you to do just that. It fits onto the saw horses with locating dowels, and as you hold the work piece with your knee and left hand, you can take a good shaving off a long wide board without too much trouble. I keep this next to my bench hung on a 'French cleat'. See page 331.

Small shooting board

This is probably used more frequently than any other jig in my shop. Every end grain cut is finished with a couple of quick shaves with a plane, just for good measure. This shooting board works with the bench hooks and so several dimensions need to match. The support for the wood is the same height off the bench as the bench hooks and the sliding fence matches the back stops on the bench hooks. This allows longer lengths to be supported as the ends are planed. Having shot the end grain of the parts to be dovetailed, you'll find accurate marking out of the tails and pins much easier than running your pencil or knife over the uneven and ridged saw marks left over from cutting to length. See page 343.

Miter shooting board

This is for trueing up a 45 degree miter, as used in the corner of a picture frame, or perhaps an architrave around a door. Technically, you don't need this jig for the projects in this book, but once you have one of these you'll be surprised how useful it will become. However, you will need it for trueing up sawn cornice, and also for making the bevel shooting board. It's part of the full set of shooting boards, and a full set is worth having as this will give you the greatest flexibility in your cabinetmaking. In the next part of the course, you may want to embellish a door panel with an applied molded profile, and you'll learn how to do this using a miter shooting board. See page 349.

Bevel shooting board

The good old 'Donkey's Ear' as it was called. This is a jig that would guarantee a perfect fit for molded profiles round plinths or facing up work. The traditional joiner would fit skirting boards to perfection very quickly with a Donkey's Ear and a sharp plane. My preferred variant seen here, allows for easy work holding, particularly on longer lengths, as they just lay flat on the bench, supported by a bench hook. I haven't seen this type elsewhere, but I'm sure it can't be an original design. See page 361.

Bench hooks

I always like to have a set hung up near my bench. For all accurate cross cutting work, the marking knife, square, tenon saw and bench hooks are assembled. Whether I set up 2 or 3 bench hooks really depends on the size of the work piece, or if I'm cutting tenon shoulder lines. Either way, the very fact that you can get a good grip on the work and hold it dead steady gives you a lot of control when crosscutting. See page 379.

Chapter 9
General work holding devices

I probably use the equipment listed in this section more than most of the other jigs and devices in this book, save perhaps a couple of shooting boards. The vise jaw protectors have saved my nice oak vise jaws from all manner of wear and tear, or more accurately, irreparable damage!

Apart from the saw horses, I hang these items on the wall to keep them out of the way, and within easy reach. Making this equipment is all good practice as some of the methods may be new to you, particularly the compound angles in the saw horse leg joints. However, I'm sure you'll find it all very useful as you see how the various devices work together.

The saw horses, clamp bar guides and caul clamps all fit together. Ideal for cabinet making!

Vise jaw protectors

I like the flexibility of doing the odd small metal work job at my woodworking bench from time to time. I'm quite often working with plane irons, brass plate, threaded bar, etc., so I use a second set of jaws to make sure my woodworking jaws don't get chewed up.

Prepare the plywood

I won't give a materials list for this, as you just need a couple of plywood pieces and some quadrant as shown in the photos. This is a quick and simple project with no tricky bits. As with all projects involving plywood, it's best to start off by planing all the saw marks off the edges with a bench plane. I also put a slight chamfer on all the edges and corners as well. You'll need a sharp and finely set plane for plywood. Either plane the two jaws separately or clamp them in the vise as a pair.

TOP TIP: Always skew the plane, heel down and toe up, to chamfer plywood. It will cut smoother and quicker.

Mark and cut the quadrant

Fitting quadrant on two sides allows you to install the jaws quickly every time you need to use them.

Put both plywood rectangles in the vise so they rest on the two tubular slides of the vise, and clamp them up.

Take two pieces of quadrant, rest them on top of the wooden jaws and mark a line where they need to be fixed. While you are at it, mark the position of the vertical quadrant, as shown in the photos on the right.

You could miter the pieces of quadrant at the corner, or just give one of the pieces a round over. To mark the round over, butt up the vertical quadrant against the long piece and draw the curved shape of the vertical piece onto the underside of the horizontal quadrant.

Cut the vertical piece to length with a dovetail saw. Next, round over the end of the quadrant. The quickest way is to take a ¾" chisel and just pop the end off, which will take most of the waste off in one go. Finish it off with a flat file, sweeping an even curve to match the line you marked, as shown on the opposite page, top left.

Clean all the saw marks from the edges of your plywood.

Give every edge and corner a slight chamfer.

Choose the best position for the quadrant...

...and mark up ready for cutting and fixing.

Round over the quadrant, or miter the corner.

Drill holes and the pins won't split the quadrant.

A good smear of glue is all you need.

Line up the quadrant with your pencil marks.

Pull the pin out at the first sign of trouble!

Use a punch to sink the heads in a little.

Fixing the quadrant

These jaws are going to need to last, so I recommend you glue and pin the quadrant to the plywood.

Take a $\frac{1}{16}$" drill bit and drill four holes in the long horizontal pieces and two holes in the short vertical pieces. Keep the holes $1\frac{1}{4}$", or so back from the ends. Splitting the quadrant is what we are trying to avoid and drilling small pilot holes pretty much guarantees this won't happen.

TOP TIP: Always drill though into scrap wood rather than your bench top!

TECHNICAL POINTER: Drill at something like a 70 degree angle as shown, this helps the heads of the pins to sit flush with the curved surface.

Run a fine bead of glue onto the underside of the quadrant, and then pin it in place, on the lines you marked out.

TOP TIP: Whenever you use panel pins, ALWAYS have a pair of pincers on hand. This will stop you from ever trying to straighten a bent panel pin and risk splitting the quadrant.

Punch the heads in just below the surface with a nail set.

After a light sand down with 120 grit sandpaper you're ready to stain up and seal!

Finishing

In principle, most shop made equipment will benefit from some colored dye and a protective finish. The wood dye is really just for aesthetics. See page 394 for more information on wood finishes.

Don't over do the wood dye!

Coloring with wood dye

Use spirit based stains to mix up a color you are happy with and then add some white spirit. Use a fixed recipe if you want to exactly reproduce what you have mixed.
I have a jar labeled 'Standard Bench Brown' which is what most things around the workshop get covered in when I don't want just pale wood showing. Keep your mix in a jar with a good seal. Brush it on sparingly so the surface is well covered but not glistening wet. If you just dip your whole brush in the jar, it will be far too much so just touch the bristles into the dye to start with. You are aiming for an even coat that dries very quickly. Any runs or puddles are a sure sign you have used far too much dye.

TOP TIP: If you have any doubt about your ability and experience with wood dye, have a clean cloth on hand and as soon as you have stained the whole item, quickly rub it down to remove all excess dye from every surface and all the corners. This will speed up the drying time but will give a lighter final color than omitting this step.

The short brush for the sealer...

Leave this to dry thoroughly. This could take between 30 mins. and 4 hours depending on the temperature and humidity of your shop.

Protective coating

I like a hard protective coating on anything that's going to get a lot of use. There is a wide range of products you could use. I'm going to recommend that you use a clear, cellulose sanding sealer for a few reasons. It has a low surface tension when it's sufficiently dilute, so it covers and spreads very easily. It dries to form a clear hard shell that resists oil, white spirit and alcohol (from shellac). The best thing is that unlike varnish, it dries very quickly. When using it have plenty of ventilation as the fumes are noxious.

TOP TIP: Keep your cellulose sanding sealer in a jar with a lid that you can fit the whole brush in. That way, you never need to clean the brush. This principle applies to any other product you may use frequently.

...allows the brush to live in the jar!

Work quickly and plan how you are going to let it dry before you pick up the brush. I like to do edges first and then the back, resting the good face downwards while the back dries, usually in about 10 to 20 minutes. Then reverse the jaws and seal in the good face, watching out for runs on the edges.

My vise jaws drop down lower than the main screw of the vise.

My vise

I fitted a set of fixed wooden jaws to my vise (made from 1⅛" solid oak) that not only overhang 2½" to the right, but also protrude down by over 1" past the bottom of the casting, as you can see in the photo here on the left.

For this reason, I made my secondary jaws the same shape by cutting out a recess.

The wooden vise jaws have been on this vise for years, and they still look fairly new. The reason for this is that the vise jaw protectors have been used for all my hacksaw work, steel filing, cutter shaping, etc., and from the photo below, they certainly look like they've seen some active service.

I used an auger in the corners to make it easier to turn the corner.

I allowed for the extra depth of my vise jaws, so I could remove this part.

My 'not so new' vice jaw protectors are obviously doing their job!

Saw horses

Over the past 20 years, I have made several different types of saw horses, sometimes in a real hurry. They have mostly been rough and ready, fired together with heavy screws and plywood. I even made a two-legged set once that just leaned against a wall, and with a heavy plank between them, doubled up as a work access platform. The set that lasted the longest were jointed and braced like the ones shown here. These are not the rough and ready type and so I have every confidence that these will last you many years.

"I have every confidence that these will last you many years."

The splay of the legs is combined with a shouldered housing joint, but the joinery is not difficult. The hardwood brace is snugged up tight under the cross member preventing any sideways movement and these features make the legs totally rigid.

The dimensions I've given work fine for me, and I certainly would not want them any smaller. If you want to scale up the whole job, or lengthen the cross bar, go ahead, but either way you are going to a need a strong set of saw horses for making the cabinets we work through in *Working Wood 4*.

A matched set

These saw horses also form part of a matched set of workshop devices, designed to fit together. You'll see how some clamp guides (page 211) and a large shooting board (page 331) fit onto the saw horses (but not at the same time), so bear this in mind if you change the dimensions drastically. You need a minimum of two of these, three is ideal and four is even better.

The clamp bar guides fit straight into location points in the saw horses.

What you'll need

Planed timber:

2"x 3" softwood - 4 pieces at 21" long.

4" x 3" softwood - 1 piece, 28"

1" x 2½" x 6" hardwood - 2 pieces

Also:

Wood screws: 2½" No.10's - Qty: 16

Exterior wood stain and a brush.

Procedure

We're going to go through the procedure for cutting and fitting one leg joint in detail, but in practice, you'll need to repeat all the steps with all eight legs as you go. You'll find it an advantage to carry out all similar operations at the same time, rather than systematically cutting and fitting one leg at a time.

Mark and cut the leg shoulders

The shoulders on the legs actually bear the whole vertical load that you will ever put on them. Conversely, without these shoulders, the fixing screws would rack and shear with excessive loading.

1. Stack your legs together flush to the tops as shown, and mark a line 3" down from the top.
2. Set your Sliding Bevel to a slope of 1:4, and mark 2 legs as 'left' and the other two as 'right'.
3. On the left pair, mark a 1:4 pencil line sloping down to the left.
4. On the right pair, mark a 1:4 pencil line sloping down to the right.
5. You have just marked the shoulder lines, so square a short line down at each side as shown.
6. Having defined your shoulders, you now need to mark out the depth of the cut before you take out the waste wood.
7. Set your marking gauge to ½" and run a gauge line around, with the stock on the same face as your shoulder line.
8. Don't forget the end grain!

Mark the first line 3" from the top. All shoulder lines will slope down, away from this line.

Remember for all your leg joinery, the right pair will be the mirror image of the left pair!

Mark the depth using a gauge, then run a pencil down the line to make it easier to see.

That's the leg marked out!

Start with a knife cut...

9. To ensure a neat shoulder, create a knifewall with a marking knife and a shallow chisel cut along the length of the knife line.
10. Now take a good sharp panel saw or tenon saw, and cut right down to your gauge lines.
11. If the grain is straight I like to split the waste off with a 1" chisel.

...and form a knifewall.

TECHNICAL POINTER:
Never split the wood right on your gauge line, but instead stop a 1⁄16" or so above. You run the risk of cutting too much off or splintering out wood fibers well below your gauge line, which you really want to avoid.

Saw down to your gauge lines with a panel saw or tenon saw...

...then split out most of the waste with a chisel.

Pare down close to your gauge line, steadying the end of the chisel with your thumb. This will give you plenty of control. Work slowly and carefully and of course, you'll keep your left fingers and thumb safely behind the cutting edge at all times.

For the finishing cut, set your pattern-makers router right on the gauge line. Take steady, sweeping cuts keeping plenty of pressure on the left hand side of the router as this will guarantee a final surface, totally parallel to the reference face. If you don't have a pattern maker's router then simply pare down with a wide chisel.

Any small marks left by the router can be levelled off with a sharp float.

Set out and cut the parallel housing

The sides of the housing are parallel, but the depth needs to increase towards the top of the cross member, so splay the legs out.

On the top of the cross member mark a line 4" from each end.

Now offer up the leg to line up with 4" line on the cross member and the leg shoulder tight up against the underside.

With a sharp pencil draw a fine line down both sides of the leg to indicate where the housing is to be cut.

Square these pencil lines across on both the top and underside of the cross member.

Hold your work in the vise and pare down close to your line.

The wide sole makes this job easy.

A float is also a good smoothing tool.

Hold the leg to coincide with the 4" pencil line (on the front face of the 4" x 3"). Mark the housing.

Mark all the leg housings, joining the lines across the faces, and mark the depths as described.

For each leg, make a knife nick on one side...

...and then the other side. You can just see the ⅝" depth line on the underside of the cross member.

Next, you'll need to mark the depth of the housing which, remember, is deep on the top and shallow on the underside. Using the marking gauge set at 1¼", score a fine line on the top between the two lines squared across in the previous step. Set the gauge to ⅝" and repeat on the underside.

To accurately define the side walls of the housing, offer up the leg again and make a knife nick each side as shown.

"...mark the depth of your housing which, remember, is deep on the top and shallow on the underside."

Angle the knife slightly towards the waste as you make the first cut.

The knifewall is next.

For a good tight fit, you'll now form knifewalls on both sides of the housing, using a marking knife, sliding bevel and chisel as shown.

What you can't see in this photo sequence is that I'm actually marking and cutting all four housings at once. It's always more efficient to carry out all similar operations at the same time.

As you saw down, repeatedly check the depth of the saw cut to make sure you don't go deeper than the gauge lines.

TOP TIP: If you have a knot in the housing, the best way to tackle this is to put several saw cuts right through it. You will then be able to chop through the knot with your chisel without tearing out too much grain at the full depth of the housing.

Cut the side walls of the housing, 1¼" deep on top, ⅝" underneath.

A few saw cuts will deal with a knot in the housing.

Don't break out the back edge...

...switch around and come from the other side!

The gap you can see is supposed to be there!

The next stage is to close the gap - see overleaf.

All four legs and housings need to match up.

Pare the waste out to get a reasonably flat bottom to the housing. Work carefully down to your gauge lines. Don't use a float again for the final finish and don't get it looking beautiful as there is a little more work to do yet.

A trial fit will tell you all you need to know. You are aiming for a snug fit on the sides of the housing. The leg should not at this point meet the bottom of the housing all the way across. There should be a triangular gap as you can see in the middle, right photo.

With the housings completed, the top of the cross member should now look like this. (Bottom, right.)

Compound angles - two stages

The legs fit into housings which we've cut parallel at first. To get around the geometry of a two directional splay on the legs, the housing needs to slope in two directions. This could be cut in one stage, but for the purposes of a clear explanation, I've shown the job in two separate stages.

After you have completed the first housing you may well want to cut out a few steps and cut the other three compound housings in one go.

TECHNICAL POINTER: If the leg is too tight, do not be tempted to drive it home with a mallet and a block of wood. The legs need to come in and out a few times during the next steps and all you will do is breakout the top surface of the wood. If a leg is just a little too tight, set a sharp plane to take off a fine shaving from one side of the leg and go for a succession of trial fits until you are happy.

Cutting the compound angle

Without wanting to cloud this process with an explanation of 3D geometry and intersecting planes, suffice it to say that to get a perfect fit in the housing you need to compensate for the splay in two directions by following the next steps:

With the cross member in the vise, fit the leg so it sits well in the housing, just touching the inside edge.

With a pencil and square draw a line parallel to the inside of the leg. It will probably be around 3⁄16" tapering to nothing. Mark an identical triangle on the other side of the housing.

Use these lines to guide a series of saw cuts (I'm using my dovetail saw in the middle photo).

Carefully chop out and pare down to your new lines.

You can see in the photo, bottom right, that I have finished cutting housing 'B' but only marked housing 'A'.

The leg should now fit very well, as seen from above. That is all there is to it. There is one more adjustment to make for a perfect fit - trimming the leg shoulders as shown opposite.

Mark a line parallel to the leg, tapering to nothing, from right to left in this photo.

A series of saw cuts is a good way to release the waste and mark the depth.

Start to chisel out the waste...

...working down to the lines...

...for a good snug fit.

This is the next gap to close.

Mark the undercut with a ruler or try square.

Pare the end grain of the shoulder at an angle.

The small gap from the top photo has now been closed completely.

Adjust the shoulders

With the leg fitted in place, there should now be no gaps except for on the inside of the leg shoulders.

This should only be a small gap so scribing an off set line, perhaps a little more than the thickness of a try square blade, will serve as a guide. You can then undercut the shoulder with a chisel, as shown in the photo, bottom right.

A sharp chisel will peel off fine wedges of end grain leaving a cleanly cut surface . Don't actually cut the shoulder line or you will create a visible gap.

For a final fit, put the leg back in the housing and check all around. There should now be no gaps in the joint. At least, that's the theory anyway!

The next part of the process is to fix the legs to the cross member. As we are not making fine furniture right now, a handful of heavy screws will do the job, so we need to mark out where they should go.

Mark and drill the screw holes:

Heavy steel screws are a good choice to fix the legs on place. For some reason my father keeps jars of old slotted screws, probably from the 1950's, and he likes to use these instead of the modern pozi-drive, or Phillips head screws (I guess he's never going to throw them out!)

I always go for modern cross head screws, as they have a very high tensile strength and I can put them in quickly with a cordless drill.

To mark the holes start by transferring the shoulder line to the outside face of the leg. Use a pencil and a sliding bevel set to 1:6. This approximates to the splay of the legs with the measurements given.

From the corner, mark a line at 1:4 with a pencil and sliding bevel.

Parallel to this outside line, mark two further lines. The first 1" higher and then a second 1½" further up, as shown.

Mark center points on the top two lines to indicate where to drill the holes.

Note: If all this measuring and alignment seems a bit much, just grab the drill, grab the screws, and stick 'em in wherever seems good to you.

To make sure the screws go directly into the cross members, the holes in the legs need drilling at the same angle as the 1:6 line in the photo (middle right). You may find it easier to put the leg in the vise so as this line is vertical, and then drill straight down.

Countersink the holes so that the screw heads will be slightly below the surface.

"...my father keeps jars of slotted screws, probably from the 1950's..."

Start by transferring the shoulder lines onto the outer face.

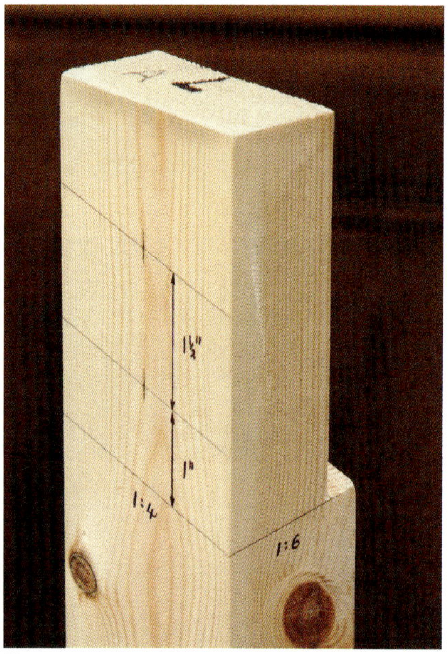

The angles and distances are shown here.

Drill the holes parallel to the 1:6 line.

Countersink the holes.

Get the leg pressed in tight and fit the screws.

This is what the saw horse should look like now.

TECHNICAL POINTER: If you hold the cordless screwdriver directly in line with the axis of the screw, apply a steady pressure and go easy on the trigger, you will not spin the screw driving bit in the screw head and mince up the driving slots, which is a common mistake. Also, chose a slow speed gear, which is function of every cordless drill I've ever used.

The hardwood bracing needs to fit tight into the corner, so measure the angle...

...and mark it onto the top of the bracing.

First trial assembly

Before you put the screws in it's absolutely critical to make sure that the leg shoulders are pushed home tight. Tap the end of the legs with a mallet to seat the joint good and tight.

Now fit the four legs, but don't sink the screws in too deeply or you'll splinter the top face when you take them out again.

With the saw stool on your bench, give it a quick look over to see how you've done. At this stage, very few mistakes are correctable, so if you have any glaring errors you'll need to just live with them, or re-make a leg perhaps.

If you have little gaps in the leg housings for one reason or another, don't worry about it. You will build in plenty more strength over the next few steps that will compensate for this.

The hardwood bracings

I've chosen hardwood for these parts for strength. Steel plates would be just as good, but then there's the extra weight. Plywood would work, but I recommend that if you can get your hands on some oak, ash or something just as strong, go for the hardwood.

Shape the top

The acute angle between the legs and the cross member is reinforced by the bracings. As a load is applied from above, the force tries to close this angle and so the hardwood bracing has the effect of preventing this if it's fitted good and tight into the corner.

With the saw stool upside down on the bench top, put the bracing in place against the legs as shown, and set the sliding bevel to the acute angle.

Transfer this angle onto the end of the bracing with a sharp pencil line. This now indicates the wedge of wood you are about to remove.

Set a marking gauge to the depth of the depth of the wedge.

Mark this depth along the face of the bracing.

It's important to get this angle very close to what you want, so a way to do this accurately is as follows:

1. Plane a chamfer down to your gauge line.
2. Using a soft pencil, run a dark line about 1⁄16" from the top edge.
3. Plane off the wedge, almost down to your gauge line and halfway through the pencil line at the top.
4. Set your plane to take a fine shaving, and take the last few shavings with care working right to your gauge line. Take out almost all of the pencil line.
5. Try the bracing in place. If you are going to have a slight gap (and I mean only a whisker) make sure it's right in the corner, as you can close this up when you clamp and fix the bracing later.

Set your gauge and...

...mark the guide line for your plane.

Run a soft pencil down the top edge. You will know if you've touched this line with your plane.

Plane a steep chamfer down to your gauge line.

It's then very easy to remove the waste.

The top of the bracing should now fit nicely.

The ends need cutting off now, so scribe the first side with a pencil to give you the correct angle.

Scribe the ends

Now you need to scribe the ends of the bracing to match the leg angles, so line up the bracing with the legs and draw the first triangle that needs to be sawn off.

As the bracings need not reach the edges of the legs, mark the other end of the bracing about ¼" back from the edge. This will allow ⅛" each side when it's fitted centrally.

Turn the bracing the right way up and on the chamfer you planed in the previous step, mark a fine pencil line using a sliding bevel set at 1:4. This is just an aesthetic point. You could just saw it off square, but it won't look as neat.

Cut down the lines you have marked with a dovetail saw and keep the off cuts, they'll come in handy later.

Use a block plane to smooth out the saw marks on the end grain and then put a light chamfer on all the edges that are not against the legs.

...and mark the top and bottom at 1:4.

Saw down the pencil lines, keeping the offcuts.

"...keep the offcuts, they'll come in handy later."

I've tidied up the end grain with a block plane, and put a chamfer onto the outside edges.

9 General work holding devices

On the outside face, mark the drill holes at about ¾" from the corners.

Drill into some scrap or into fresh air.

Mark a line where the bracing comes to. This is important.

Drill the holes

To drill the holes, start by marking cross hairs with a pencil about ¾" in from each corner. I just use my fingers as a guide.

Put the bracing in your vise to drill the holes. It will give you more control and make it easier to eye in a vertical hole.

Just before you move on, put the bracings in place one last time, and with a soft pencil mark a line clearly on the underside of the cross member.

Countersink the holes in the bracings to take No.10 screws. They are now ready to fit, but set them aside. We'll sort the legs out next.

Marking a line using a thin ruler as a spacer allows for planing flush after sawing.

Mark all the tops, all the way round.

Remember the off cuts I suggested you keep?

You can mark all four sides using the offcut.

...and saw off the tops and feet in the vise.

Mark and cut the legs

To mark the tops, use a sharp pencil and a 6" steel rule. The thin steel rule acts as a spacer, so after sawing the tops off you've still got some leg to plane down flush. Go around three sides of all four legs.

To mark the feet I have a nice trick. Stand the saw horse on the bench top, making it good and steady with a wedge placed under one foot if needed.

Next, take the offcut from one of the bracings, and use this as a spacer to scribe around all sides of all of the feet. (Bottom left photo.)

Unscrew all the legs and put them in the vise in turn, sawing off the tops and the feet, remembering to cut on the waste side of the line.

Suffice it to say that you need to put a heavy chamfer on the underside of all the feet. This prevents the wood splitting as the saw stool is dragged across rough ground.

Cross member shaping

From each end measure down 1½", square a pencil line across, and in the dead center drill a hole through measuring around ⅞" to 1", depending on the dowel size on hand. Use a square to ensure you go through at 90 degrees. Keep the square ⅛" or so away from the auger or you'll scratch up the square.

On the end grain of BOTH ends, measure 1½" from the underside of the cross member, then join this up with the line you marked when the bracing was in place, shown in the large photo on previous left hand page.

Choose one end or the other, but NOT both. On the end grain draw two lines, each 1½" from the edge and parallel with the hole you drilled. Join these lines up with the edges of the hole. See the middle right photo.

Take a dovetail or tenon saw and remove the central section of wood.

The hole and notch detail make these saw stools more versatile as you'll see when you progress onto making clamp bar guides (page 211) and a large panel shooting board (page 331).

On BOTH ends, saw off the triangular shaped wedges on the underside of the cross member.

Use a block plane or a No.4 to tidy up the saw marks.

Start by drilling a hole in each end as described.

Join up the lines ready to saw off the underside.

Join the lines to the hole on ONE end, not both!

Saw out the waste to form a notch.

Saw off the underside of each end.

Clean up the saw cuts.

Chamfer every edge, except inside the housings!

Filing and chamfering

I'd strongly recommend that every edge and hole get a heavy chamfer at this stage.

Use a small bench plane to chamfer every edge on the cross member (apart from the housing edges, of course!).

Using flat and round files, you will be able to smooth off every part of the notch and the round holes. (Middle photos.)

Final assembly

Make sure you have given the sides of the legs a reasonable chamfer before you screw everything together again.

Hold the assembled saw stool across the bench with a clamp and then plane off the tops of the legs, as shown in the bottom left photo.

Again, the final finish on the tops of the legs will come up well with a sharp low angle block plane.

To fix the bracings, clamp them tight up against the cross member using a wedge, as shown, to stop the clamp from slipping. (Bottom, middle.)

Finishing

For an even, dark brown color, mix up the spirit based stain and apply a light coat, working fairly quickly. I'll often use this as a base coat before brushing on water based, high build, protective wood stain.

Use both flat and...

...round files, to smooth off the edges.

Plane the tops off flush and then...

...screw the bracings in place.

With the wood finish dry, they're ready for use!

Clamp bar guides

Clamping up a cabinet on your bench is far from ideal. For a start you'll need to move it straight away or you can't use your bench. Also, depending on where your bench happens to be and if the floor happens to be dead flat, there could be a slight twist in your bench, which you will then build into anything you clamp to it during assembly and gluing.

One good way around this is to do your clamping and gluing up on a pair of saw horses. The clamp bar guides shown here allow you to fit a pair of strong clamps to the top of your saw horses, and with a single wedge get the clamps dead parallel, not dead horizontal. Close to horizontal is good, but parallel is mission critical.

The glued up cabinet, shelf unit, table top or side panel can then be clamped up dead flat and rest in that position until the glue sets.

When you go through the following instructions, bear in mind these guides are being made to fit a pair of long sash clamps that I use frequently. Make sure you take the dimensions of your own clamps into account.

I've used a wedge to get the clamp guides absolutely parallel.

The steel bar rests in the guides, and the locating dowels allow the guides to fit nicely into the saw horses.

What you'll need

Pine Batten 1½" x 1¼" 2 pieces, 36" long.

¾" Dowelling - 1 six inch piece.

Procedure

Check your clamps:

The long steel bars of the sash clamps need to fit into a set of slots, so the first job is to make sure that the slots you are going to cut are wide enough for the clamps you are going to use. I've got less than ¼" in width so I'll cut ¼" slots.

Set out your slots

Mark out both guides at the same time, so put them side by side and measure 5" on either side of your center line (shown dotted in the photo, middle right).

Take a large pair of dividers and having set them for a 3½" spacing, step out points to mark the edges of the slots closest to the center of the work piece. Square lines across both pieces exactly on the points you have stepped out.

Now set a small pair of dividers to your required slot width (¼", in my case).

Use the dividers to mark an offset measurement on each of the previous lines, always stepping a mark away from the center of the work piece in order to maintain an even spacing.

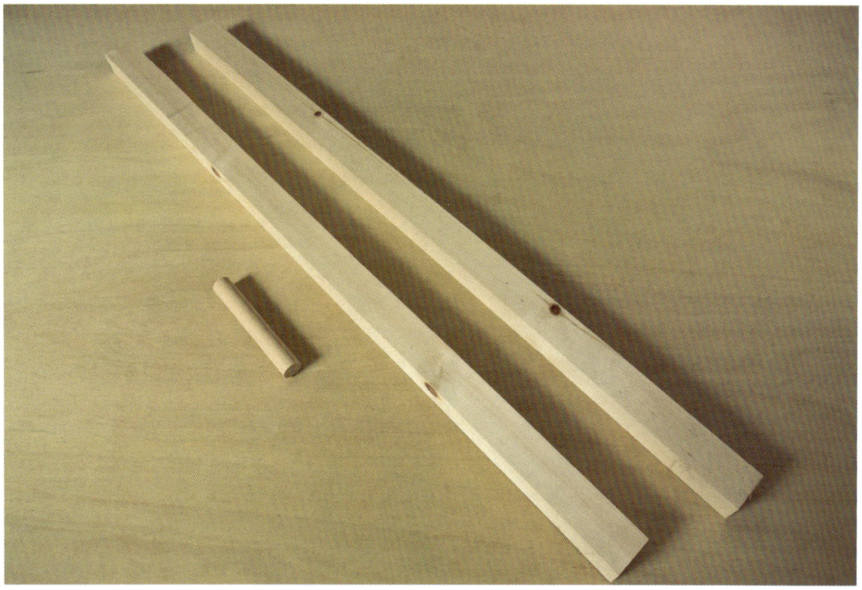

Two lengths of wood and a piece of dowelling is all you need.

Check the thickness of the steel bar first.

Find the center, and mark off 5" each side.

Step out the 3½" marks, from the 5" lines.

You need a little more than the steel thickness.

Mark out off set marks from the 3½" points.

Knife across the pairs of points for a clean cut. In this case it's just good practice, not essential.

Cut the slots

Using a square and a marking knife, define the slots with a good knife cut on each side in order to create a neat edge. Take the lines over the edges with a pencil and mark out the depth of the slot, which can be around ⁵⁄₁₆".

Saw down the sides of every slot on both pieces and pop the waste out with a small chisel.

You can tidy up the bottom of the slots with a small router if you have one, otherwise just pare down to depth with a chisel.

To finish off, give all the edges and corners a good round over with a large file. This will prevent damage to the guides as you're putting in and taking out the clamps.

Mark out the slot depth, around ⁵⁄₁₆"

Saw down to your gauge lines...

...and chisel out the waste.

A small router is handy for this sort of thing.

Round over all the edges and corners.

Fit the guides to the saw horses

This is a simple case of measuring the spacing of the hole and large 'V' notch in the saw horses directly onto the guides.

With the hole and the 'V' notch marked on the underside of the guides, allow a bit of clearance by positioning the dowel hole a little further away from the extremity of the 'V' notch mark. This just helps the guides drop into position quickly and easily.

TOP TIP: To drill the holes for the dowelling to a depth of ⅜", first mark the auger with a black pen. Do this by rotating the auger and touching the nib against it as it rotates. It's then very easy to see how deep the hole is as you progress.

Chamfer the dowel before you cut each piece to length. You may find it's much easier and safer than using a sharp chisel on a short piece of dowel. Pare down onto a piece of scrap.

A good chamfer helps the dowels locate into the saw horse easily.

Glue the dowels in place and hold them in place with a spring clamp.

Place the saw horse centrally on the underside of the guide.

You need a bit of slack in the system, so mark the dowelling about ⅛" from the end of the notch.

I like the old marker pen trick. You can easily see this mark when the auger is rotating.

Run the auger in reverse at first, then drill to depth for a clean hole.

Put the chamfered end in the hole to mark it for length, cut it off...

...and glue the short dowels in place, chamfer facing upwards. Hold them with spring clamps until the glue has set.

Chamfer all the edges and corners with a bench plane.

Stain up the grooves first...

...and then stain up the other surfaces.

Finishing

Plane a good chamfer on the ends of the guides and sand them down, cleaning up any glue from around the dowels.

Now, I can't abide seeing bare pine anywhere in my shop once it's being used for a purpose, so I use a standard brown stain on almost everything I make for the workshop.

When it comes to staining up the guides, apply a liberal amount to the slots first and then go back and do the easy bits, brushing it evenly but sparingly.

Eye in the clamp bars, and level up the guides using a wedge. This will allow you to glue up with no twist.

Caul clamps, clamp bar guides and saw horses - all work together!

For larger work, just make a longer set of guides to suit the job in hand.

Using the clamp bar guides

These are very easy to use and work very well as long as you remember to use a wedge to get the guides totally parallel.

The clamps sit in the guides allowing you to get the work flat and straight as the glue sets. You can see here I'm using the caul clamps (page 219) to keep the board joints aligned as the glue sets.

Caul clamps

The word 'caul', as recorded in R.A Salaman's excellent 'Dictionary of Woodworking Tools', is defined as "A piece of flat or curved wood used for holding down a veneer or other material while the glue sets."

From a historical point of view this is a good definition, but in many workshops today the variety of uses for clamping cauls goes way beyond veneer work.

Cauls are traditionally curved on the underside allowing pressure at the edges to be transferred to the center of the clamp. Combining this simple design element with adjustable clamps at each end, creates a very versatile holding device. When gluing up boards into wider panels, these clamps keep the joints perfectly aligned, and this is the main use I have for them.

The way this works is fairly simple: One side is straight, and the other side is bowed slightly. This means that when tightened, the middle part closes first and considerable central clamping pressure is maintained even when the edges are nipped up tight. A uniform clamping pressure prevents any slippage of joints near the center, which can be a problem if the cauls are both straight.

The right size and design of caul clamp will easily hold a wide board perfectly flat and true while you carry out some operation requiring absolute flatness, such as marking out dovetails (shown on facing page), or housings, etc. There is no better way to bring a pair of wide boards together, ready to mark out for a joint, than clamping both components absolutely flat beforehand.
If you have had to deal with wide boards that have a slight cup, you'll know exactly what I mean!

The dimensions I give are not critical, but what follows in this section will kit you out with a pair of caul clamps that will not only be adequate for the cabinet work in *Working Wood 4*, but will cover a whole host of other projects.

"When gluing up boards into wider panels, these clamps keep the joints perfectly aligned, and this is the main use I have for them."

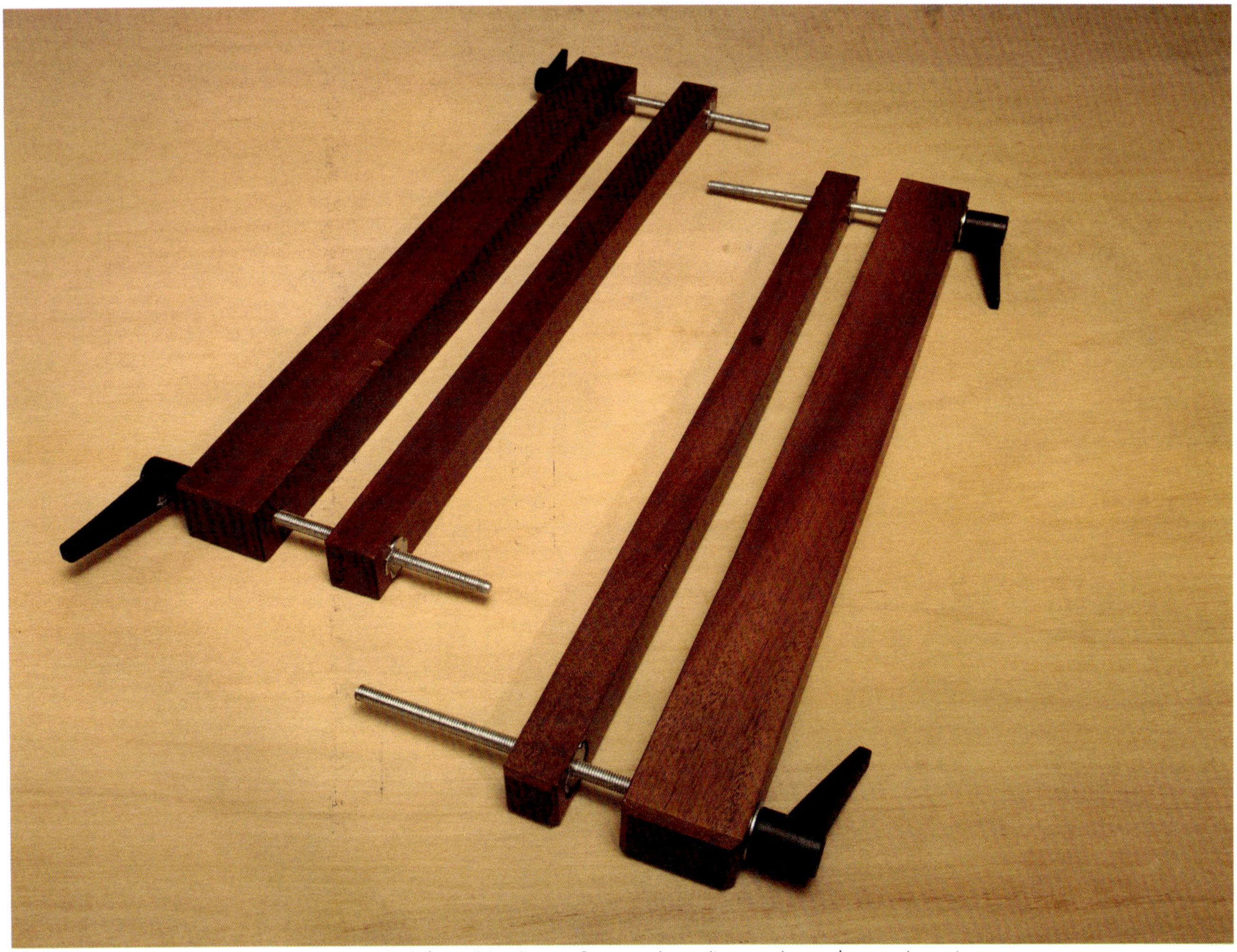

I've shown a matched pair here, but you may find it's useful to have a few sets, depending on what you've got planned.

Mark out the curve as described below.

Plane down to the lines, always working away from the center.

Check the curve by sighting down the pencil lines.

Prepare the clamp bars

In order for the board or other work piece to be clamped tight in the center, we need to mark and plane a reasonable 'curve' onto the underside of the top clamp bar.

Mark the middle of the bar and then, using a soft pencil, mark on a taper from the end, finishing at the middle.

I use my fingers as a guide and just rotate my wrist steadily until the pencil slips off around the middle. It seems an inaccurate method, but it really works!
Repeat the same on the opposite end of the same face.

If you sight down the bar, you should see the dull grey pencil line now looks like it's curved along it's length. Put the bar in the vise and plane off all the waste down to your pencil line.

Don't try to plane a fancy curve, a dead straight taper from the middle to the end in both directions is ideal.

What you will need:

Hardwood:

2 pieces, 2" x 1⅝" x 22"

2 pieces 1⅛" square x 22"

¼" Threaded rod, 2 at 18"

4 Lever handles (¼" thread)

8 'T' nuts and 4 washers

After planing to your lines, check the curve looks even.

Relieve all the corners in a few passes with a plane.

Chamfer the ends evenly, all the way round.

That will do nicely!

The lower clamp bar needs no special attention.

Gently take a fine shaving off the sharp edges along the length of both bars, holding your plane at a skewed angle.

The next job is just to put an even chamfer on the ends of the planed stock, as shown in the photo on the left. Anything from 1/8" to 3/16" will do. It's not important.

You are now going to mark up for drilling the holes, so you need to be absolutely clear about this: The holes must be marked on the narrow faces of the larger of the two clamping bars, and the curved face (and reverse) of the other, smaller clamp bar.

Sharpen up the points on your gauge, if you have not done so already.

Mark out the right spacing for the holes.

Mark the holes

Accuracy is very important for the next step, so I'd recommend you polish up the pins on your marking gauge so you can see them very clearly.

Now set your gauge to 1" and mark a short line on all the ends, referencing against the end of the planed wood.

Find the dead center using your gauge. This is a quick technique and is much easier than you may think:

Start by estimating the center and on the short line you've just scratched, make a tiny point, mark from both sides. Chances are that there will be a slight discrepancy between the two points, however it's now very easy to estimate the center between the tiny marks with a high degree of precision. If you don't get it spot on this iteration, then one more will get it right.

The photo on the left here illustrates how the pin is centered between the two point marks.

Find the dead center by making pin point marks from both sides.

I like working with cross hairs.

A Forstner bit will drill a flat bottomed hole.

Mark the centers on both faces at each end using a short line. Centers need marking on both large and smaller clamp bars, and must be aligned perfectly between the pairs of bars.

The cross hairs you now have will allow you to drill a small pilot hole ($\frac{1}{8}$" is just fine). Don't drill all the way through, just halfway at this stage. Keep the drill as perpendicular to the work piece as possible, in all directions.

When you turn the wood over and drill holes from the other side, go all the way through, but go slowly and carefully. This way you will 'pick up' the previous hole and this will help steer your drill straight out of the first hole.

With the pilot holes drilled through both top and bottom bars, set the larger of the two clamp bars to one side.

Choose a wide bit which is going to suit the 'T' nuts that you've sourced, and using the $\frac{1}{8}$" hole as a guide, drill a short ($\frac{3}{16}$") circular pocket for the 'T' nut to fit in. I'm using a Forstner bit in both photos, as it gives a smooth, clean cut and a remarkably flat bottom to the recessed hole.

A pillar drill can be used for improved accuracy.

TECHNICAL POINTER:
Perpendicularity is mission critical. If you know you are going to really struggle to drill straight, use a pillar drill or go talk to your neighbor if he or she has one.

SAFETY: If you choose to use a pillar drill, make sure everything is clamped, locked and fully tightened in place before you start.

The 'T' Nuts need to be fitted on both sides of the 1¼" square bar, so drill a clearance hole for the threaded sleeve of the 'T' nuts to fit into.

A trial fit of the 'T' nuts will assure you that all is going well, and a firm push will make small marks where the angled teeth will be located.

In a softwood you would not need to do this, but with a hardwood it's best to drill out shallow ⅛" diameter holes to seat the teeth into. The middle left photo shows the locations of the holes.

With a firm tap using a hammer, fit and seat the 'T' nuts into both sides, at both ends of the top clamp bar, and then try some threaded rod.

The ⅛" holes in the larger of the clamp bars needs to be followed through with a clearance hole for the threaded rod. If you are using ¼" threaded rod, you'll need to drill clearance holes at least 5⁄16", or the clamp bars will jam as you try to move them apart once assembled.

Drill the clearance hole from both sides, as this will make the drill less likely to wander off course.

Drill small holes for the 'T' nut teeth.

Press the 'T' nuts in and tap them home.

TOP TIP: If you struggle to get the threaded rod through both nuts, you need more slack in the system. The 'T' nuts do not have to be seated good and tight, they just need to stay in place. Take the rod out and go through from the other side. As you approach the depth of the first nut, put the clamp bar in the vise and give the rod a good wiggle, with a slight 'stirring' action, then take it all the way through. Now back it out and go back through from the other side.

Give the rod a good 'wiggle' before going through the second nut. You don't want everything tight!

Make up the clamp rods

Measure and cut four lengths of threaded rod, using your newly made set of vise jaw protectors to hold the rod.

Use a fine toothed junior hacksaw, as the narrow saw blade will just fit into the thread and will cut smoothly.

It's important to use a small, smooth file to remove the burr from the end of the rod, and cut an even chamfer as a 'lead in'. This will help the rod to go into the nuts without jamming or an awkward cross thread.

To fix the handle to the rod, just put a good blob of superglue (cyanoacrylate) on the threaded rod and screw it in quickly, as far as it will go. It does not even have to be really tight.

Cut the rods to the same length of around 8" to 9".

A junior hacksaw will leave a tidy finish.

This saw cut needs a neat chamfer...

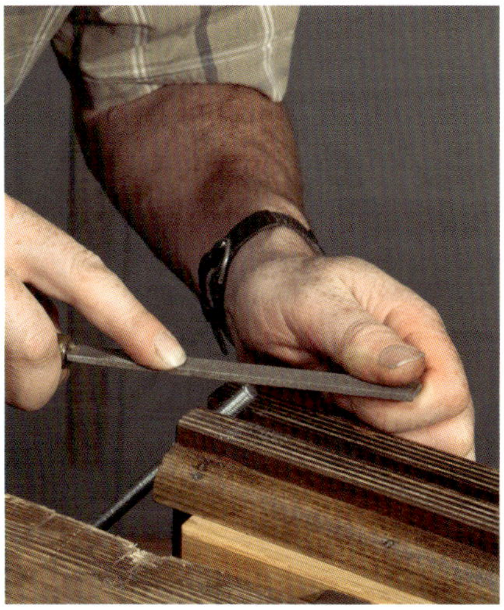

...so use a smooth file at 45 degrees.

Create a nice, smooth 'lead in' for the thread.

Use superglue to fix whatever handles you have.

Give everything a good sand down...

...before brushing on a coat of sanding sealer.

Use the sanding sealer liberally, but don't let it run!

Assemble the caul clamps, making sure you have a washer between the handle and the wood. Check the handles turn easily, and they're ready to use!

You can see how the caul clamps will keep the boards flat.

Finishing and assembly

Try putting all the parts together and if they fit well, take the whole lot apart again ready to sand down.

Sand everything smooth with 120 grit sandpaper and then either go over the surfaces with a vacuum cleaner or just brush down well with a soft brush to remove the fine dust.

Use a fairly thin cellulose sanding sealer to seal up the finished clamps. Brush it on liberally but not too thickly. Apply it to one face first and give it a few minutes to dry. Once you are happy that the solvents have evaporated, turn it over onto a pair of thin sticks so as not to pick up dust off the board you are working on. Apply the sealer liberally to the end grain but watch out for runs.

Chapter 10
Bench work holding devices

Holding your work still on your bench is a big deal. You don't want it to move, shake, wobble or slide. I have in the past propelled the work straight off the end of my bench, plane in hand and airborne plank underneath. A more reliable bench stop was the obvious solution. The interesting problem is that we need to not only hold a good variety of shapes and sizes of wood, but we need to be able to hold them in different orientations. Working on edges, wide flat faces and end grain all require different work holding devices.

Today a whole array of different work holding systems are available to buy, some fairly simple and some, how can I put it - overly complex! Traditional devices were always made by the woodworker and so I'd like to introduce a set of work holding devices that are simple, easy to make and very useful.

There are lots of different ways to hold your work to the bench.

Adjustable bench dogs

These bench dogs are great for holding wide boards on your bench top. The work piece is held against the dogs by a pop up vise dog. There are many benefits to using these.

- The dogs live in your bench top - You'll never loose them.
- They are quickly adjustable for height, from ⅛" to 1".
- There are no large holes to loose things down.
- You can fit as many as you like, almost wherever you like.
- You can easily pop them out and clean out the sockets whenever you want to.
- They stay at any height you set them at, held by simple springs.

"They stay at any height you set them, held by simple springs."

You pop them out using the notch...

...and tap them flat when you're done.

What you'll need

1" x ⅞" x 2½" planed oak.
As many as required.

2" Pieces of old hacksaw blade.

Cut the mortises

Decide on the number and spacing of the dogs. Start near your vise and put in a couple for bench stops, and probably four right by your vise. I have a set all the way along my bench top spaced 18" apart.

You are going to cut a 1" square mortise hole into your bench top for every dog, stopping ½" short of the underside of the top. Mark the positions you want your dogs and measure in 1½" from the back edge of your bench top. Use your square and knife to define the edges of the mortise hole, and then create four short knife walls as shown.

Deepen the knife walls to about ⅛" and then with a sharp pencil, find the center with diagonal lines from corner to corner.

Accuracy is important for the auger hole, so use a nail punch to carefully punch a shallow circular socket, dead center, to start off the auger hole.

> **TOP TIP:** *Screw a support block to the underside of the bench top, and put the auger through this as well. This will prevent breakout as you mortise down to the correct depth for the hole.*

Plan the positions of your dogs.

Start with a knife cut, then a knifewall.

Mark the center.

A center punch keeps the auger from drifting.

To prevent breakout, make a support block...

...and fix it under where the auger will emerge.

Drill down plumb vertical...

TOP TIP: *Stop as soon as you have 'started' and check with a square. After a couple of rotations, stop and check again. You are only going to drill this hole once, so you may as well get it right.*

Use a ¾" auger to take out most of the waste, taking care to go through perpendicular to the bench top.

First chop down using the bevel facing the edge. This makes it much easier to lever out the waste in a tight space. You may then need to drop down a size and do most of the work with a ¾" chisel.

As you go down deeper, cut slightly towards the center of the auger hole. It is then a very easy job to pare the hole out to the right size once you are down to the right depth. The converse is obvious, in that if you get wider going down the hole, you are going to have a sloppy fit which will be very tricky, but not impossible to fix!

Stop ½" from the underside of your bench top. Pare out square and straight once you are happy with the depth.

...and don't let it lean over when you first start off.

Use your knifewall as a guide and start to...

...chop out the waste. However, make sure...

...you lean the chisel in slightly as you go deeper.

Cut the spring pockets

At this point you need to decide the direction of force on the dog. For example, the end stops need to resist a force applied in the direction of the length of the bench top, however the other dogs along the bench top need to resist a force applied crossways to this.

So, looking at the dogs running down the length of the bench top, I would cut the spring pockets into the right hand side of the mortises, as viewed from the bench front. The rule is this: The spring pocket must be cut at 90 degrees to the applied force, which is what I'm doing in the photo here on the right.

Using a ½" chisel, somewhere around ¼" from the top of the hole, chop out a shallow pocket, say 1⁄16" deep and about ¼" long, so that it looks rectangular, as you can see in the photo, middle left.

Make the springs

Hacksaw blades make great springs, cutting blades, and all sorts of tools. Choose a worn out hacksaw blade and cut the end off square using the 'nick and snap' method, shown in the next step.

Slide the square ended hacksaw blade down the hole until you reach the bottom of the mortise, and pencil mark a line corresponding with the spring pocket you have just chopped out.

To cut the blade, simply 'nick' the back edge with a good pair of tin snips (metal shears in the US), and then just bend it right on the nick. It will snap easily.

Chopping out a shallow spring pocket prevents the spring from being lifted out as the dog is lifted.

This is all you need.

Mark the top of the pocket you have cut.

One good snip on the edge...

...and it will snap as you bend it!

Place the spring on some scrap, and...

...hammer the middle until it curves nicely.

The top of the spring should sit in the pocket.

Take your oak and measure off the hole depth.

Make a series of saw cuts after cutting it to length.

To make it into a spring it needs a slight curve beating into it, so get a block of scrap softwood and a cross peen hammer. Start tapping the blade in the center, slowly working away from the middle in both directions.

Despite the high carbon content, you will permanently deform the shape. Keep going until you have around ⅛" gap underneath when flipped over and placed on the bench.

Try it for size in the mortise hole, it should fit snugly.

Make the dogs

Your hardwood stock needs to be slightly under 1" x ⅞", so try this in your mortise with the spring in place, and check that it slides in and out without too much slop or jamming. If it jams then just plane off a whisker or two until it's about right. If it's a sloppy fit, you may need to source some more hardwood stock of appropriate dimensions. Sloppy is what you don't want!

Slide the planed stock into the mortise until it stops, then mark and cut it to length.

The dogs are lifted out using a screwdriver, the end of the blade locating into slots cut into the dogs. Cut a series of shallow slots in the side opposite the spring. A dovetail saw is ideal for this. Make the first slot somewhere between ⅛" and 3⁄16" from the top and then cut a further three slots about the same distance apart.

The saw cuts allow the dog to be lifted with a screwdriver, but you still need to chisel a notch out to allow you to lift it out of the bench top.

You can see how the notch allows the screwdriver to 'pick up' the first saw cut.

Cut the lifting notches

I use a flat screwdriver with a ¼" blade to lift the dogs, so I cut a notch dead center opposite the spring pocket with a ¼" chisel. If you chop down at 45 degrees and take out about 3⁄16" of bench top, your screwdriver should line up nicely with the first lifting slot.

> *"I use a flat screwdriver with a ¼" blade to lift the dogs out..."*

Finishing

Give the dogs a fine round over on top using just 120 grit sandpaper, and a general sand down. I used dark oil based stain and a light coat of furniture wax to help them pop in and out easily.

Having a good set of adjustable dogs made all the difference to me and I hope that you'll find them equally as useful!

Bench stop

You will need a dog on the far left hand side of your bench as shown here.

This stops a board shooting off your bench while you plane it flat.

This bench stop is rock solid and can be tapped into the bench when I'm done.

TECHNICAL POINTER: *As this dog acts as a bench stop, the force on it is sideways, so put the spring and spring pocket at the back of the socket, unlike the rest of the dogs where you put the spring at the side of the dog.*

My vise had no pop up dog when I bought it 20 years ago, so I just cut a housing in the front wooden vise jaw, and dropped in a piece of old file. The cast iron was easy to drill and thread so I used a brass wing nut resin fixed to a threaded brass rod, as a means of holding the dog at the required height.

I always use a little packer when using the pop up vise dog so that the work piece does not get damaged.

This is a shop made pop up vise dog. The wing nut is glued to a threaded bar, and locks the height.

TOP TIP: *Always have as much of your work piece on the bench top as possible. This may mean you have not got enough travel in the vise to hold it, so just use a batten as a packer to increase the travel.*

I always use a packer so as not to damage the work.

If the work is too narrow to reach the vise dog, pack it out with a batten.

Bench hold downs

Continuing the theme of simplicity, these particular workshop aids are a firm favorite of mine. Made traditionally by the local blacksmith, the design for the bench hold down clamps we are about to look at has been used for centuries by woodworkers the world over.

Their function relies on the two simple principles of leverage and friction. From one sharp tap on top, the arm reaching onto the work piece acts like a lever, forcing the round bar hard against the side of the hole. As the bar gets jammed hard against the side of the hole, the subsequent friction grips it in place. Every tap with the hammer causes more leverage, more friction and hence more clamping force at the end of the arm.

I always keep a pair of hardwood wedges on hand, and I place these between the hold down and the piece of work. They perform two functions. Firstly they prevent the metal bruising the work and secondly if you orientate them correctly they create a quick release mechanism for the hold downs. A gentle knock sideways rotates the arm of the clamp down the tapered wedge and the clamping pressure is released.

They are surprisingly simple to make, however you will need a strong vise to bend the ⅝" steel bar. If you don't have access to a heavy engineering vise, there are plenty of other ways of doing this. I have bent significantly thicker bars than this around the tow hitch of a tractor and even in a municipal road drainage grid without much difficulty or indeed any damage. (I was right out of options for that one!) You could also use a steel scaffolding tube, sledge hammered into the ground, or two lengths of steel pipe as levers, and so on. We'll look at how to heat up and hot forge the end into a flat, well shaped gripper. However, you could choose to do this with a bit more effort as a cold forging job, with repeated hammer blows. Mild steel is easy to work and will deform and spread to some extent without applying heat.

Failing any of that, you could just cut a flat on the underside of the arm with an electric grinder and finish it off with a file. So, seriously, there is no 'right' way to do this. Bear this in mind as you read through.

SAFETY POINTER: *Working with hot metal has inherent dangers, and using considerable body force to bend metal could cause injury. So please read on but take your own decision as to whether this project is appropriate for you. It is interesting to know how these clamps are made, but they are readily available to buy, and that will be the better option for some folks.*

I recommend using mild steel for these clamps simply because it's very cheap and there is absolutely no benefit in using a more expensive, higher carbon steel. You could use bright bar which is clean to work with and has been drawn through a die, so it has a very uniform thickness, but there are no real benefits compared to the cheaper black bar I'm going to use.

Make a few of these, two is the bare minimum, but three is ideal.

What you'll need

Mild steel round bar ⅝" diameter. One 20 inch long piece per hold down

Tools

- Engineering vise (not essential - find an alternative if you need to).
- Large hammer.
- Hacksaw.
- White chalk or marker pen.
- Coarse file and smooth file.
- 4ft Scaffold tube (as bending lever).
- Propane gas torch (not essential - mild steel can be beaten into shape even when stone cold, heating it up just makes it a lot easier!).
- Anvil (not essential, but if you are going to shape steel with hammer blows, you'll need a solid lump of steel - Offcut of steel girder, railway track, etc.).

Procedure

Measure 20" on the bar, mark it with chalk or a marker pen, and saw it off with a hacksaw. You could use an electric grinder but a hacksaw will do it in less than a minute.

Measure 10" and chalk that onto the bar. Place it vertically in the vise with the 10" chalk mark level with the top of the jaws.

For the first and main bend, choose a strong hollow section steel tube such as steel scaffold tube, heavy water pipe, gas pipe, etc. I happened to have some heavy box section steel, but find something that will work safely, without breaking or bending as it will exert quite a lot of leverage.

Slide it over the steel bar, take a very firm grip and pull it down towards you.

"...find something that will work safely, without breaking or bending..."

Put the steel in a sturdy vise, and saw off a 20" piece.

A new blade will slice through the soft steel.

The 10" mark must be at the top of the jaws.

Get yourself a good lever and make sure that...

...your vise is fixed to the bench properly!

Keep bending the steel until you are somewhere near 35 degrees below the horizontal.

Keep going until you reach about 35 degrees below horizontal. You may have to reposition the tube a little further from the vise so it does not get pinched.

When you are done, this photo on the left is what it should look like.

There are two things you need to do now before you take it out of the vise:

Firstly mark a series of 'X's on the vertical portion in the vise.

Secondly, measure 5" from the back of the bar onto the front bent part and make a mark. Do this before you forget.

You now need to reposition this in the vise with the 'X X X' section facing directly forwards in the vise and the 5" mark level with the top of the jaws. See the photo, bottom left.

The next step is to bash the vertical part backward in the vise until it's about 90 degrees in relation to the 'X X X' part. It's a noisy business, the vise will shake and you'll need to concentrate to avoid injury.

With that done, it's time to heat up the steel!

This is what you are aiming for.

Mark up a line 5" from the vice jaws.

Now change the orientation of the steel in the vise. Notice the new position of 'X X X' marks.

Beat the rod until it's at 90 to the 'X X X' part.

The Gripper

The gripper is normally beaten out wider than the rest of the section to allow a greater area to hold the work. If you do not have the facility to do this, just move on to the section below where you saw off the excess and file it to a round. It will still work fine.

If you have access to a propane torch and an anvil (or alternatively a small piece of railroad track or heavy I section steel beam) you will be able to heat up the steel to then flatten and spread it. This does have a functional value but is also an aesthetic feature.

To speed up the process and conserve gas, some kind of heat reflector is really helpful. This doesn't need to be elaborate. Here I'm just using an old disposable saw that I have bent, but if you do this then be careful. Bending them too far can suddenly make them snap without warning.

SAFETY POINTER: *Before you start heating the steel, first rehearse that you can beat the hot steel safely. It is vital to get set up right before you start as the steel will cool down quickly. Clear your work area, get you hammer ready, wear some good leather work gloves and safety glasses. Figure out if you are going to need help to hold the steel while you beat it. Do you need a second pair of hands and a set of tongs? Even if you've never done this sort of thing before, with the right preparation you can work safely and effectively, but give this serious consideration.*

The process is deliberately what I would describe as "rough and ready"; achievable with a minimum of equipment. Your local blacksmith would of course have far superior facilities! Keep the heat on until the steel is glowing red hot.

Heat up the horizontal section, where it levels out after the bend.

Keep the heat on until it's glowing red hot.

Quickly transfer the steel to your set up for flattening. Get some help for this bit if you need it.

Once it reaches red hot (the color red), take the bar out and get beating. You haven't got any longer than 10 seconds! I am lucky to have an anvil onto which the bent bar fits nicely.

This is now flattened in the places I want, and also it's cooled down too much to work it any more without considerable effort!

Back into the vise. The arm is ready to be sawn to length, to about 6" from the back of the bar as shown.

TECHNICAL POINTER: *If you can't heat up the steel, you can still beat a good flat face on the end even when it's stone cold. This will take you some time but it will work providing the rod is held properly and you have a surface to beat the steel on that won't move, break or deform.*

This looks 'well beaten' to me!

Place the hold down back into the vise...

...and hold the 'X X X' section 6" from the jaws.

Saw off the steel right by the jaws.

Catch it before it drops onto your toes!

The planish

Again this is a design feature that is not absolutely necessary. The change in profile of the arm as it's flattened, or planished, gives it a bit more strength (in terms of resistance to bending), but most of all I just like the look of it. Cold working this steel is only possible because of the low carbon content of mild steel, but it still takes a good amount of careful bashing. I've mentioned careful bashing as you don't really want to leave edge marks where the lump hammer hits the steel at a jaunty angle.

Final shaping and filing

Clean up the top of the gripper with a file if you need to. I like to do this just so it looks neater.

To form a nice rounded profile on the end of the gripper, find something small you can draw around with a marker pen. I used a circular flanged nut that you can see here.

Either saw or file the corners off. I always use a saw when I can because the piece you cut off with a saw equates to steel that you don't have to slowly turn into iron filings to remove.

Give both sides of the curved section a good flattening, or planishing.

To round the end over, I used a flange nut as a template.

Saw off what you can, as it's quicker than filing.

Finish the end off with a file, giving it a good chamfer...

...so it looks like this!

Give the other end a little chamfer.

Using a hold down with my sticking board.

The final finish and chamfer on the gripper is definitely a job for a file.

The last job is to put a little chamfer on the end of the stem. Nothing should leave your workshop with a sharp edge or a burr on it.

Fitting the hold downs

I'm using 16mm steel, which approximates to ⅝" in US size. The holes in your bench top need to be a whisker larger than the steel so that the hold down will slide in and out nicely.

I'm going to break with convention here and turn to metric, as it's a lot easier to talk about what I actually do, and the measurements I actually use!

I happen to have a 16.5mm blacksmiths' drill which I use as a reamer, after first going through with a sharp 16mm auger. The extra 0.5mm of clearance is all I need for the hold downs to drop in and out easily, yet still hold the work when tapped into place. For most of us our bench is a functional item, so drill holes in as you need to, keeping them away from the vise and the edges of the bench top. If you are fanatical about organized layout (I'm just a little that way inclined), then drill the holes in a regular spaced pattern for neatness. There is some science to the ideal spacing, but it depends on so many factors that you just need to take your own decision here.

I hope that was a load of fun. One thing is for sure, you are not going to wear them out or break them!

TOP
MABEL

Extra bench leg

I have seen a vast array of solutions for holding long panels and boards in the vise, from the elaborate to the 'barely works' basic. One thing is for sure, some sort of device is a necessity. I have used plastic milk crates upside down, saw horses and battens G-clamped to the end of a panel as an extra leg, so my tendency is to go for the simple rather than the complex. I built myself a new bench a few years ago and decided to invest some time in a functional but simple 'extra leg' for the front of my bench.

This design of device is not permanently fixed to my bench, I just fit it when I'm doing the kind of work that calls for it. The key design features are:

- The board support is easily adjustable.
- The leg can be easily moved closer to, or further from the vise, on either side.
- The leg extends all the way to the bench top and is the same thickness as the back jaw of the vise, so that it will hold the work parallel to the bench top.
- The board support has a top sloping inwards, preventing the board from working it's way off and dropping down.
- When not in use, it can be removed quickly and stowed out of the way.
- Simplicity: It's easy to make, and even easier to use!

Note that the design of this bench leg fits a bench with a front apron, such as the European workbench, the construction of which was covered in the previous *Working Wood* series. If your bench is of a different design, you can probably just adapt the idea and make something similar that works with your bench.

"One thing is for sure, some sort of device is a necessity."

There is not much to this device, but it's very handy!

The holes are essential for adjusting the height of the support block.

Materials

Planed softwood

4" x 2" -1pc at 38", 1pc at 12"

4" x 1" -1pc at 18"

2" x 2" -1pc at 6"

1" diameter dowel -1pc at 12"

Plated steel screws: 8 x No.10's at 3", 6 x at 2"

PVA Glue

Wood stain.

Procedure

Fundamentally, this device has to be made to fit your own bench. For this reason, pay attention to which distances and measurements are relative to your particular workbench. In fact, I'd recommend you become familiar with the whole project before you start. That way you can prepare the materials in advance and get your wood down to the right size before you start on the making.

Prepare the leg and the spacer

The thickness of the 2"x 4" leg needs to correspond to the front face of the rear wooden vise jaw. Measure this before you start and get the difference to within ¼" if you can. Less difference is better and if you are stuck, you can get away with more but it's really not ideal.

There are two key lines to mark on the leg before you start the layout: The bench top height and the underside of the apron. Holding the 2"x 4" leg vertically against the apron, mark on the bench top (less a bit, as you want to be under not over) and also mark on the bottom edge of your apron.

Cut the leg to the right length, and tidy up the top with a block plane.

Clean up the top of the leg with a block plane.

The front face of the leg needs to line up with the rear vise jaw like this.

Mark the height of the bench top and the underside of the apron.

From the midpoint of the foot and the spacer mark 45 degree lines as shown here.

Saw off the waste, and then chamfer the foot but not the spacer (top piece) as shown.

TOP TIP: *A reminder for tidying up end grain - Put a small chamfer all the way around as it stops the edges from breaking out and splintering. I usually alternate between chamfering and end grain planing for a job like this. Alternatively, just plane towards the center from all edges, then chamfer the edges when you're done.*

Measure the apron thickness. The spacer needs to be planed down to be a fraction *thicker* than the apron. Add more than 1⁄32" but no more than 1⁄16". If you go too far and plane the spacer down to the same thickness as your apron, or thinner, the leg will not fit on. If this happens, then start again from scratch. Don't rely on using a packer during assembly.

On the foot of the leg and one end of the spacer, find the midpoint and mark on a 45 degree line on both using the try square.

Saw off the waste and tidy up with a block plane. Cut a substantial chamfer on the underside of the foot, but leave the spacer with barely any chamfer, As shown in the left hand photo.

These 'half miter' cuts allow the leg to go in and out easily with out jamming.

The orientation is up to you, but I prefer the leg to go in anti-clockwise, so I have the half miter on the foot to my right as I look at the vise.

Mark and drill the adjustment holes.

To set out for the holes, project a level line from the steel tubes of your vise, onto the front face of the leg. This is a reference line for your first hole.

To mark a series of holes I use a home made 'pencil gauge' much like a marking gauge, but it just gives you a clear pencil line to work to, and no score marks to eventually plane or sand out.

Set your pencil gauge to 1½" and run two lines the full length of the leg, on the front face, as shown in the middle left photo.

Use your ¾" dowel rod as a template and draw on the position of your first hole on the right hand pencil line, with the top of dowel just touching the reference line you marked earlier.

The hole centers are marked off quickly and easily using a large set of dividers. Set your dividers to a distance of 2½" between the points before you start and tighten them up so they can't move.

Find the center point of the circle you have drawn, and then use this center point to locate the first leg of your dividers.

You can now step up and down in any direction making sure you always step onto the *alternate* pencil line as you go. Do not stay on the same line.

Mark the height of the steel tubes of your vise.

Mark lines 1½" from each edge.

A pencil gauge leaves a very visible line.

Use the dowel to set out the first hole...

...then step over to the other line for the next mark.

Alternate back and forth across the lines.

Mark cross hairs on every point.

Drill through at every mark. (See Top Tip!)

Cross from one line to the other with every step, as you can see in the top right hand photo.

In the foreground of this photo, you can see the vise reference line, the first hole drawn around the dowel and the pencil line indicating the bottom of the apron. Take a square and a pencil, and convert the pin points made by the dividers into cross hairs.

TECHNICAL POINTER: *Whenever you mark a hole to be drilled, whether in wood, masonry, drywall, bathroom tiles, or anything else, always use clear cross hairs. Don't try to work to a single dot as the first thing you will do is completely obliterate your reference point with the drill, leaving you guessing where the hole should actually be.*

With your holes clearly marked put the leg in the vise, either way up is fine, and using a try square as a guide carefully drill all the holes at 90 degrees.

TOP TIP: *Don't push hard, just concentrate on steering, particularly the first ¼" to ½" of the hole. Don't break through all the way, stop when the small thread of the auger emerges, and then reverse the work piece so you can drill from the other side to make a neat hole.*

The next step is rather tedious but just has to be done. Take a round file and carefully chamfer every hole you have drilled on both sides. If you don't do this, the adjustable support will frequently jam on the tatty wood fibers, and will break out chips of wood from the front face during normal use, neither of which are ideal.

Drill the spacer

When using heavy screws and relatively thick stock, I always pre-drill the work piece being fixed with a clearance hole. This ensures that the component being fixed is pulled really tight against the adjacent part, as the screw thread can't grip it and jack it off leaving a gap.

Now that the leg is peppered with holes, in an orderly fashion, you need to make sure that you fix the spacer into solid wood, locating the screws away from the holes you have drilled.

Put the leg on the bench top with the front face downwards. Check before you start that the half miter on the spacer is on the opposite side to the leg. Line up the half mitered top of the spacer with the reference line you marked earlier indicating the bottom of the apron. Use the pencil gauge to mark screw lines 1" from each edge on the spacer, and then transfer the best positions for the screws (in between the holes) on to the screw lines. Do this for both screw lines, and mark up your cross hairs. Drill and countersink ready for fixing.

Fitting the sliding wedge

The leg is held in place for everyday use by a tapered sliding wedge that you simply knock back and forth with a mallet to loosen or tighten the leg against the apron.

The wedge needs to press against the apron, so the position of the sliding wedge is very important. Find the two adjustment holes just above the apron line and with a square, mark across the top of the lower one and the bottom of the upper one, thus defining a space where you can drill through without intersecting either of the holes. Check the geometry on the opposite page.

Arrange the leg as shown in the photo with the front face towards you and transfer these new lines onto the uppermost edge as shown. Use the dowel as a template and position it dead center between these lines, and oddly enough, make sure the dowel overhangs the back edge a little.

Line up the spacer as described, and set out screw holes going into solid wood, missing every hole!

Countersink after drilling clearance holes for each screw.

Look carefully at the lower apron line and position the dowel between the holes as shown.

With some scrap alongside the mark, drill a hole leaning out of the leg, and into the scrap as shown.

This is the result. STOP before you break out at the bottom of the hole, as you can then...

...set up in the vise a second time, and drill into scrap. This will give you a very neat exit hole.

This is where you will drill the hole to accept the wedge. Find the center of the hole and mark it with cross hairs.

TECHNICAL POINTER:
Make sure you are drilling through at 90 degrees to the length of the leg, or you may risk wandering off slightly and intersecting one of the adjustment holes. If this happens, you may need to face the fact that the only way to fix it, is to start again from scratch, so be careful.

Clamp the leg in the vice with a piece of scrap behind where the hole is to be drilled. After checking you are on target, with part of the auger cutting the scrap, lean the drill towards you slightly so you are drilling into the scrap at a slight angle as shown in the top photo.

As you drill through, the auger will progressively cut more into the scrap as you go deeper. Stop drilling when the thread of the auger just emerges underneath. When you take it out of the vice, this middle photo shows you what it should look like.

To finish off the hole, put the leg in the vice with the scrap behind the hole, clamp it up and cut the last bit out with the auger.

To emphasise the geometry

The bottom photo shows a 'cut away' section of the hole I have drilled. You can see three important things very clearly:

1. The hole started off partly in the waste.
2. The fact that the top of the drill was leaning towards me as I drilled, has given me an inclined hole, progressing further into the waste as I drilled down.
3. The hole is drilled right between the other holes, and does not intersect them.

Slide in the dowel so that 1" protrudes, making sure it can go no further by using some packing against the dogs. Plane off all of the dowel that is above the surface of the leg. The dowel should have a clear and visible taper now.

Take a file and chamfer both ends of the tapered dowel.

Assembly

Plane a good chamfer all round the 4" x 1" back plate.

Line up the top of the spacer with the apron line on the leg, clamp in position and screw it down tight.

As you fit the back plate, you'll need to avoid hitting the screws already in the spacer. So use a similar method as before to carefully avoid them, i.e. mark and transfer lines, drill and countersink in suitable locations.

"...you'll need to avoid hitting the screws already in the spacer."

With the dowel sticking out about an inch, plane the whole top surface flush with the leg.

Align the top of the spacer with the apron line...

...clamp it up, and screw it in place.

Plane a good chamfer on the back face of the 4" x 1" back plate.

Fix the back plate with 2" No.10 screws. Plan to miss the other screws!

With the back plate fitted, you can then check the action of the wedge. This photo shows the 'unlocked' position.

By tapping the wedge forwards a few inches with a mallet...

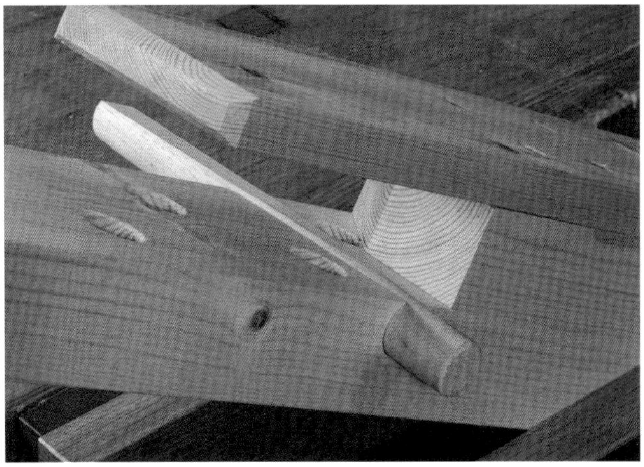

...it moves into the 'locked' position, gripping the apron nicely.

Check the action of the wedge

Place the assembled leg in the vise with the wedge in the 'unlocked' position.

Tap it through a few inches with a mallet.

You should see the wedge reduce the size of the opening as it's tapped through to the 'locked' position.

Support block

Take your 6" piece of 2x2 and drill a hole in the center, about 1" from the top. The hole is to accept the short dowel that will lock the support block into the adjustment holes in the leg.

Measure the length off, so the dowel protrudes the same distance as the thickness of the leg. Cut it to length with a dovetail saw.

Mark the top of the block at a slope of 1:6, taking the lines all the way around. Saw the wedge off the top and then tidy up and chamfer with a block plane and a file. You can't do this before you drill the dowel hole as the auger would just burst out the short grain fibers on the sloping cut.

Mark the center about 1" from the top, and drill through.

Fit the dowel in, mark it for length and cut it off. (It must not protrude through the leg!)

Saw the top off at a slop of 1: 6. This helps hold the work piece against the leg, stopping it from moving.

Put a saw cut into the top of the dowel, and prepare a wedge to hold it in place.

Apply glue to the surfaces, and tap the wedge in as shown.

Plane the wedge and dowel flush, and you are ready to fit it together!

In the same fashion as the stool legs were fixed in the last series, put a saw cut into the top of the dowel. You can then fix the dowel into the support block with a wedge and glue, tapping the wedge in gently.

Saw off the wedge and plane the work flush.

Check the block for a good fit in a few adjustment holes. If it's a little tight, give the dowel a light sand down and try it again.

Give the support block a coat of the usual brown stain.

Fitting

If you have chosen the half mitered foot to be on the right hand side of the leg (when looking from the front), then you install the leg by holding it at 45 degrees (twenty minutes to two on a clock face). You then rotate it counter clockwise with the back plate behind the apron until it reaches vertical.

A gentle tap of the wedge towards the vice will then lock it in position.

To remove the bench leg simply repeat the above steps in reverse order.

Make sure the leg fits well before you stain up. Incidentally, the position of the support block in the photo, coincides with the support tubes of my vise. I've marked a line across the leg as an easy reminder for me when I want the block to be the same height as my vise.

"A gentle tap of the wedge towards the vice will lock it in position."

If it all fits properly and the sliding lock works you can sand down and stain up next.

Finishing

With an extra leg, you'll find you can support most boards and panels that you ever need to put in the vise.

Stain up the leg and support block. Wax makes the block easier to move.

I'd recommend a good sand down of everything followed by a spirit based stain over all the surfaces. Follow this with a light coat of furniture wax. Nothing else is really necessary as it's not a device that needs to take a lot of punishment.

Using the extra leg

Above is an example of how you can use this device to support your work. By moving the support block right up, it will also carry a long board, again with the other end in the vise jaws.

4-12/1815C
A84-12
-12/485F

Sticking boards

To address some terminology first, sticking boards are not sticky. The name comes from the term 'sticking', which refers to the decorative molding applied around the inside of a frame to hold a panel in place. The more labor intensive approach was to use 'stuck' moldings where the molded profile was worked onto the solid stile or rail of a cabinet door or frame. So, making 'sticking' to apply to a panel was a common job, which required the use of a work holding system, so that the wood could be worked on with molding planes, rebate planes, etc. The work holding method traditionally used was known as a 'sticking board'.

It takes the form of a sub table, usually held to the bench with a pair of hold downs. You can see this in use in the photos on the right.

The thing about a sticking board is that it is there to serve a single purpose: To hold your work. Screw stops into it, pin extra support battens to it, make 45 degree sloping holders to screw to it, basically do anything that seems like a good idea to hold your work. In the photo here, you can see my basic sticking board has a 45 degree holder fixed to it, with a lower support (the work piece is resting on this).

I frequently change mine about, depending on the work I'm doing and I keep all the bits that go with it in a bundle, sitting in a box screwed to the wall.

The general method to hold work on a sticking board is to fit a screw to one end of the board, gently tap the work against the screw so it bites in, and then fit another screw at the other end. I use a cordless drill, as it's just very quick to put screws in and move them.

Vintage sticking boards can very rarely be found these days, as folks clearing out granddad's shop would probably chop them up for firewood, not realizing they were part of a system to be used with the more obviously valuable molding planes that they may be stored with.

You are going to need one of these for the practice exercises on page 132, where you can try out making some moldings.

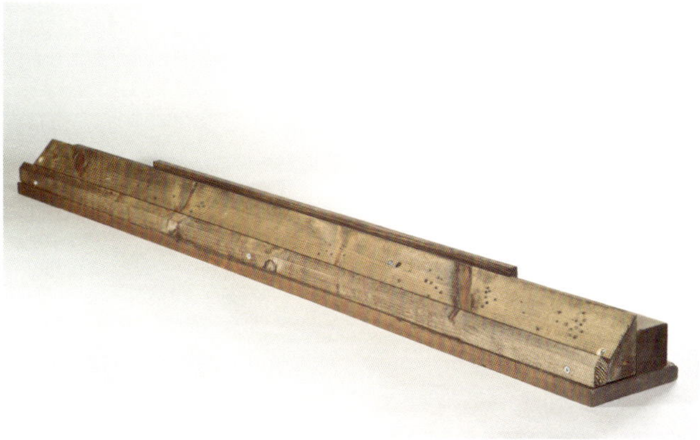

It's a simple and adaptable device.

It's great for molding work...

...or grooving with a plow plane...

...and you just need a few screws to fix the work down.

Long bench clamp

This bench clamp is similar to a device written about by Joseph Moxon, famous for writing in detail about the practices and principles of various craft based professions in the mid 16th century. ('Mechanick Exercises' printed 1683.) The 'Moxon vise' sat on the bench, held down by sprung steel clamps (hold downs - page 239).

My version is just the same, but a lot longer. The extra length allows two boards to be clamped together and planed simultaneously, which is ideal for jointing panels and boards for cabinet sides, table tops, etc. This may seem to be a rather cumbersome device and if you are prepared to do a lot of clamping to the bench with hand screws, you could manage without it. However, if you've got the space to store one of these and the time to make it, you'll find that it makes all sorts of jobs much easier. In the next part of the *Working Wood* course we'll be using this a lot, so you could wait until then to see how much it's used before you decide to make one yourself.

The front clamping bar is curved, so the middle of the work is gripped tightly, as well as the ends.

Materials

Planed hardwood

4" x 2" 1pc at 52"

2" x 2" 1pc at 52"

Plywood

¾" x 8½" x 52" 1pc (apron)

½" x 8½" x 52" 1pc

Hardware:

½" 'T' nuts - 4pcs

½" Threaded bar - 2pcs at 11"

2 Winding handles

Check for square...

...and for absolute flatness.

Flatten and straighten first

The hardwood 4x2 is in the part that everything fixes to, and therefore is the most important component to get totally flat and straight. The best advice I can give you here is to choose the straightest, flattest and most uniform piece of wood that you possibly can.

It's worth making a quick check for square in a few places. Even if you buy planed timber, it may not be accurate.

Take your straightedge and check for a hump or a hollow along the length. Make sure you have a good light source so you can see any gaps easily.

This piece of oak had a slight hollow in the middle so I've marked a few squiggles with a soft pencil so I can easily see how much is coming off, and from where.

This piece was not perfect so I've made some pencil marks where I need to plane it down a bit.

Work steadily at the high spots and then flip the wood over and do the same on the other side. Generally speaking, if you've taken both ends down on the hollowed side, when you flip it over, it's the middle that needs the attention as there's probably going to be a slight hump to take out.

Checking for twist is important. Use your winding sticks (page 293), again with a good light, to check for any twist. With a well chosen piece of timber, any corrections should be minimal and fairly quick. We will look in more detail at how you straighten out your stock in the next part of the course.

The pencil lines show me where I'm planing.

Eliminate all twist by checking and planing.

I've marked the depth of the recess.

The Forsterner bit leaves a neat finish.

You need to drill out for the threaded sleeve.

Choose the right diameter bit and drill to depth.

Finally, go all the way through with an auger.

With the rod in place, tap the 'T' nut home.

"...mark up both sides of the hole before you start, so you can drill from both sides."

Drill the holes in the 4 x 2

There is no practical requirement to inset the 'T' nuts into the wood, but I like to do this just to make it look neater. I'll show you this extra step first in case you want to do the same.

TOP TIP: *If you want to eliminate the risk of going off course when drilling the through hole, mark up both sides of the hole before you start so you can drill from both sides, or use a pillar drill.*

As you will have done making the caul clamps, select the correct diameter of auger (I'm using a Forstner bit, as it cuts a nice flat bottomed recess) and mark on the depth you require. One 'T' nut is fitted to the back of the 4x2, and another to the front plywood apron. This is to make them 'captive' (unable to move or come out) after the threaded bar is wound through.

Around 2" from the end of the timber mark cross hairs dead center on the face edge and drill the recess.

The threaded sleeve also needs a recess, so measure and select an appropriate cutter and then bore this out to the right depth.

The threaded rod needs to go all the way through so select a long auger, perhaps 1⁄16" oversize relative to the threaded rod (clearance is always good), and bore through dead straight.

In the photo, bottom right, the 'T' nut is being fitted into the back of the 4x2, as the plywood apron needs fitting before the second recess is cut into it.

To seat the 'T' nuts, thread the rod through the nut, but not so far that it protrudes, and then tap the nut into place as shown. The rod guarantees that the nut seats properly at 90 degrees to the hole.

Repeat this process at the other end of the 4x2, or 2x4 if you are in the US!

Fit the plywood apron

With the hardwood held firmly in the bench vise, drill, countersink and pilot drill into the 4x2 to fix the plywood apron down. Use a clamp to help you hold the plywood in position while you screw it together.

TECHNICAL POINTER: *Do not put any screws too close to the area 2" from the end of the work piece. You will be fitting another 'T' nut here.*

Screw the apron piece to the oak 4x2 timber.

Fit the front 'T' nuts

Remove the 'T' nuts you have already fitted into the 4x2 (don't worry, they will go straight back in again), and place the work in the vise with the long holes facing you. Now bore through the back of the 4x2 oak, into the plywood with the same auger you used to drill the long holes.

Keep going slowly until the thread of the auger just pops through.

Stop immediately to switch augers, and bore out a recess for the 'T' nut as you did before. Don't forget to use the second auger to widen the hole for the threaded sleeve.

You already have a hole in the 4x2, so just carry it through to the other side.

TOP TIP: *If you ever need to use an auger to widen a hole, the usual problem is that there is no wood to center the point in because there is an existing hole! To get round this, tap in a small wooden plug, and pre-drill a small central hole in the plug. The point of the auger will now pick up the pilot hole allowing you to bore out as required. You simply knock out the plug when you are done.*

Stop as soon as you hit daylight, then go in...

...from the front of the apron to form the recess.

As before, fit the rod into the 'T' nut before you tap it home, as this will help keep it straight.

You could use a heavy socket as a drift.

Fix the ½" plywood to the underside of the 4x2.

To set out a curve in the clamp, bend a piece of batten to the right shape, holding it with 'G' clamps.

Use the threaded rod again to center and align the 'T' nut into the plywood.

TOP TIP: *If you want to tap the 'T' nut without any danger of leaving hammer marks in the wood, use the right sized socket from your tool box as a drift. The steel should be tough enough to take a reasonable beating without denting or shattering.*

To finish assembling the main body of the jig, clamp the ½" plywood base board to the underside of the 4x2 as shown, and screw it down in the usual fashion.

TECHNICAL POINTER:
Do not put screws into the area where the threaded rod goes through. This will foul up the operation completely!

Make the long clamp bar

It's very important for the clamp bar to be curved on the inside. This is an important design feature that allows the work piece to be held rigidly during normal use. With this in mind, the first job is to set out the curve on the clamp bar.

The most simple way to set out a long even curve (and this works for patios, driveways, arched brickwork and pretty much anything else really) is to use something long and flexible enough to adopt the shape of the curve you need. In this case, a thin pine batten will do the job. Using a series of packers, clamps and wedges, set out a curve along the length of the hardwood.

TOP TIP: *Mark the curve on both sides of the 2x2 hardwood. This makes it easier to plane down to the final size and shape accurately.*

You are aiming to take about $\frac{3}{8}$" off each end and nothing off the middle so use these measurements as you set up the curved batten.

You could remove the waste in a variety of ways. I chose my rip saw as I just happened to have recently given it a good sharpening.

The saw marks come out easily with a hand plane. I used my Stanley No.5½ for the extra width and weight.

TECHNICAL POINTER:
Always keep a close eye on the flatness of the planed surface, checking with a try square repeatedly, and of course work from the middle towards the ends or you'll be going against the grain!

Drilling the clearance holes is next, but don't rush this in your eagerness to get done. Carefully transfer the hole centers onto the clamp bar.

Bore through at 90 degrees, using your try square as a guide. Don't rush, get this right!

With a bent batten as a guide, scribing an arc onto the long clamp is easy.

Rip off the waste with a sharp saw...

...and plane down to the lines.

Mark the exact position of the clearance holes on each end.

Bore a clearance hole through, making sure you are at 90 degrees.

Trial assembly - I've fitted the handles and got everything in place.

Shown here are two boards, clamped side by side, getting planed up ready for glueing together.

Assembly

Fit the winding handles to the ends of the threaded rod; press and tap the 'T' nuts into place and clamp the whole jig to the table using your hold downs. Check the operation of the handles making sure they are not stiff. I should point out here that you need a little play in the 'T' nuts from front to back. Don't get everything all fitted together super tight or you'll need arms like a wrestler to clamp anything. You can give the threaded rods a light pass with a waxed cloth which will help the clamps operate smoothly.

Finishing

I gave the oak a coat of medium oak hard wax oil, as it brings out the wood grain nicely and is an excellent protective finish. The plywood got a coat of my 'standard bench brown', oil based wood stain, thinned down so it spreads easily.

Using the long bench clamp

The curvature in the clamp holds the middle of the boards really tight. Keeping the boards tight together is very important when you are planing long boards ready to join them together. Frequent checks with a long straight edge are also vital, as we all know how easy it is to plane a hump or a hollow on any board edge!

Chapter 11
Other devices

Along with general work holding devices, bench work holding devices and shooting boards, there are a few other devices that I'm including in this section which are well worth making. None of these devices are complex, but are very useful additions to your collection of equipment.

In this section I've included 'diagonal sticks' for measuring inside cabinet frames, a 'shooting stick', which just clips onto your plane and keeps it level, a nice pair of inlaid 'winding sticks', to check your boards are not twisted, and lastly, a simple pair of jigs for cutting tapered sliding dovetails.

On several occasions, the construction of some devices relies on the use of other jigs or aids detailed in this book, so before you start, it's always worth a quick run through any project, to see if there is anything you need to make before hand, or if you can easily manage without a device I'm suggesting you use.

Diagonal sticks

Have you ever glued up a large carcass and tried to fight your way through a forest of clamps to measure the diagonals with a tape measure? I used to do a lot of that at one time and I used to find it quite stressful. Diagonal sticks allow you to take a surprisingly accurate internal measurement during glue up and clamping, without having to worry about external corner to corner readings on a tape. It's simple to use and simple to make. Brass is a very nice metal to work with, as it's easy to bend, holds it's shape well and does not corrode. It dulls a little with time and develops a pleasant patina with use, but it will always polish up to a good shine, no matter how old it is.

What you'll need

Two fine grained hardwood battens - I'm using utile here.

½" x 1" x 27" - 2pcs

Brass plate: 1⅜" x 4" - thickness needs to be 18/20 SWG, (around 1mm)

Brass wood screw - rounded head (slotted) No.8

Diagonal sticks - They are not essential items, but just really useful!

"Diagonal sticks allow you to take surprisingly accurate internal measurements during glue up..."

The materials you'll need.

Cut the dadoes

If your stock is cut to size, this is a quick project. All it takes is cutting a couple of short dadoes and bending some brass! You are only going to cut a single dado on each stick, so just mark up one end across both lengths.

To mark up for the dadoes, draw a line across the stock at 1¼" from the end, and then a second line ⅝" away. Take these lines around the 3 visible faces on each stick, as you normally would for a dado housing.

The dado only needs to be ⅛" deep, so set you gauge to ⅛" and mark the depth between the lines.

Define the shoulders with a neat knife cut.

Place them side by side to mark up.

Mark the depth of the housing.

Define the shoulders with a marking knife.

Form a shallow knife wall and saw down to depth.

Removing the waste is simple:

- Saw down to the gauge lines with a dovetail saw.
- Peel out the waste with a sharp chisel
- Round over the edges with a square file.

One end of both sticks should look like the photo, bottom right, when you are finished.

Take the waste out with a sharp chisel.

File the sharp corners to give them a round over.

The finished housing.

For the brass band

Always treat brass with a bit of respect. Don't dink it or scratch it if you can help it. Start by setting your gauge to ⅝", and scribe a parallel line down the plate.

Next, use a fine liner black pen to draw a line adjacent to the gauge line. Work accurately here, as it will save work in fettling to fit later.

To cut the brass, clamp it in your vise jaw protectors and cut it using a hacksaw at a very steep angle as shown here in the photo, bottom left.

Saw down the black ink line, leaving the gauge line just visible.

File and polish both cut edges to get them smooth. (I say both, as you'll need to repeat this to get a second brass strip for the other end)

Scratch a fine line at ⅝".

Draw a black line on the waste side of the line.

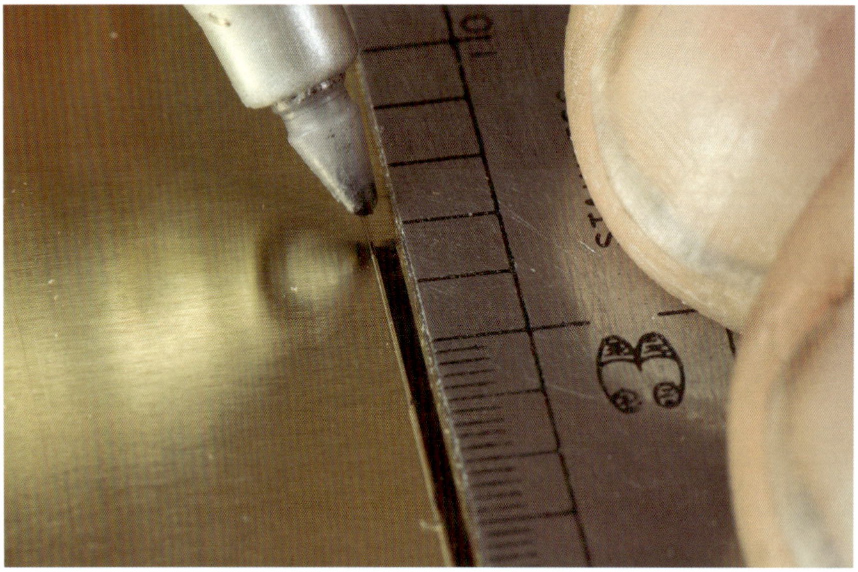

This is a close up so you can see what I mean.

Cut the brass with your saw at a very steep angle.

File the saw cut down to your marking gauge line.

As the brass strip is 4" long, measure 1½" from each end and mark this with a pen.

To fold the strip neatly, I would suggest you put it in the dado of one of the sticks and make a small packer to sit on top. The packer will grip the brass in the vise jaws.

Now place the stick, packer and brass strip in the vise so you can just see the black pen mark you've just made.

Make sure the setup is dead square, checking it before you tighten the vise fully.

Take your panel beater's mallet, and tap the brass over to a reasonable 90 degree angle. Don't bash away or you'll just beat the whole setup down lower in the vise. Gently does it!

To fold the other side over, you'll need to find a suitable spacer or packer to keep the bent leg you've just folded, from touching the vise jaws.

Measure 1½" from each end.

Place the brass in the housing with a packer...

...and clamp it in the vise as shown.

Tap the assembly to get everything at 90°.

Fold the brass over with a plastic mallet.

Use a large spacer for the next bend.

When you are happy with the set up, gently tap over the top leg to form a 'U' shape.

To finish the job off, place the second stick in the vise, on top of the first, with the legs pointing upwards, and start to bend the legs over. This forms the start of the bend. Don't flatten them down yet!

Insert a thin spacer, I've used a 6" steel rule as it's about the right thickness ($^1/_{32}$") and with this in place, tap the brass band over and down so that it sits flush.

TECHNICAL POINTER:
Without a little spacer, the sticks would be forced tight together and would just bind, making them unusable. They need to be able to slide against each other easily, even when a piece of masking tape is stuck between them.

At the opposite end to the dadoes, cut the ends of the sticks to a 45 degree bevel. The sticks, when laid on the bench with both dadoes uppermost, should have the longer side of the cut down on the bench.

You can shoot the ends to 45 degrees very quickly using the miter shooting board from page 349.

When shooting the beveled ends, notice the orientation of the dado housings in the photo below.

The second fold makes the brass 'U' shaped.

Put both pieces of wood in the vise for this part.

This spacer is VERY important ! See TECHNICAL POINTER.

Note the orientation of the housing relative to the bevel angle.

A sharp plane will leave a very smooth finish.

Saw off the brass screw with a fine blade in a junior hacksaw.

Select a drill that will give you a snug fit.

Drill the right sized hole to the right depth, and try the brass 'pin' for size.

Stop screw

To prevent the sticks from separating when you don't want them to, a small stop screw is needed. I used a longer brass screw with the thread sawn off.

Choose a drill that will give you a snug fit and drill a short hole about ¾" back from the end of the stick. As you pop the screw in, which is more like a pin now, it will prevent the sticks from sliding apart. Check the action, and if it all seems fine, take it all apart again.

Take them apart for a light sanding down...

Clean up and finish

With the sticks apart, give them a light sanding down and file any edges of the brass bands that need smoothing. Use your fingers to find the rough bits on the brass and if you need to, use a small, fine file.

It's out with the sanding sealer again! Notice that I use a pair of short, square sticks on my scrap plywood, just to keep the work off the deck as the sealer dries.

...then give them a coat of sanding sealer for protection.

Stick on a piece of tape so you can see the pencil marks clearly.

Glue and clamp up the carcass, getting everything level and square...

Using the diagonal sticks

For each piece of work that you measure, use a piece of tape on the inside of the sticks so you can make an accurate pencil mark.

Measure the inside across one diagonal and make a pencil mark on the tape.

Measure the other diagonal and make a second mark on the tape.

If you can see both marks, you need to reduce the distance of the second diagonal until you are half way between them.

If you can only see the second mark, you need to increase the distance of the second diagonal until you are half way between the pencil marks.

If both measurements are identical, the cabinet is square and the pencil marks will match up in exactly the same place on the white tape.

...then use the diagonal sticks to check the internal measurements.

Shooting stick

Why do I need one?

This is a simple device that acts as a fence for any one of your metal bench planes. In some ways it's not a conventional fence in that it's purpose is not to guide the plane at a predetermined distance in relation to the edge of the work piece. The purpose is to keep the plane at an exact 90 degree angle to the face of the work. Some people think that this is a skill that must be acquired through practice, more practice and still more practice! The real difficulty is that when trueing up boards for jointing, you need to get a 90 degree true edge all the way down a long board, and keep the plane flat with no twist, and keep it dead level with no hump or hollow. I have to admit, I simply can't do that! I can do a lot of other things reliably and consistently, but square edging a long board perfectly by eye is not on my list of accomplishments. Very few people can do this with consistent reliability.

For the rest of us

Help is at hand in the form of a simple device that I've called a 'shooting stick'. I just love easy solutions to every day practical problems. The device clips on and off your plane in a jiffy and will keep your plane at a perfect 90° to the job. I'll say no more.

The lengths of the two parts are not really important, and you may end up cutting the whole assembly down to say 5" long anyway, depending on how you want to use it. These instructions will help you get your first shooting stick made, and after that, you may want to adapt and improve the design.

This is a very simple device to make, and works a treat!

The shooting stick makes a tricky job very simple!

"Help is at hand in the form of a simple device that I've called a shooting stick."

What you'll need

Two hardwood pieces
10" x 1⅜" x ½"
8" x 1⅜" x ⅜"

Two rare earth magnets (¾" diameter ⅛" thick)

Brass wood screw 1" x No.10

Furniture wax

Polyurethane glue

Mark out first

Up to the step entitled 'Cutting corners', all the work is carried out on the longer of the two pieces.

To start, line up both parts flush at one end and mark a line on the longer piece. This marks the shoulder of the short piece, when assembled.

Set your marking gauge (or pencil gauge) to ⅜" and mark a line from the previous shoulder line to the top.

You may find it convenient to use shorter pieces, but you can always adjust the length afterwards.

Mark the shoulder onto the long piece.

Score a line ⅜" from the edge.

On this line, mark 1¼", 1½" and 1¾", corresponding to different sizes of bench plane

Square the 1¼" line across...

Now mark three holes for a brass screw, which will fit against the inside of the side of the plane body, holding it captive. I'm suggesting three holes here, as the brass screw will need to be moved towards the top if you swap the shooting stick from a small No.4 to a larger No.5 or an even larger No.7 try plane. Holes marked out at 1¼", 1½", and 1¾" will probably do the job and cover a wide range of planes. Only mark up at this stage, you'll drill the holes later.

Extend the 1¼" mark across the part and placing the magnet against the shoulder line, draw around it and mark the center.

TECHNICAL POINTER:
Check that the height of the sides of your plane, adjacent to the mouth, are within the range of 1¼" to 1¾" before you start. If not, adjust the screw positions to suit.

Draw around your magnet to mark the recess position.

Fit the magnets

To bore out the hole for the magnet, here's a good trick that prevents tear out.

1. Drill a pilot hole about ⅜" deep with a $\frac{3}{16}$" drill.
2. Then, set up your auger in the drill, put it into REVERSE, and 'attempt' to bore out the hole, with the auger rotating in the wrong direction.
3. The result is that all the top fibers of the wood get pushed down and the side cutting spur cuts a very neat circular groove.
4. Now select the 'forward' direction, go slowly and carefully on the trigger, holding the drill upright. You will now find that you can cut the hole very neatly with no tear out of the top surface.

TOP TIP: *With a marker pen, mark the depth of the magnets (I'm using two for extra holding power) on the polished side of the auger. When it rotates you will easily be able to check your depth as you now have a clear reference line.*

TECHNICAL POINTER: *Bore out a little deeper than you need to, not much, perhaps $\frac{1}{16}$" or less. If you don't do this, there is a risk that when you fit the magnets with glue, they won't go in far enough to sit flush with the front face. Check this first with a Vernier, using it as a depth gauge.*

With the hole bored out to the right depth, tidy up the bottom of the hole with a narrow (¼" - ⅜") chisel.

You need a really clean cut here, so drill a pilot hole for the threaded part of the auger to locate in.

Mark the depth on the auger.

Run the auger backwards, then forwards!

You will still need to clean the bottom of the hole out with a ¼" chisel.

Wax up a cabinet scraper, so the glue won't stick.

Spread the polyurethane glue evenly.

Wait for it to froth up a little before you put the magnets in and...

...clamp it in the vise.

Here's a good method for glueing the magnets in, so that they sit flush with the front face:

1. Take a cabinet scraper and give it a good coat of furniture wax. This prevents any excess glue from sticking to the metal.
2. Next, place the magnets onto the well waxed steel plate and squeeze some polyurethane glue into the socket. Spread it fairly evenly with a matchstick sized piece of scrap.
3. Give the glue a moment to start to froth a bit (the moisture in the air starts the setting reaction) and then locate the magnets in the recessed socket, still attached to the scraper, and press them home.
4. Clamp the set up in your vice. Note: The central snail (thread) from the auger hole I made, actually popped out of the back a little, which is not an issue, but the expanding glue will ooze out of the hole onto your vise jaws. You can just see the piece of paper that I put in the vise to prevent the glue from touching the jaws.

Clean up and shape the top

When the glue has set, drill out the three holes you marked previously. I'm using a small pilot drill for the brass screw, and the holes are about ³⁄₈" deep. With the pilot holes drilled, go ahead and clean up any escaped glue.

To round over the top, find a suitable sized washer to draw around, as shown in the photo, middle left.

Simply take the corners off with a coping saw, and smooth the surface with a single cut mill file, as shown in the photo at the bottom of this page.

Drill three small pilot holes for the brass locking screw.

I've used a large washer as a template.

A coping saw will take the waste off quickly...

...and a single cut mill file will smooth down the saw marks.

Mark 3⁄8" on to the short piece.

Draw a 45 degree line...

...and saw the corner off.

Use about this much glue...

Cutting corners

This is just a small detail that helps you to fit and remove the shooting stick easily with no fiddling about. Take the shorter of the two parts and mark 3⁄8" from the top and the side edges.

Join the lines up, using the 45 degree part of your try square stock as a reference, and saw off the corner.

Assembly

The choice of glue here is up to you. I like polyurethane glue as it sets very quickly.

Apply and spread some glue.

Clamp the assembly in the vise, being very careful not to get any slippage as you tighten up. Slippage is definitely a drawback with polyurethane glue. It acts as a very effective lubricant in any joint you are gluing, unless you use the trick we looked at on page 334, i.e. apply a thin film to both sides and allow it to froth and go slightly tacky before you press the parts together.

...spread it evenly, and...

...clamp it in the vise to set.

Pre-thread the screw holes

A nifty trick when you are fitting brass screws into hardwood is to use a hard steel screw, driven in and out a few times with a cordless drill, to pre-thread the pilot holes. It acts like an engineers tap. If you then drill a very shallow clearance hole, (about ⅛" deep) as shown in this photo, the brass screw will go in straight and easily. I've cropped the screw to length with pincers so it does not protrude through the wood. The reason for this extra care is that brass is very soft. Given that the screw will be moved, perhaps frequently depending on your work patterns, it pays to make sure that you never have to use much force to put it in or take it out.

I'll mention this again later on, just to remind you, as it makes such a difference!

Pre-thread the holes first.

Saw the brass screw to the right length.

Seal it up

After a good general sand down (120 grit will do), seal it up with a light coat of sanding sealer, and when it's dry, apply a good coat of wax polish, buffing it to a high sheen.

After a good sanding, apply a coat of sanding sealer.

One last dab of wax

Chose the plane you want to use with the shooting stick (I'm going for the No.5½) and fit the brass retaining screw into the hole that best suits the shape of the casting, in this case the middle position. Put a dab of wax on the screw before you wind it in, as this will allow for easy removal and re-positioning.

With the screw in the middle hole, it will clip on to my No.5½ plane.

Clip the shooting stick on as shown, sliding it into position and adjusting the screw as required.

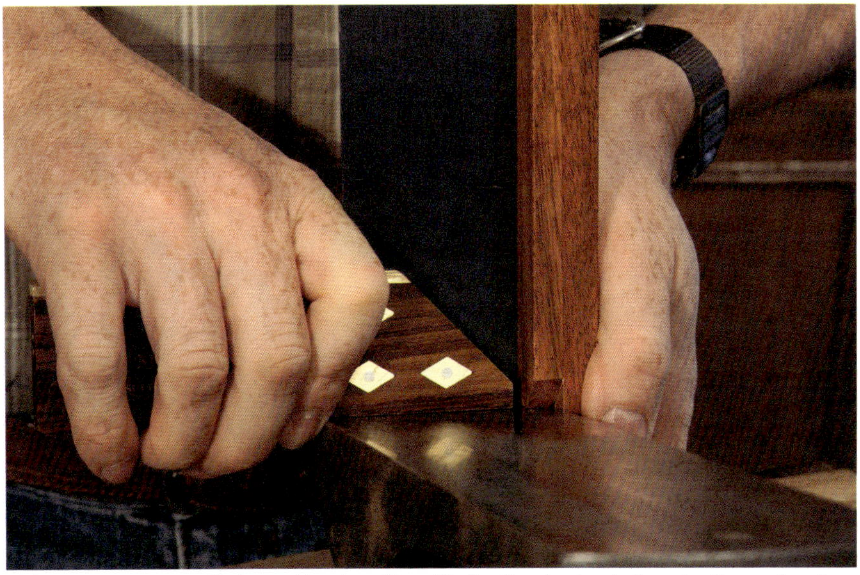

If this is not square, rectify the problem by taking off a few fine shavings before checking and sealing.

Keeping the shooting stick against the work, all I have to do is push the plane forwards!

Check for square

Clip the shooting stick onto the plane as shown, and check for square using the try square against the sole of the plane.

If for some strange reason, you don't have a perfect 90 degree angle, pop it in the vise and take a few fine shavings off the face shown registering against the blade of the square, in the middle photo. Depending on which way you need to correct the angle, you will need to either take shavings off near the screw or near the end, making sure the face is flat with no humps or hollows. Check again and when you are satisfied, sand down, re-seal and re-wax as required.

Using the shooting stick

Now that you know for sure that the shooting stick is set up square, I'd recommend you use it with metal planes about the size and length of a Stanley No.5 or No.7 try plane. For this long board, I've moved the screw to the top position and fitted the Shooting stick to my No.7. You can see here that when it's clipped on, it just requires a little sideways pressure on the stick to keep the sole of the No.7 absolutely flat and at 90 degrees to the face.

You'll also notice the long level in the background. I always use this when square edging a board as I can check for humps and hollows as I go. As you approach what you think is a truly flat and perpendicular edge, back off the iron in the No.7 to take the finest shavings. With a sharp, well adjusted iron, you should be able to take full length shavings.

Winding sticks

These classic workshop accessories are very simple in concept, but in use are remarkably accurate. They are used to sight down a length of timber, with one in the foreground and one at the far end. It will be obvious if there is a twist, or wind in the timber as the white lines will be out of parallel.

I've chosen a design that includes a contrasting inlay against a fumed, dark oak background to make the lines more visible. The key consideration is to select a very stable wood so that over time these measuring tools don't twist or bend themselves. A good many coats of sealer increase the stability throughout the range of seasons.

For this design I suggest choosing some good looking oak with straight grain, as this will make cutting the inlay slots much easier. You'll need to get a couple of pieces of white or very pale inlay ready before you start, and check that your slot cutter (page 42) is going to fit the inlay first. We will be covering shop made inlay later in this series, but for now I suggest you buy some in from a supplier.

The contrasting inlay stands out from the dark oak.

"It will be obvious if there is a twist or wind in the timber..."

Just look straight down the timber - Are those white lines absolutely parallel?

11 Other devices

Cut the slot

It's up to you how far from the edge you want to fit the inlay, I went for a little over 1⁄16", so my cutter was set to this distance from the stock. As you sight down the board, the light and dark stripes make it very easy to spot if they are not parallel.

Holding the oak stick in the vise, slowly cut out a slot, working from the end facing you, and going further and a little further with each pass. Keeping the stock tight against the work is your main concern. Take small shavings until you feel you have absolute control of the process.

The inlay slot cutter makes short work of cutting the narrow groove.

TECHNICAL POINTER:
Make the first pass over uncut wood nice and light, just taking a fine shaving.

As you progress down the stick, go to your full depth (set on the cutter), and then switch the work holding in the vise to allow you to reach the far end.

Hold the work in the vise and go with the grain.

Check for a good fit - you don't want it too tight!

Fit the inlay

With the slot cut cleanly and carefully, try a piece of inlay for a good fit. I'm using a piece of shop made inlay so I know it's going to be a good fit.

To glue up, have your burnisher handy, a clean cloth and some PVA. Put a small blob of PVA on the cloth and run the bottom edge of the inlay through a couple of times. Do a visual check for the glue, it should look reasonably even all the way down.

Starting at one end, feed the inlay into the slot and start to stroke it in slowly, in long even passes, getting firmer as it sits deeper in the groove. Finish off with a good, hard press, all the way down, which should seat it firmly in the slot forever! If there is any excess glue, wipe it off quickly and rub the work clean.

Pull the inlay through a little glue on a cloth...

...and smooth it down with a burnisher.

Trim the inlay flush with a block plane.

Into the shop made 'fume box' or 'smoker'. It does not have to be elaborate, as you can see!

TOP TIP: *If you would rather not use ammonia (I wouldn't blame you!), you could soak the oak in ebonizing shellac for a week or so. Shellac is good as it's not water based and so won't swell and distort the wood.*

You can use a plane to trim the inlay flush, pretty much straight away. I put the kettle on, had a nice cup of tea, and then got back on the job. The glue was obviously not set rock hard, but that inlay was not going anywhere.

Fuming the oak

The reason for fuming the oak is to make it much darker, so that the contrast with the inlay is even greater. The tannins in the oak react with the ammonia and darken the wood, deeper and deeper below the surface. The longer you leave it fuming, the darker and the deeper the color will be. The exact set up you use for this is entirely up to you. The main thing I want to introduce here is the process. Ammonia is pretty horrible stuff. Don't get near it if you are asthmatic or have any kind of breathing condition. The fumes will make you choke, even if you are fit as a fiddle.

A typical set up needs to include the following:

1. An airtight sealed compartment of some description, large enough to accommodate the work plus an extra allowance for the circulation of fumes within the compartment. Yes, that explains the large refuse sack and the shopping basket!
2. The work must be suspended so as not to rest on solid supports, or the color change will not be evenly distributed. That explains the fine wires you can see.
3. There must be a waterproof container, placed inside the compartment, which contains the ammonia liquid. That's what the plastic tub, under the sticks is for.
4. When the ammonia is introduced, you need to be able to close the compartment quickly and efficiently. I just grab the neck of the sack, pull it tight, and roll it up, keeping it in place with some weights. It's not high tech, but it works!

What a color difference! The next morning, the oak was really dark, but the inlay had not changed color.

Leave the set up to 'fume' for as long as you like. I'd recommend overnight for a dark oak, and a couple of days for a very dark shade of brown.

Now, when it comes to taking the sticks out, I would suggest you take the whole set up outside into the yard, and hopefully there will be a breeze blowing. Hold your breath, squint a bit, and just get the bag open, then quickly get out of the way. Let the fumes and fresh air mix a bit before you retrieve your nice dark winding sticks. That's what I do every time, as I can't stand the smell of ammonia. For this photo, I waited until the smell of ammonia was very weak, and then brought the setup back inside my workshop.

The sanding sealer makes them look stunning, and seals the grain against moisture.

Sand and seal

After letting the sticks 'breathe' for a day or so (yes, it really does take this long to lose the pungent aroma), give them a good sand down and a coat of sanding sealer. Look at the lovely color of these guys. Just wait until we get onto the inlaid cabinet doors in the next series, they're going to be beautiful!

Sliding dovetail jigs

The tapered sliding dovetail joint is one of the most underrated joints I have ever come across. I don't know how many biscuit joints, dominoes, screws, glue and lengths of baler twine you'd need to get a housing joint as strong as a tapered sliding dovetail joint.

Cutting a tapered dovetail or the housing it slides into are not exceedingly difficult processes, getting them to match perfectly is the crux of the matter!

Just imagine if both of these operations could be carried out by hand in a simple and organized fashion that just works every time. If you are quickly losing interest here because you can do this with a router and 'ain't gonna change', you may be interested to know that this method works for any thickness of timber panel, joining any width of timber panel and could just be quicker than using a router?

I am only writing this because I know the complexity of set up you need to get high tolerance routed parts to match beautifully. You need a separate set of matching jigs for each combination of widths and thicknesses, and matching cutters and template guide rings. If you are cutting the same exact joint, day in day out, a router will do the job nicely, but that probably does not apply to most of us.

This joint is the best and strongest for holding solid wood side panels together using a shelf, and if you decide to make the following simple jigs, you could have a whole load of fun cutting and fitting shelving into your projects using techniques that you thought were way out of your league! In the next part of the course, this joint is going to get plenty of use as we put together a very traditional cupboard, using very traditional bench joinery.

A typical set up for cutting a dovetail on the end grain.

"You could have a whole load of fun... using techniques that you thought were way out of your league!"

These two jigs make cutting and adjusting the joint (if required) a straightforward process.

What you'll need

Three pieces of sapele mahogany, utile or maple

1¼" x 4¼" x 21" - 1pc

1¼" x 2" x 21" - 1pc

¾" x 3" x 21" - 1pc

3 Brass wing nuts (¼" or 6mm thread) and washers, brass threaded bar

Pozi-drive wood screws.

Sanding sealer

Wax polish

Set out to saw up your stock

I'd suggest that you arrange the pieces as shown in this photo, labelling them similarly to avoid confusion. You'll notice here that I'm pointing to a line on part 'C', drawn square across ¼" from the top and marked onto the piece marked A-B. The small mark you make on A-B is important for the next step.

Set your sliding bevel to 1:7, and with a sharp pencil, draw a 1:7 line across the end grain from the small mark you made in the previous step. This indicates the line you are going to saw down to create two pieces out of one.

We now need to score lines down the length of A-B on each face, corresponding with the 1:7 line on the end grain. So which tool is the best for the job? If you choose a small marking gauge, it will work fine, but the farther out the point is from the stock, the more chance there is of wobbles and errors.

I prefer a panel gauge, as the wide sliding stock gives me a much longer, and therefore more stable, reference edge to slide against the work piece. Fine adjustments are made by giving the bar a gentle tap, which moves the stock very slightly towards, or away from the marking pin. Run a pencil down the scored line left by the panel gauge, as it's really important to see the line clearly.

Arrange the pieces as shown. The line I'm pointing to is also marked onto the adjacent piece 'A-B'.

Mark a 1:7 line across with a sliding bevel.

For a parallel line, you could choose either,...

...but I'm going to use the panel gauge for ease of use. Gentle taps can be used to adjust it in or out.

I'm going to saw the piece in half using a panel saw, but a tenon saw starts easily on the end grain.

TOP TIP: *Starting off with a tenon saw will cut the end grain easier than a panel saw.*

Saw down your lines with the work piece held in the vise.

TECHNICAL POINTER:
Frequently swap the orientation of the work piece in the vise, as it's important to saw from both sides. By doing this, you will get a very accurate saw cut and save yourself a lot of planing in the next step.

Cut from both sides, alternating as you go.

Clean up the saw cut, and take fine shavings...

With the two parts separated, place them in the vise and take off a few shavings to get the surfaces flat and smooth.

TECHNICAL POINTER:
You need to get both pieces to match up perfectly when B is laid on top of A. This means constant check for gaps, using your try square as a straight edge on the front face.

Check the front and back faces for gaps. I am pointing at the faintest whisker of a gap, which should come out with the next few passes of a very finely set plane.

When you are confident that parts A and B match up very nicely, apart from a good sand down and a coat of sealer, Part B is finished!

...until both pieces match perfectly.

After planing up, the gap between both pieces should be nearly invisible.

Match the angle

The next step is to plane down the top of part C to match the angle planed on top of part A. Set part B to one side, as it's finished apart from sanding and sealing. Plane off the shaded area marked on part C

This is a straightforward business as you don't have to work to a very high degree of accuracy on part C. Just get it pretty close. Don't plane any more off part A!

Cut the slots

As the work piece is 21" long, and I want 3 slots, I measure in 2" from each end and mark the center. These marks indicate the center lines of the slots.

Set your marking gauge to ⅝", and mark points on the slot center lines as shown.

These points define the extremities of the slots, so drill through into some scrap, using the six marked points as hole centers.

TOP TIP: *If you have a drill press/pillar drill, this will speed the job up and guarantee accuracy.*

Saw out the waste with a coping saw, just like the sliding fence project on page 329, and carefully file all three slots smooth.

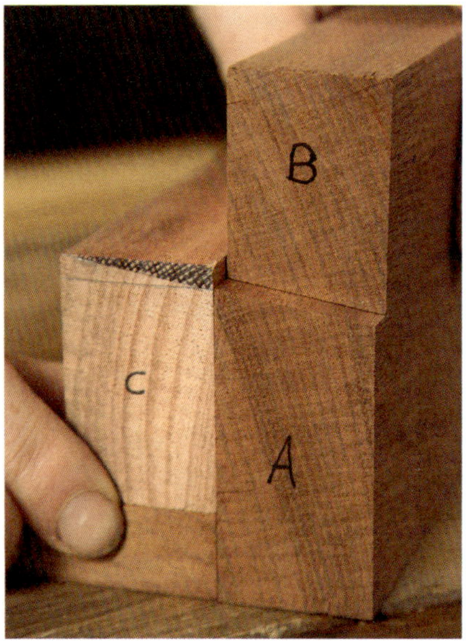

The next job is to plane off the hatched area...

...to match up with part A.

Measure 2" from each end and mark the center. These are the slot positions.

Mark ⅝" from each edge.

Drill through into some scrap.

Don't break out the edges with a file!

Mark the center of part C onto the baseboard.

Mark the center all the way along.

On the line you have just marked, draw cross hairs for 4 clearance holes.

Screw it together

On the end grain of the base board, mark the mid point of part C as shown in the photo, top left.

Set your pencil gauge to this mark, and draw a line down the baseboard to show you where the screws should go.

Mark positions for 4 screws and drill clearance holes, countersinking the underside of the base board.

With the clearance holes drilled, assemble the baseboard and part C as shown in the photo, bottom left. Use clamps to hold the work together, and tap everything to align the front face flush, all the way along. With the parts aligned, and clamped, invert the assembly so you can drill and screw the underside of the base board.

TOP TIP: *Use an angled wedge as a packer to protect the top surface of part C. This will make the set-up much more stable!*

Drill pilot holes from the underside of the clamped up assembly and screw the parts together from underneath, holding part C in the vise as shown.

With all the drilling complete, align the pieces and clamp up, ready for...

...fixing together with screws, driven in from the underside.

Fit the brass rods

I have marked a line on part A (sorry, the letter is obscured by the ruler), which is the depth of the hole I want to screw the brass rod into. This gives me a total length of threaded rod of 2½", allowing enough sticking out to fix the wing nut and washer.

I can now drill the holes through part C, into part A, at the very bottom of the slots. Drilling a hole for the rod at the bottom of the slots will enable the front of the jig to be raised when in use. The clamps stop the work from moving around as I drill. You'll notice that the chuck is about to hit the base board, so obviously, with the holes started, unclamp Part A and drill it separately to the right depth.

TECHNICAL POINTER: *The brass rod needs to cut it's own thread into the hardwood, so drill an undersize hole. The exact diameter of the hole needs to be determined by some trial and error in some scrap hardwood. Too tight, and you'll never get it to screw in. Too loose, and you'll strip the thread as you tighten up the wing nuts. Bear in mind, you will insert the rod by putting it into the chuck of your cordless drill, and then simply winding it in, using a low gear for high torque.*

So, we know we need 2½" of brass rod per hole and we have 3 holes, so we need 7½" of rod. I've marked off 8½" to leave me some extra to grip in the chuck of the drill when I wind in the last piece.

TOP TIP: *The easiest way to mark threaded rod for length is to use a piece of tape, just as you would for a drill bit, to gauge hole depth accurately.*

I'll cut the brass rod off in situ. It's going to be around 2½" long after I've cut it.

Drill holes through the very bottom of the slots, going in just enough to mark the positions.

Use tape on the drill bit to mark the depth.

Wind the brass rod in carefully so as not to strip the wooden thread you're forming.

Saw the rod off, allowing ⅜" of protrusion.

Repeat with the other holes.

With all 3 holes drilled to the correct size and depth, hold part A in the vise and slowly fit the brass rod using the cordless drill.

For every rod you insert, test it for a fit through the slot and cut it to length in situ.

Repeat this for all 3 rods.

Finishing

Assemble the jig to check everything goes together as it should and then ease the corners and all the edges with a light sanding.

Finally, take it all apart, leaving the threaded rods in place, and apply a good coat of sanding sealer. Don't forget to include Part B as you apply the sealer! I like to have a door open for ventilation when using sanding sealer, which is fine unless it's the dark depths of mid winter! I'd rather a cold workshop than a warm shop full of solvent fumes!

Fit the jig together with the wing nuts when the sealing coat is dry. See page 307 for full instructions on the use of these jigs.

Assemble the jig and check it moves and locks.

Take it apart to give it a coat of sealer.

Re-assemble the jig, and it's finished!

Chapter 12
The tapered sliding dovetail joint - cut by hand

The right jig makes all the difference!

This relatively complex joint adds strength and rigidity to shelves and dividers used in case work, and before the invention of wood screws and modern glue, furniture makers knew the benefits of trusting their reputations to such a strong interlocking joint.

The strength of a dovetailed joint has been exploited for centuries, to great effect in countless examples all over the world. It's quite common to find tapered sliding dovetail joints in older pieces, but it's interesting to note that these are usually barefaced (i.e. only one side is dovetailed). It is very uncommon to find pieces where the maker has hand cut a tapered sliding dovetail, with both sides of the joint cut at the dovetail angle. Even for the skilled traditional maker, to get a good fit is a technically challenging operation and for this reason the hand cut variety of the joint has mostly fallen into disuse.

Added to this challenge is the problem of slight natural curvature that exists in even the most stable of planed timbers, and so you realize why you don't meet many folks who regularly cut and fit these joints by hand.

Instrument makers commonly use the joint to join a neck to the body, but again, I suspect not many joints are entirely hand cut.

It's true that a router and a set of jigs and templates will enable the user to produce a machine cut joint, which would probably work well, but the question is this: How do you cut this joint reliably, efficiently and entirely by hand?

The wing nuts allow you to adjust the bar, setting the exact taper you want to cut.

The function of the jigs

I'm a big fan of workshop jigs and aids. I make them on a regular basis, sometimes out of curiosity but usually out of necessity. The jigs I use for hand cutting the TSD joint are fairly simple to make by hand, but even quicker and easier on a table saw (or band saw) and surface planer. Both jigs rely on a smooth sliding surface, sloping at a 1:7 gradient, acting as an accurate guide for your chisel. All the chisel work with these jigs is in a paring action, prizing or slicing the wood fibers. The first jig (larger of the two shown below) is used for working on the end grain. It has to be adjustable so you can move either end up or down, according to the taper required. This jig allows you to cut a tapered dovetail profile right onto the end grain of your shelf, dividing panel or drawer back.

The second jig (part 'B' on page 302) is a piece of hardwood with a 1:7 slope on one face. This is used to create the dovetailed sides of the housing. This jig is also adjustable, as it's simply held to the work with a pair of clamps. Adjustments are made by tapping the jig up or down, as it's clamped to the work piece. Making the jigs is surprisingly straightforward and is described fully on pages 299 to 305. I've used a method of slots and brass wing nuts for the adjustment, but any design is fine, so long as it works!

"Two simple jigs make hand cut TSDs a breeze. One is just an angled piece of wood, the second is an adjustable and lockable guide."

Start off by preparing your wood, shooting it square and to the right length.

Mark on the shelf positions.

Measure down 1/8" from the top mark.

Continue the 1/8" line all the way across.

Mark where the housing will stop.

Sizing up the joint

The precise dimensions for the tapered sliding dovetail joint are worked out 'on the fly', but there are a few principles that will maximize the joint strength.

1. Cut the depth of the dado housing about one third of the thickness of the side piece.
2. Make the back end of the tapered dovetail (on the shelf) full shelf width. This may give you a shoulder width of between 1/8" and 1/4" depending on the thickness of the side pieces.
3. Make the front end of the dovetail between 1/8" and 3/16" less than the back, depending on the shelf thickness. This will produce plenty of taper and keep the front of the shelf as strong as possible, as well as making the job quicker and easier than cutting an unnecessarily steep taper.

Layout

Before starting, make sure the board ends are a perfect 90°, using a shooting board.

The joint is laid out such that the top of the shelf fits into a dovetailed housing cut at 90 degrees to the board. The underside of the board always has the taper cut into it. On assembly, the shelf can be seen to rise upwards as it is tapped gently towards the front of the side piece, travelling up the inclined taper and finally locking tight, flush with the front face.

Layout the shelf positions first, and then layout the upper shoulder lines for the dadoes, about 1/8" in from each finished shelf position. Extend these lines all the way to the front of the side pieces, as this defines the uppermost side of the tapered housing after assembly.

For a stopped, tapered sliding dovetail, mark the end of the dado 5/8" back from the front edge of the side piece, and leave the gauge set for marking up the mating part.

Mark the housing depth

Using either a wheel gauge or a marking gauge, mark the depth of the housing on the back edge of the side piece, aiming for around 1/3rd of the thickness of the side piece. Again, leave the gauge set ready for the next step.

That is the first part of the layout completed on the side piece. It's now time to layout and cut the tapered dovetail, after which, we will measure and cut an accurate tapered housing to match perfectly.

The tapered dovetail

Tapered dovetails are formed on both ends of the shelf, and the convention is that the taper is cut to the underside of the dovetail. For this reason, the first shoulder cut on the upper side of the shelf is cut parallel, with no taper. However, both shoulder lines can be defined at the same time. The shoulders need to have a minimum depth of about ⅛", increasing to around double this amount on the underside of the shelf, at the front, on account of the taper.

Dovetail layout

The shoulder lines on the shelf define the depth of the dovetail. Back off the wheel gauge by a whisker (around 0.5mm in metric, which is less than 1⁄32"), and mark on the shoulder lines on both sides of the shelf. This little bit of clearance will ensure the dovetail does not 'bottom out' in the housing before the shoulders fit tightly. Mark the shoulders lightly and then deepen the lines with a square and marking knife.

The first cut

Hold the shelf in your vice and using a sharp chisel, pare out some of the waste, evenly all the way along your knife line, with the chisel held at around 20-25 degrees.

Mark the housing depth on the sidepiece.

Mark a slightly shallower depth on the shelf.

Define the shoulders all the way round, apart from the back edge, which needs no knife cut.

Form a knife wall, all the way round, and then place the shelf into a pair of caul clamps.

Hold the work in caul clamps, and set the jig up to work on the end grain.

Set the jig so your chisel barely touches the front edge...

...then just work your way along, slicing out the fibers. Release the fibers with a knife cut.

After forming this knife wall, place the shelf into a pair of caul clamps and hold these down securely to the bench as shown. Make sure you have the top side of the shelf uppermost before you start.

TOP TIP: *I always use the first jig in conjunction with a pair of caul clamps, and a couple of long bench 'hold downs'. The caul clamps have two important functions. Firstly, they get the work off the bench, holding the shelf at the right height. Secondly, they clamp the board totally flat, an prerequisite for this operation. However, if you haven't got these special purpose clamps, you can do the same job with a few stout battens, half a dozen G clamps and a few sash clamps.*

You are going to cut the non-tapered side of the dovetail first, so you will set up the jig absolutely parallel with the top face of the side piece.

With the first jig clamped to the bench, raise the bar so a chisel just barely removes any waste off the front edge, equally on both left and right edges of the shelf. Lock the bar in position.

Pare off the waste, holding the chisel down firmly onto the sloping top of the adjustable bar, using this as a reference face to work your way along.

The cut should be parallel with the top surface of the shelf, dovetailed due to the 1:7 slope on top of the bar, but definitely not tapered! Progress along the full width of the board, holding the chisel firmly against the jig while still allowing it to slide as you pare off small bites. A quick wipe and a polish with some wax may help the chisel slide over the adjustable bar easily.

If you need to release the parings at the end of the cut, just use a marking knife to sever the fibers. Clear them out of the way and take a second knife pass if you still need to go a little deeper.

The ⅛" shoulder line you have created will correspond with the ⅛" line you squared across, in the bottom left photo on page 309, the idea being that the shelf will be positioned exactly where it is supposed to be when assembled. (See the photo, top right.)

A marking knife will release the fibers.

The shoulder should be about ⅛" deep.

The second cut

Take the shelf out of the clamps and turn it over with the underside uppermost. You will now cut the tapered side of the dovetail.

> **TOP TIP:** *Make sure that you have clearly marked up the front, back, top and bottom of each end of each shelf. Check this regularly, as it would be very disappointing to cut one taper sloping one way and the other taper sloping in the opposite direction!*

Saw the shoulder down to a depth of 3/16" at the front, running the cut uphill slightly to a ⅛" depth.

Mark the depth of the dovetail shoulder at ⅛" on the back edge of the board, but on the front edge, increase the depth of the shoulder to around 3/16". This will produce the tapered profile.

Define the knife wall as before, but this time, take a dovetail saw and cut carefully towards the ⅛" and 3/16" marks on the back and front edges of the shelf respectively. The cut will of course be sloping slightly uphill towards the front edge of the shelf.

Sawing the shoulder is not a job to be rushed. Go steadily and carefully with your saw. A larger toothed tenon saw will work, but it will have a tendency to jump and skip as you saw across the grain. Sticking to a dovetail saw will make the job slower but more controllable, and the fine set and narrow kerf will give you good results.

This is the front edge of the shelf. You can see I've sawn down about 3/16" ready for the chisel work.

Set the jig and check your chisel will pare the shoulders to the correct depths of 3/16" and 1/8".

The taper is formed quickly and accurately. You can see I've marked the back so I don't get it wrong!

Set the jig up, initially estimating the height of each end of the cut, then use a chisel on the jig to precisely intersect the marks.

Again, pare the waste away until the side of the dovetail is smooth, even and critically, matches up with the depth marks.

A stopped dovetail

Transfer the stop mark from the dado to the end of the dovetail. I used the same setting on my pencil gauge for marking both.

Form a knife wall on the front edge and saw off the waste, taking out the pencil line completely. This will make sure your shelf can be adjusted to finish flush with the front face of the sides. Sawing on the wrong side of the line will stop the shelf before it's flush.

Pare down the saw cut shoulder to give a neat finish.

TOP TIP: *You can 'dish' out the middle of the stopped shoulder very slightly, as this will guarantee the joint is tight at the edges, instead of riding high on an accidental bump in the center. I mean VERY SLIGHTLY, and don't accidentally touch those knife cut edges.*

You need a stopped dovetail so mark it up...

...saw off the waste, and...

...trim up the stopped shoulder.

The dovetailed housing

This method assumes you are able to quickly, easily and accurately hand cut a dado housing or stopped dado housing. The first stage is to cut a tapered housing, which is really just as easy as a parallel housing - similar layout method, same process and the same tools.

Procedure 1
Mark and cut the dado

You should have already marked up the shelf positions and the uppermost side walls of the dadoes. As my design for this particular shelving unit incorporates a back panel, I need to mark out the width of the shelf on the side piece.

So, the back of the shelf is a known position in the housing, and the front position is also known, as we have already marked it up as a stopped dado.

The first job is to transfer the width of the dovetail from the front of the shelf to the stopped end of the dado, towards the front of the side piece.

The width is easily measured with a digital Vernier , which can be locked off so as not to move. When you are happy that you have got the gauge tight in down to the narrowest part of the dovetail, and you're happy that you have an accurate reading, lock it off with the thumbscrew.

Register one side of the Vernier gauge precisely on the ⅛" shoulder line (see bottom photo). Make knife marks to indicate the width. Put a circle around the knife marks with a soft pencil, so you can easily see where they are.

Repeat the measurement for the back of the shelf, and transfer this width onto the back of the side piece, at the point where the shelf stops.

TECHNICAL POINTER:
Remember, make the knife mark where the shelf ends, not on the edge of the side piece!

Looking at the back edge, mark the position of the shelf as it will be when it's in place.

Measure the width of the dovetail, right down at the shoulder, then...

...simply transfer the measurement to the point where the dado stops.

Pick up the knife nicks, and cut a knife line for the non-tapered side using the square.

For the tapered side, just pop a wedge in, adjusting it so the knife nicks line up, then knife across.

Cut the dado

On the side piece, the uppermost shoulder cut is at 90 degrees to the board so you can form a knife wall in the usual fashion.

However, on the other side we need to form a knife wall that is not at 90 degrees, and runs precisely between the marks we set out with the Vernier gauge. The easiest way to do this is to get a fine wedge and place it in between the stock of your square, and your work piece, as shown in the middle photo. This will kick the square out of 'square'. You simply adjust the wedge, and slide the square up or down the work piece, until the blade of the square exactly matches the Vernier knife marks. Deepen the knife lines from the stop mark all the way to the back of the side piece.

TECHNICAL POINTER: *For the first 1/8" of depth, you must use a marking knife to deepen the side walls, and a chisel to take the waste out. If you chop down with your chisel from above, you will move the side walls out from the lines, and I guarantee your shelf will then be a sloppy fit, and you really don't want that!*

You can see both knife lines here.

Form a knife wall on both sides...

...going down vertically, as for a regular housing.

When you have a good depth of sidewall, switch to a chisel and chop out in the usual fashion. Clean up with a hand router, going right down to the depth mark you made earlier.

Procedure 2
Create the dovetailed side walls

So, with your stopped, tapered housing cut to the correct depth, you now need to cut the dovetailed sides of the housing. The dovetailed shape is formed by under cutting the side walls, forming a housing that is wider at the bottom than near the surface. However, it's very important not to get carried away paring at the walls, or you may actually widen the whole housing. A good trick to prevent this from happening is to run a soft pencil down both sides of the housing, right along the top edge.

If you ever make a slight mistake and take off a whisker too much, you will instantly see what you've done without ruining the whole job.

Undercutting the housing could not be easier. Start by running your Stanley No.71 cutter down the sides of the dado, set to the right depth, slightly undercutting the side walls.

With you work held vertically in the vice, clamp on the second jig. Tap the jig until a chisel placed on the sliding surface just kisses the top fibers of the dado. Remember, don't go taking off those pencil lines! Make sure both ends are aligned perfectly and lock the clamps down.

Chop down when you have ⅛" deep knifewalls.

A router will finish the dado to the right depth.

Run a dark line along the top edge of each side of the housing. A soft pencil is best for this.

Clamp the second jig onto your work, arranging it so the chisel barely touches the pencil line.

If it looks like you are about to slice into the pencil lines, slacken the clamps and adjust the jig.

That's better! You can just about see the pencil line is not being touched.

The jig allows you to guide your chisel along at just the right angle, for both sides of the housing.

Don't forget to use packers with the clamps or you'll risk damaging the outer face of your work.

With a sharp chisel held firmly against the sliding surface, start to peel off the fibers with a sideways slicing motion, or alternatively with short, controlled stabs forwards.

In the middle photo, you can clearly see the pencil line that I have not touched (so far) as I start to work my way along.

If you attempt this without first giving your chisel a good sharpen, you are going to be frustrated very quickly. A sharp chisel will slice effortlessly sideways through softwoods or if you are using a hardwood, short 'bites' are best. Repeat the process for the other side of the housing. So that's it, your tapered dovetailed housing is finished!

There may well be a few minor adjustments, but a trial fit will tell you all you need to know.

Trial fit

Take the side piece out of the vise and slide in the shelf. If cut correctly, the shelf should start to tighten about an inch back from the front face when thumped in gently with the palm of the hand. If this is the case, closing that last inch is best done with a few gentle taps with a rubber faced mallet.

If the shelf stops further back, pop the side piece back in the vice and clamp on the second jig once more. Set it up carefully, so as to allow a little more to be pared off all the way down the housing. Use the pencil lines inside the housing as a reference for how much you take off. A try out with a chisel will tell you if you've got the alignment the same as before. It's then easy to judge the thickness of waste peeled off by a chisel cut.

The relationship between how much to take off and how far forward the dovetail moves along the housing depends on the angle of the taper. In practice, the shallower the taper angle, the less you need to take off to close the joint by a given distance. It may take a couple of goes to gradually creep up on a perfect fit, but with a little practice, the whole process can be carried out quickly and efficiently. You will work out the effect of paring off a certain thickness of the housing sidewall, and by simply observing how far the shelf moves forwards in relation to the waste removed, you'll soon be having a lot of fun with excellent results every time.

TECHNICAL POINTER:
This is a joint where glue is not a strict requirement. With the back panel fixed in place, the shelving joint cannot slide apart with or without glue!

You will be very surprised at how strong and solid this joint is. No biscuits, pocket screws, nails, string or even glue! It may be old fashioned, but it works!

Chapter 13
Shooting boards

Shooting boards have been used for centuries by woodworkers, as a means of guiding a hand plane. The most common operation is trueing up the end grain of a sawn board, but variations exist for all manner of purposes. This is almost a subject area in it's own right, but for our purposes, we are going to look at how to make and use four different shooting boards.

I will quite often use a heavy wooden badger plane (a left hander!) with a shooting board, as the width of the cutting iron, skewed iron and extra weight allow 2" thick end grain to be trued up with relative ease. (See photo opposite.)

Other variants are designed for 45 degree miter or bevel cuts and we'll look at these too.

The function of a shooting board remains the same, regardless of the arrangement of the angles, fences and sliding track. In principle, a hand plane is placed on it's side on the sliding track, the wood is held firmly against a stop, and provided that the plane is adjusted correctly (page 244 of *Working Wood 1&2*), the edge will be easily 'shot' (trued up) to the desired angle. The most frequently used angled cuts are 90 degrees, 45 degrees on the miter, or 45 degrees on the bevel. If you ever need to make wooden hoppers or beehives, you'll find a shooting board can be easily knocked up to allow you to shoot a compound miter, ready for dovetailing. (Note: The compound geometry dictates the need for both left and right hand devices.)

Although the angles and configuration are dictated by the basic purpose of the shooting board, the scale of the device is really down to the size of the work piece you need to fit on it. Bear in mind that you always need some 'run in' and 'run out', so it's best to incorporate this in the design dimensions. I have a huge shooting board that is a skeleton frame of batten and plywood, allowing me to shoot over 2ft of end grain. I have several smaller shooting boards in daily use, depending on the type of work I'm doing.

We'll look at a large 90 degree shooting board first, as this can be used to make parts for the other shooting boards. It's designed to fit onto the saw horses from page 193.

A sharp plane will cut thin ribbons of end grain.

"The function of a shooting board remains the same regardless of the arrangement of the angles, fences and sliding track."

General construction considerations

The challenge in making any shooting board is in having enough patience and perseverance to get it made to a high enough level of accuracy. A shooting board that is reasonably close to 90˚ is quite useless, as you will build the inaccuracy into every cabinet you make. Doors won't shut properly and things just won't line up as they should. Be very aware of this before you start, and be fully prepared to adjust or remake any critical part as many times as you have to, to get the angles spot on.

An important part of the design is an adjustable fence. This may be crept forwards a fraction as required. My justification for sliding fences is simple. If you know that you are going to break edges out at the back of the cut with every swipe of the plane, this limits the way you can use the work piece. You never want broken out edges on show. The alternative is to use a piece of sacrificial batten every time you shoot end grain. Either way, it's an issue you have to address.

You can use a bench plane (as I mostly do) to finely trim off the end grain of your work, both reducing it to the correct length and giving you a perfect 90˚ in two directions simultaneously. There are also specialist planes with skewed irons that tackle the end grain with even greater ease and efficiency. By all means get yourself one of these if your budget will stretch that far.

The great benefit of using an accurately made shooting board is the fact that a high degree of precision is possible without a lot of effort.

A modern chop saw can also give very accurate results, but I think the end grain would still need planing as well, depending on where the work piece was to be used. Hopefully, as you work through this section, you can pick and choose what you want to make and also pick up some pointers on how to work to quite a high level of precision. This is probably the most demanding set of devices you'll need to make, only because if they are not dead true, they are a waste of space.

> **TECHNICAL POINTER:** *With all the shooting boards in this section, you can always use a 'sanding plane' on any work with unsupported fragile edges, molded work and the like. The sanding plane will not break out any end grain edges and can be used across the grain, with the grain and against the grain at any angle. We'll have a look at this device first and then make the sliding fences.*

I do a lot of rough cutting with a radial arm saw, but the end grain usually looks better planed up.

The brass knobs are tightened to tension up the cut pieces of machine sanding belt.

You could not do this with a plane.

You can get a nice crisp corner...

...on small molding sections. The molding shown here is about 1¼" thick.

The sanding plane

This, of course, is not a plane at all, but it will take the place of a plane, when a plane can't do the job. When you need to miter a fancy molding from two directions, so as to meet on a corner, a bench plane is going to struggle to get a crisp result when used with a shooting board. A device such as the one shown here on the left, will allow you to get a perfect miter straight after the molding (sticking) has been cut with a fine saw. Two grades of sandpaper (60 and 120 grit) will quickly shape the molding even if the saw cut is slightly awry. This sanding plane can to be used with all of the shooting boards in this book, but I use it mostly on the miter and bevel boards, for cornice and plinth molded stock.

There is a very thin strip of hardwood glued to the lower section of the body (on both sides), which prevents the shooting boards being abraded. I have used cloth sanding belts from a belt sander as they are tough and flexible, unlike sandpaper, which will crack and tear easily.

Every sliding fence needs to have a very solid fence support behind it.

Sliding fences

All the shooting boards in this section have sliding fences fitted to them. The reason for this is that a razor sharp plane is going to eat away at the fence, ever so slightly. If it doesn't do this, it's because there's a gap behind the work piece where the wood is not supported, and it's likely that you are going to get a little breakout from the back of the cut, each time you plane. Alternatively, the iron could just skim the end grain of the fence, which is ideal but a heavier cut from your plane will slice more of the fence off in proportion to the protrusion of the iron. When the iron is then set back in for a much finer cut, the difference in protrusion is equal to the area of unsupported fibers on the back of the work piece. That is of course, unless you can advance the fence a little to compensate for the amount removed by the heavier cut.

The sliding fences have about an inch of travel before you need to move the screws to a new position. There is every chance the fences will last a long time before they need replacing. A well-made set of shooting boards should, for this reason, still be around for the next generation, and will be just as accurate as the day they were made.

TECHNICAL POINTER: *A piece of sacrificial batten will work equally as well, so long as you remember to get it aligned perfectly for every part you shoot.*

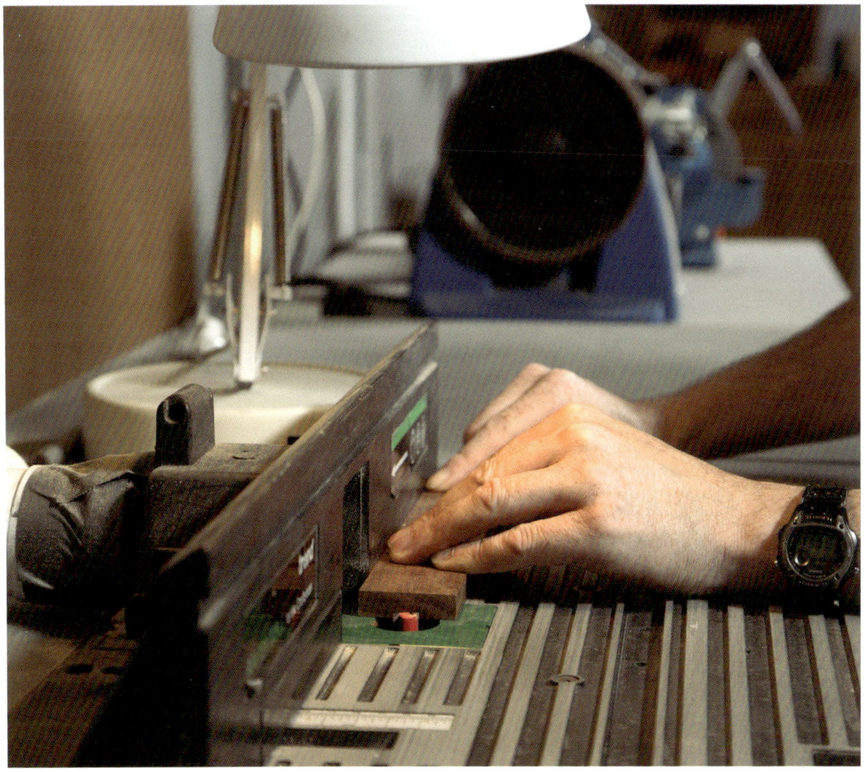

A router will do the job very nicely.

Six sliding fences will be required for the shooting boards in this section, so it's best to make them all in one go.

Now, I have to say, you are welcome to use an electric router for this job, but below is an account of how to get excellent results fairly quickly without one. If you do choose to use a router, an important note on safety is to at least make sure that it's bench mounted, inverted and guarded correctly with good extraction. I've removed the guard in this photo for clarity. When it comes to choosing wood for the fences, select some with a fine grain texture.

In the photo below, you can see how I've matched the slot size with the washers I'm using. The two woods you can see here are Iroko (left),hand cut, and an African hardwood called Ekki cut with an electric router (right).

Two recessed slots. Top left was hand cut and on the right, machined with a router. (Iroko and Ekki are the woods.)

Materials

Hardwood (for 6 fences)

½" x 1¾" x 10" - 6pcs

Brass screws and approx. ½" diameter washers.

Some material is cut off one or both ends of the sliding fences for some of the shooting boards, and the width is also adjusted to suit.

Cut the groove

With a square, mark lines across 3" from each end. These lines denote the positions of the fixing screws and the length of the stopped groove.

Set a mortise gauge to your ½" chisel.

Lightly score on the lines to define the groove. Mark from the end to the second line, as shown in the photo, middle right.

The depth of the groove can be marked on with a wheel gauge like the one shown below, or alternatively use a cutting gauge as it will give you a sharper line than a normal marking gauge. Set the depth to a fraction above the brass washer, placed over the screw as shown below.

This line serves as a reference for the depth cut when using the hand router.

Square across 3" from each end.

Set your mortise gauge to your ½" chisel.

Mark the lines for the groove as shown.

Set the gauge to just above the washer.

Mark this depth measurement onto the end of the work piece.

Set up with the work held securely, and chop out a series of cuts, going to the correct depth.

Trim the sides of the recess...

...carefully!

Now secure the work piece using a hold-down clamp, and butt it up firmly against one of your bench dogs. Starting at the far end, work backwards with your chisel taking small even chops, prizing up a little after each cut. Try to keep the depth even by striking the chisel with steady, even mallet blows. How hard you hit the chisel determines the depth of cut and each chop should produce the same sound, if you are consistent. Listen to your progress as well as keeping a watchful eye on the size and shape of the chips.

You may be aware that in Britain carpenters and joiners are still called 'chippies' because traditionally they would produce small chips of wood every time a door was hung or hinge rebate cut, for example.

With the chopping out of the way, tidy up the edges with your marking knife and a straight edge. All you are doing here is shaving off the fluffy edges so the sides look neat. A lot of care is required for this task, so go slow and steady.

Set your good old Stanley No.71, or similar hand router to the correct depth and then shave all the uneven chop marks completely out of the bottom of the groove.

Clean up with a sharp hand router.

This shows the finish before and after the hand router.

The finished groove.

The photo above illustrates exactly what a sharp hand router will achieve, very quickly!

The finished groove should look like the photo, top right. However, if it still has marks visible from the previous chopping, just go ahead and drop the cutter of the router down a whisker and shave some more off. If you end up a *little* deeper than you intended, it will not cause a problem.

Cut the slots

Take your brass washers and mark their respective positions, as shown, running a pencil around the center holes.

From the edge of the center holes, mark off about an inch from each one and run these center lines around the work piece, over onto the back face.

Use the brass washers to mark out the hole centers.

Mark a second set of points 1" from the first set, as shown.

Transfer the marks over the edge, and mark up the back as well.

Use a center punch to indent the exact hole positions on the front and the back.

Drill through from both sides...

...and remove the waste with a coping saw.

File out the slots, being careful of the back edge!

Check the depth with a screw and a washer.

TOP TIP: *For accurate pilot holes, use a small nail set to punch shallow indentations on the exact center points you've marked. By doing this, you'll find the drill has much less of a tendency to wander off course as you start to drill the holes.*

Drill though with a 3⁄16" drill going in dead straight, but only just over half way through from each side.

Saw out the waste between the holes using a coping saw.

TECHNICAL POINTER: *To clean up the slots, incline your file very slightly so you only file a little over half of the surface inside the slot. Neglecting this will guarantee you'll splinter the back of the slot and end up with quite a shredded mess. If you work only from the front, it won't be seen. However, best practice is to work neatly, even on parts and places that won't be seen.*

Clean up the slots with a file. You may be able to discern a slight gap between the file and the front face of the slot. I did not want to risk the situation outlined in the technical pointer above, so I filed the slots from both sides.

Check the screws and washers fit nicely with the screw heads below the front face of the fence. This looks about right, but be prepared to go a little deeper if you need to.

Make six identical fences ready for the shooting boards.

Large shooting board

This shooting board fits onto the saw horses, allowing you to get right above the work. Cleaning up the saw marks after cross cutting a wide panel or table top is a job that is easily accomplished with this.

There is a logical order in which to make the different shooting boards in this set. This first one is absolutely key to get right. If you can get this shooting board made accurately, you can then use it to make many other parts for the other boards. If you get it wrong then you will end up multiplying your errors. There is only one corner that you need to spend a lot of time on, so it's worth getting it as good as you possibly can. Do whatever you need to check for square. Use straight edges, levels, an engineer's square or any other trick in the book to get this right. If you work carefully and methodically (and your measuring tools are accurate) then you should be fine, so all the best with it!

"...it's worth getting this as good as you possibly can."

The heavy timber shown here is the fence support. This has to be solid!

This is a very stable set up, steadied by the use of heavy dowels.

Materials

Plywood

¾" x 28" x 28"

½" x 24" x 24"

Hardwood

1½" x 2¼" x 22" - 1pc

½" x 1¾" x 12" - 1pc

1 Sliding fence (page 326)

¾" dowel - 1pc at 6"

Brass screws and washers.

Cutting up plywood

I'll take this opportunity to start with a top tip for sawing up the plywood on your saw horses. I thought I'd cut up the boards outside as it was a nice sunny day!

Mark your cut and start to saw through as you would normally.

However, when you've got about half way through, clamp a short batten across the cut with a pair of G clamps. This does two things:

1. It stops most of the vibration in the board that normally causes the saw to jump and judder.
2. It also acts better than a second pair of hands, as the board remains rigid right down to the last stroke.

It's now back to the workshop, to a sturdy bench!

Support the board on two saw horses. Stop half way through the cut, and...

...clamp a batten across the saw cut. The job suddenly becomes much easier!

Plane a perfect 90°

The first operation is to remove all the saw marks and flatten off an edge. You can grip the board in the vise, using the extra leg (page 247) as a support, or some other good method of work holding. The downward pressure of the hand plane is going to cause the board to move unless it's fully supported.

> **TOP TIP:** *File a small chamfer on the corner before you start planing. This prevents the corner from breaking out as you take full passes all the way across.*

On the underside of the edge that your plane is going to run against, plane a small chamfer to act as a dust groove. This will prevent your plane from being diverted off course by trapped dust when you use the shooting board.

File a little chamfer on the corners.

Plane a small dust groove on one edge.

Get the first edge very flat and square (The shooting stick from page 283 is great for this!)

Mark a clear line down the board, and plane up the edge to a perfect 90°.

Check the edge using a straight edge, a good level or the blade of your large square. The shooting stick (page 283) is very useful for this.

Once you are happy with the edge, square a fine line down at a perfect 90 degrees. Plane down to your line to get the corner very close to the 90° that you want.

You are going to use this device as a reference for many other operations, so the 90° corner needs to be very accurate. There's a good trick for this using sanding sealer.

Plywood will cut fairly well with a sharp plane, but for a glassy smooth finish, thin down some sanding sealer with a standard thinner and give both edges of your chosen 90 degree corner a light coat.

Mark the corner clearly (I've used a red marker pen here) as you want to make sure it's easy to identify. The sealer should dry very quickly.

The sealer binds up all the loose end grain fibers of the plywood, so you get a glassy smooth finish, not a flat and furry edge.

TOP TIP: *Give the sole of your plane a quick wipe with a waxed cloth as it will give you a very smooth cutting action.*

Thin down the sealer a little, and then...

...brush it on to the edges, ready for a final planing when it's dry.

Now set your plane to take very fine shavings, and using the shooting stick whisk off fine shavings from both edges, checking again with the square until it's about as accurate to 90° degrees as you can possibly get it.

You will get a good finish but your plane iron will need a quick sharpen up as sanding sealer blunts the iron a lot faster than wood, even when it's thinned down to 50% strength.

Laminate the boards

The next step is to laminate both pieces of plywood together. Draw around the ½" thick top board, to indicate where the glue is to go on the baseboard. Notice the red mark on the corner to remind you where the 90° corner is. (Photo below.)

TOP TIP: *Get all your caul clamps, 'G' clamps and any other sort of clamps ready to use, and plan where they are going to be placed. Only then think about getting the glue out!*

Check with a square and a straight edge, every few passes.

A few fine shavings should be all you need to take off.

Mark around the ½" plywood board - this will show you where the glue needs to go. The red dot is just a reminder for me of which corner is 90°.

Spread the glue evenly, and then, if you are using PU glue...

...clamp it up when it's finished frothing, but is still tacky.

"It's really important to understand the characteristics of different glues."

Spread the glue evenly and fairly thinly, making sure you avoid any blobs near the edges. I'm using polyurethane glue for speed and strength.

TECHNICAL POINTER: *It's very important to work quickly and spread the glue on without being too fussy and hesitant, as this will allow it to start to react in a reasonably even fashion across the boards. Do NOT just whack it together as soon as you are done. Instead, allow the glue to froth a little for a couple of minutes.*

Then, imagine you are using a one-shot contact adhesive, and carefully bring the pieces together. Straightaway, get the clamps on, keeping the boards flat, and squeeze the edges tight together, and the middle! I've used a temporary pine caul to clamp the middle tight. Waiting too long is even more disastrous, the glue has to be sticky and tacky or it will no longer stick - meaning you need to start over again. *(See page 389 for more on PU glue).*

Some PU glues will react very quickly, literally within minutes, and other varieties could have a much longer length of time before the initial frothing starts to occur. It's really important to understand the characteristics of different glues. Just reading the instructions is not good enough. In a cold, dry workshop, the setting time could be five times longer than in a warm and rather humid shop, regardless of the manufacturers instructions.

So why let the glue expand before bringing the parts together?

This has the effect of preventing the glue near the edges from frothing up, expanding, and oozing sideways into the very corners you have worked so hard to get flat, smooth and a perfect 90°. You don't want the small dust groove to fill with frothing glue, as it can be difficult to remove neatly.

Fix down the fence support

Take the clamps off and inspect the edges. If the last step was carried out successfully, there should be no frothy glue bulging out from the join. If you do notice some, just carefully trim it off with a marking knife, but take care avoid damaging the edges.

The fence support needs to be screwed in place so mark it's position as shown.

Mark the screw holes. Four of them should do.

Drill clearance holes for the screws. Countersink the underside of the base board.

TECHNICAL POINTER:
Make sure the fence support is a whisker back from being dead flush. Feel it with your fingers and give it a little tap with a mallet, with the clamps in place, until it's where you want it. Do not let it protrude past the ½" plywood it's clamped up against.

Plan where the fence support is going to get fixed, then...

...plan where the screws are going to go.

Drill clearance holes for the No.10 screws. Tight holes could cause the screws to jack the support up.

Countersink the underside, so the screw heads finish up a little below perfectly flush.

Clamp the fence support hard against the ½" plywood, before...

...you drill the small pilot holes through the larger clearance holes.

Apart from the front face that supports the fence, relieve all the edges with a chamfer.

In order to fix the fence support super tight against the back edge of the top board, clamp it loosely in place with G clamps, then using a batten as a spacer, clamp the timber tight against the plywood, before fully tightening the G clamps. (Top left photo.)

You'll need to pre-drill the hardwood to avoid the risk of snapping the screws. Then put in the screws before you take the clamps off.

Using a block plane and chisel, take off the sharp corners from the fence support and make sure that the base board edges are all planed and sanded.

Make a small indent where the fence fixing screws need to go. (As far forward as possible!)

To fix the fence in place, mark through the slots with something sharp and pointy. I used a sharp brass screw (as in the photo left). Pre drill pilot holes for the screws and then just fix the fence to the fence support, holding it tight with the brass washers. Position it flush with the edge of the ½" plywood, and then cut and fit the permanent packing piece alongside it.

TOP TIP: *To drill the pilot holes, you may find it easier to dismantle the fence support beforehand, and then screw it back in place when you're done.*

The packer needs to be the same thickness as the fence.

Fit the location dowels

With the shooting board upside down on the bench top, place your saw horses upside down on it, close up to the edges. Make sure the cross bars (4x3) of the saw horses are running at 90 degrees to the fence. This reduces the chance of a wobble if you hit a knot or take a heavy cut. Mark the hole positions as shown. In this photo on the right, the fence is sitting in the well of my bench, and the saw horses are about 1" from the side of the base board.

Mark the dowel position around ¼" further out towards the edge of the open notched end of the cross bars. This allows the large shooting board to locate very easily as you place it on the saw horses, as it won't be a super tight fit.

Drill a pilot hole dead center of the dowel position, and remove the waste with the auger to about ⅜" deep.

TOP TIP: *To mark a ⅜" line round the dowel, use your finger as a guide and simply rotate the dowel in the direction shown. This is a quick and easy trick that is reasonably accurate.*

Mark the hole positions and the notch positions, but make sure...

...the dowel position is marked ¼" back from the end of the notch.

The extra clearance this gap provides makes the board much easier to locate.

Drill down about ⅜" and clean the hole out.

Hold the pencil steady and rotate the dowel.

This line shows you where to pare down to. (Not the depth of insertion!)

Round over the pared end - this aids location in the saw horses.

Saw off about 1" of dowel...

...and make another 3 more.

Pare down the end of the dowel to give it a good taper. Keep your fingers well out of the way when paring, and have a board underneath to protect your bench top.

Give the dowel end a good sanding to smooth it off.

Cut about 1" of the dowel off in the miter box and make another 3 more short dowels in the same way.

Glue the dowels into the base board, with the rounded taper facing upwards.

Hold them in with a clamp whilst they set. Once the glue has set, pare off any excess glue with a sharp chisel.

I've used quick setting PU glue, and...

...spring clamps to hold them in place while the glue sets.

The finishing touch

Give the whole board a good coat of sanding sealer, paying particular attention to the edges and corners.

Give the fence and fence support a light coat of thinned down sealer. The first time you adjust the fence, you may need to unscrew it in case the sealer has formed a slight bond in the gaps.

When it's dry, which should only take 5-10 minutes, try it for size on your saw horses. You'll find the saw horses are a good working height and provide a very stable platform to work on.

One knee and a hand keep the set up and work piece steady.

As the board end is shot, the grain appears darker where the end grain has been planed.

The corners and edges get more wear and tear, so give them a heavy coat of sealer.

Thinned down sealer is better than a thick coat on the fence.

Check everything fits as it should.

This large shooting board is great for wider boards.

Small 90° board - bench top

This shooting board is the everyday workhorse for squaring up the ends of your stock. With medium or larger pieces of wood, it works in conjunction with the bench hooks, which are cunningly designed to the same key dimensions. See pages 321 and 322 for my comments on shooting boards, planes and the 'sanding plane'. Before the advent of circular chop saws, the shooting board was the No.1 method for fast and accurate squaring of planed stock. A well made shooting board, used in conjunction with a sharp, well set plane, will give you results that look better than anything machine cut. Of course, if you are in the realms of high volume production, nothing is going to beat the speed and efficiency of a sharp, well set chop saw, let's not kid ourselves!

At the risk of sounding archaic, I like to use a shooting board for trueing up stock in small quantities, and I totally rely on one for trueing up stock so large that it won't fit onto the table of my radial arm saw. This is a relatively easy project and won't take you too long to make.

"At the risk of sounding archaic, I like to use a shooting board for trueing up stock in small quantities."

A small shooting board could be the most useful device you'll ever make.

What you'll need

NOTE: Don't cut plywood to these dimensions before checking your bench top, see below!

- $\frac{3}{4}$" Thick marine grade or similar quality plywood 17" x 13"
- $\frac{1}{2}$" Thick marine grade or similar quality plywood 13" x 10"
- $\frac{5}{8}$" x 1" x13" - 2pcs hardwood
- $1\frac{1}{2}$ x $2\frac{1}{2}$ x 10" - 1pc hardwood
- Sliding fence plus fixings (2 brass screws $1\frac{1}{2}$" x No.8's plus 2 x $\frac{1}{2}$" washers). Page 324
- 8 x Wood screws $1\frac{1}{2}$" No.8's (steel)
- Sanding sealer
- Polyurethane or PVA glue
- 000 Grade wire wool
- Furniture wax

The materials for a small, 90 degree, bench top shooting board.

Check your bench top dimensions

Before you start on any glue up or squaring your boards, just check the general layout against your bench top. The critical issue is that the base board when centered on the bench top has enough overhang to fit the stops that hold the shooting board on the bench top. I've got about $1\frac{1}{2}$" of overhang on both sides so I know this will work.

Center the boards on the bench top as shown, and check you have around $1\frac{1}{2}$" overhangs.

TOP TIP: *Use a small piece of masking tape on your bench top, and mark the center on this. It's easy to see the mark, and you just peel it off when you're done!*

Square up first

Set up the large shooting board and use this to square up the $\frac{1}{2}$" board.

Take extra care over one of the corners. Get this absolutely spot on and mark it up. (I've just used a red dot, as shown in the bottom photo).

Get one corner absolutely square, just as you did in the last project, and mark it up.

Laminate the boards together, just as before, and...

...clamp up when the glue has finished frothing.

Laminate the boards

Just as before, mark the baseboard, spread the glue, and clamp the assembly together with your caul clamps.

With the glue set, plane up the base board square, again using the large shooting board.

Fit the fence support

It's the standard procedure of pre-drilling the base board, and clamping the fence support in place (a whisker back from being flush, remember!), tight against the plywood. Screw the fence support in place before you take any clamps off.

True up the base board.

Drill clearance holes for 3 fixing screws, countersinking the underside.

Clamp the support in place, before...

...drilling pilot holes and driving screws in.

Fit the fence

Just like in the last project, pilot drill and screw the fence in place. No extra support packer is required as in the large shooting board, because the whole fence is slowly advanced towards the cutting edge as it is shaved down with use.

Fit the stops

Mark the positions of the stops allowing a little clearance (I've used a small steel rule as a spacer), so it won't be a tight fit as it's used.

Square across from your marks and indicate clearly where the stops are to go, i.e. on the outside of both your lines.

Give the stops a quick chamfer on three edges before you fit them.

See how the fence has been trimmed a little as I gave it a quick 'try out'!

Mark the position for the stops, but...

...include a little slack (steel rule as a packer).

Square the stop positions across the underside.

Chamfer 3 faces of the stops, as shown.

Drill and screw the stops in place, and check for a good fit on your bench.

As with most of the jigs and devices, I'm recommending a coat or two of sanding sealer to finish.

The bench hooks provide essential support for longer pieces.

Seal up to finish

After a sanding down, it's out with the sanding sealer again to give the shooting board a measure of protection against the rigors of workshop use.

This shooting board can be used to clean up the saw marks from many of your work pieces. The only criteria is they must be thinner than the height of the fence, and fit on the board in such a way that you can take a shaving easily. Larger pieces or wider boards are a job for the large shooting board, on page 331. Having both sizes of shooting board is very useful for efficient clean up and squaring of your work.

The bench hooks (page 379) shown in the bottom photo, are designed to support the work as it is being shot or sawn to length. The one at the far end of my bench allows me to mark up and cross cut a lot of smaller stock on my bench. I then simply pick up a plane and shoot the end to a perfect 90°. The finish on the end grain is a good indicator of how sharp your plane is.

Miter shooting board

A miter shooting board gives you lots of options for fitting and fettling all manner of work. I'd recommend that you make yourself one of these. It's a standard piece of kit for any cabinet maker.

"...it's very useful to be able to shoot a miter from either direction."

The design I've chosen allows both right and left handed operation, as sometimes it's very useful to be able to shoot a miter from either direction. I have to say that this is a reasonably heavy construction and you may get away with something much lighter, depending on what you intend to do. The fence supports are set into, and held in place by plywood triangles, making them very rigid. On occasion, perhaps when shooting thick stock with a heavy wooden plane, the fence supports may have to withstand quite a severe wallop (especially if the iron is set out too far, by mistake!). It's reassuring to know you are not going to damage the device or lose out on accuracy, even by accident.

In terms of workflow, it's unusual to shoot less than four miter cuts in one set up. For example, a simple cornice molding around the top of a cabinet comprises two short side pieces with a single miter one end, and a middle piece, with miter cuts on both ends.

On pages 357 to 359, there are a few examples of how this is used, including a method for working with complex molded stock.

This is a very solid piece of equipment, and is designed for right and left handed miter cuts.

What you'll need

¾" Plywood rectangles

24" x 13" - 1pc

14" x 10" - 1pc

Plywood triangle- 17" along the hypotenuse, 12" for each short side. I've run the grain in the same direction as the long side of the triangle to make it look neater. This needs to be a very good 90 degree corner, so get it prepared before hand.

Hardwood for stops

¾" x ¾" x 13" - 2pcs

For fence supports

1¼" x 2½" x 14" - 2pcs

2 Sliding fences (page 326)

½" x 1¾" x 7" - 2pcs

Brass screws and washers

Zinc plated steel screws for assembly

Accuracy

In much the same way as we spent a while making sure that our reference edges on previous shooting boards were a perfect 90 degrees, in this instance we need to produce perfect 45 degree angles. The process for this is iterative, in the sense that it's a process of checking and finely adjusting. For the material dimensions given, this method should work well and I'd encourage you to spend the time closing the smallest of gaps.

Get the 45°'s perfect

Take the smaller board and measure 2" in from each edge on opposite corners. Draw a line at 45 degrees between these points using the miter square. Saw down the line with the work piece in the vise.

TOP TIP: *Start the cut with a tenon saw, as the finer teeth will be less inclined to jump off course as you start the cut. Switch to the panel saw and hold it at a fairly steep angle for a smoother cut.*

The materials for the miter shooting board.

Measure 2" in on opposite corners, and join the marks with a pencil line.

Start with a tenon saw, then...

...switch to the panel saw.

Arrange both pieces and check for a gap.

You need to work on both pieces, so...

...clamp them up and plane down as required.

Check for flatness, then...

...check to see if the gap has been rectified. There must be no gap, and the pieces must be square.

Plane the saw cut edges fairly smooth.

Arrange both pieces on the bench top as shown in the photo, top left, using the large square as a reference. There is a considerable gap that you can see here, and this needs to be closed accurately to a high tolerance.

Notice that the gap is in the foreground, meaning a few shavings near the pencil lines at the back and the middle will need to be removed.

To do this, take both pieces and set them vertically on the bench, getting them flush and square before finally clamping them together.

With the pieces clamped together, place them in the vise, tighten up and take a few light shavings as required. Keep you plane flat and work carefully.

Use a straight edge to check you have not hollowed out the middle, or rounded the ends over. This may take a few attempts, each time setting up and checking back in the vise, out of the vise and so on, until you are totally happy with an even, tight fit, all the way around and on every edge.

TECHNICAL POINTER: *Always work on both parts together. Don't ever plane just one piece down, thinking it would be easier. If you do this, you'll end up with one piece at less than 45°, the other at more than 45° and you'll never spot the error because they will appear to 'fit' together beautifully! The very fact that both parts are identical is they key to achieving the high degree of accuracy required.*

Get ready to fix the board

Now that you are happy with the 45° angles, place the matching triangles onto the base board as shown, and draw lines to indicate roughly where they are going to go. An accurate set up at this point is not required, you are simply marking up for drilling a bunch of holes. In this photo, I am drawing a line along the REFERENCE EDGES of the matching triangular pieces.

Do the same for the fence supports and, as before, this is just an indicator as to where they are going to be fitted.

You will also need to drill a pattern of holes to fix down the central triangular piece of plywood. In the photo below, I'm just finishing off drilling some holes for this piece.

This is what your base board should look like now (bottom photo). You can easily identify the holes for the matching triangular 45 degree pieces, the 3 holes on each side for the fence supports and the 6 holes for the central triangular piece.

Mark the positions of the triangular pieces, and...

...do likewise for the fence supports.

Drill clearance holes for the fixing screws.

With the base board drilled, this is what it should look like.

On the REFERENCE EDGES (opposite page), plane a dust groove on both triangles.

Fix down one triangular piece first (I'm using the second triangle as a packer to support the work).

This is where you need to line up the REFERENCE EDGES very accurately, Use a square, and...

...allow for a ¼" gap between the triangular boards. (You can see the dust groove as a shadow.)

Set out for fixing

Just before you fix the two matching triangular pieces down, plane a small chamfer on the bottom of the reference edges of both boards. This will create a little groove for dust and help keep the plane running true.

It's very important to make sure that when these pieces are fixed down, the reference edges are 100% in line. The easiest way to do this is to clamp one piece in place first and fix it in position with the 1¼" No.8 screws.

Put the screws in pretty tight, so the boards really pull together, but don't spin the screw or it will lose nearly all of it's 'pulling power'. I am using the other piece in the foreground (yet to be fixed) as a packer to support the work.

Clamp up the second 45 degree board and adjust as required. You are aiming for a ¼" gap in the center between the reference edges and perfect linear alignment of these edges. Clamp, tap, check, unclamp, tap, check as many times as you need to but get this right, not just close!

TECHNICAL POINTER:
If the reference edges are not lined up perfectly, the shooting board will never give you accurate results.

TOP TIP: *With both triangular pieces fixed in place, put the large square inside, and up against the 45 degree edges. It should show a reassuringly perfect 90 degree corner. If it doesn't, then sorry, there is nothing you can do other than take it all apart and go back to a previous step of checking and adjusting the 45°s.*

Fit the fence supports

The fence supports need to meet at 45 degrees, so set your marking gauge to ⅛" and mark one end of each fence support as shown. As both supports meet together, the ⅛" ends will fit into the ¼" gap you left between the triangular boards in the last step.

Knife across from the ⅛" line at 45 degrees, and take this line down the back edge, all the way around

Form your knife wall in preparation for some careful cutting.

Using the knife cuts as a guide, saw a 45 degree angle, and clean up with a block plane.

With both pieces cut, the fence

The fence supports are going to meet in the center, so they BOTH need a 45 degree miter.

Mark the miter cut with a knife, and...

...mark the sides of the cut as well.

Start off with a knife wall, then...

...saw down your knife marks to remove the waste.

Clean up the sawn ends with a block plane.

The fence supports in place. I've trimmed off the front edges at 45 degrees, so they fit flush.

Mark the underside, and cut them off flush.

The large triangle will need cutting to fit.

supports should fit together as shown here on the left.

Mark and trim the fence supports so they no longer overhang at the back.

This next stage will make the whole set up incredibly solid.

Take the triangular piece of plywood and trial fit it against the fence supports. You can see in the photo, middle right, that I need to plane off a small amount, but apart from that it's a good tight fit against the fence supports.

With that taken care of, clamp the triangle against the fence supports using a packer to squeeze it in good and tight, as shown in the bottom left photo. If all still looks good, flip it over and screw it together. Don't forget you'll need to predrill the hardwood before you put the screws in.

For the 'belt and braces' approach, I put an extra screw across the supports as shown below.

Clamp the large triangle, and the fence supports, before...

...you drill and fix from the underside.

I've put an extra screw through both fence supports just for good measure.

I like my miter shooting board to be held firmly in the vise, so I'm putting stops on the underside to go from my vise jaws to the back edge of the bench top.

Make and fix these as you did in the previous project. Cut and fix the sliding fences and packers, again using the usual brass screws and washers to hold everything in place.

Sanding sealer is what I'd use to finish the job off, but if you prefer clear shellac, that will work just fine. Put some furniture wax on the surfaces that the plane will run along. Any reduction in friction here is a good thing, but do not wax anywhere else as friction between your work and the fence is helpful. You don't want the plane to continually push the work out of the way, as you slice the end grain.

I'm going to clamp the miter shooting board in the vice, as I like it to be absolutely solid.

TOP TIP: *You may choose to put an extra guide on as a runner to prevent the plane from jumping sideways as you slice the end grain. It's not a necessity, but you may find it to be a useful modification. If you put an extra runner on, you will of course limit yourself to a particular size and shape of plane, but this may be exactly what you want.*

The stops are fixed on now, so I'll put the fences and packers on next...

...which does not take long. The packers never move, but you can nudge the fences forwards.

The shooting board works well in either left handed orientation, as seen here or right, as shown below.

A reeded picture frame is easily shot to a 45 degree angle.

Using the miter shooting board

If you switch around the orientation, this shooting board will work for left hand cuts just as well as right hand operation. For longer work pieces, you're going to need to support the end of the work.

The ability to shoot a perfect 45 degree miter is vital for accurately fitting picture frames, decorative moldings, cornice, pelmets etc., and basically anything that needs to come together with a 45 degree join.

Square edged, flat stock is the easiest to shoot at 45° and this device will perform the task admirably.

Molded stock

For most decorative work however, we don't have flat stock, but rather some sort of elegantly shaped molding, full of fillets and curves.

The usual problem with shooting a molded section is that the back of the molding profile gets broken out due to the fibers not being supported. Even a super sharp plane is going to struggle in this respect with a complex molding.

This is the molding that we made on page 136, using a molding plane and the sticking board.

Using a miter box is a quick way of sawing a fairly accurate 45 degree corner.

Providing that you saw towards the molded edge, you should get a reasonably clean cut.

A miter box is a quick and handy guide for your saw.

The handy thing about a miter box, is that it will give you a 45 degree angle on a piece of stock that would be very difficult to mark up with a pencil line.

To plane up this cut, you'd either plane against the grain, or break it out, unless you did it free hand.

A few careful passes with the sanding plane will level up any saw marks. You can be surprisingly accurate with this device, working down to the finest of knife marks. This is very important when working to a measured length, as you don't want to end up with a work piece that is just too short!

The finish is not as glossy smooth as a sharp plane will give you, but more important is the fact that there are no fibers broken out at the very edges of the curve.

The sanding plane (page 323) works a treat for moldings, and when combined with this jig, you can get molded corners to come together very nicely.

It's true that the end grain of any molding can be worked successfully by holding the work piece steady and using a finely set block plane to shave off the saw marks. You can approach any delicate curves and fillets in such a way as to not break out the edges, but the point I'm making here is that you can't normally do this quickly using a shooting board.

This cornice molding is about 3" wide and 1¼" thick. The extra width allows for easy fixing onto the top of a cupboard.

Bevel shooting board

This is a fairly complex device to make, so you may want to leave this until you really need one. When it comes to mitering together plinths and facings, this shooting board is in a class of it's own. It's very easy to set up and use, and if made correctly, will give very reliable results. This shooting board is reversible, so both corners of a mitered molded plinth can be shot, from opposite directions. This is a requirement to avoid breaking out the molding.

The construction is more detailed than previous shooting boards, but the step by step instructions will get you on the right track, without ever needing to resort to machines, unless you really want to.

"It's very easy to set up and use, and if made correctly, will give very reliable results."

A bevel shooting board will allow you to shoot end grain at 45 degrees, like this example of a rebated plinth.

What you'll need

2 sliding fences (See page 326)

2 Fence supports 1⅛" x 2" x 8½"

1 Top bar ½" x 2" x 13"

2 Stop battens ¾" x ¾" x 13"

1 Bottom runner 2½" x 1½" x 16"

½" Plywood 10½" x 8½"

¾" Plywood 16" x 13"

Square the boards

Start off by squaring up both boards, using either the bench top shooting board or the large shooting board on the saw horses.

Plane a smooth bevel

The next step is to plane a 45 degree bevel on the long edge of the ½" plywood. A marking gauge is one of the best tools for laying out a 45 degree bevel. If you set the gauge to the exact thickness of the plywood, you can then score a line adjacent to the edge.

The materials you'll need for the bevel shooting board.

Shoot the plywood boards to square them up. Use the large shooting board if it's easier.

Set your gauge to the exact thickness of the plywood.

Mark the thickness onto the face, ready to plane a large bevel.

There are a few nifty tricks here - a pencil line will ensure you don't touch the front face unwittingly.

Another trick is to bevel the ends first...

...and use a rigid support behind the ½" ply.

Plane down to the line on the front face, but barely touch the pencil line at the top, as shown.

TOP TIP: *Take a soft pencil and mark a line down the back edge of the board as shown. This allows you to plane really close to the corner and instantly know if you've gone a little too far anywhere along the edge, as some of the pencil line will be obviously removed.*

Start by planing a chamfer on the very corner, between the gauge line and the back edge. Do both ends before you start and you won't split out the end grain so much. Take long, even passes the whole way down the edge, estimating an approximate 45 degree bevel to begin with.

TOP TIP: *Place a sturdy piece of plywood behind the ½" board you are working on. The extra rigidity will give you more control as you take each shaving.*

Adjust the angle of your plane to get each pass more parallel with the steep chamfer on the edge, until you almost touch the gauge line and almost touch the top pencil line.

When you get this close, back the iron off to take really fine shavings and slowly work to the pencil and gauge lines.

TECHNICAL POINTER:
The final check is to make sure that the adjacent edges are at a perfect 90 degrees to the beveled face. If they are not, spend a little more time finely correcting them on your 90 degree shooting board until you are satisfied. Only then move on to the next step.

Set up for centrality

The bevel shooting board is designed for either right or left hand use. In either orientation, the back fence needs to line up with the same fixed point. This is because this shooting board is used in conjunction with the bench hooks (page 379) that are used to support the work on the bench top.

To do this, you'll need to establish a few reference points, using the small 90 degree shooting board (page 343) as a template.

1. Firstly, ensure that your base board is the same size as the base board of your 90 degree shooting board.
2. Next, mark the dead center of your bench top, I've marked this 'B' in the photo.
3. Position the beveled board you have just planed with the left hand edge corresponding precisely with the back of the fence. This is clearly marked 'A' in the top photo.
4. The point marked 'C' in the photo is measured off from point 'B'. The distance from 'B' to 'A' is exactly the same as 'B' to 'C'.
5. It is likely that you will need to trim some of the beveled board off, to make the width correspond to point 'C'. I have shown this as a dotted line.
6. Saw this off, and plane it up straight.
7. Measure and transfer the points 'A', 'B' and 'C' onto the base board you are working on, as shown in the bottom photo.
8. These marks indicate precisely where the boards should line up, when you laminate them together.

'A' is the front of the fence support, 'B' is bench top center, and A-B is equal to B-C.

After cutting along the dotted line place the ½" plywood as shown, marking points A,B and C.

TECHNICAL POINTER: *When you plane up your sawn edge, make sure that it is absolutely square to the beveled front edge of the board you are working on. Take your time to do this accurately. The same applies to the opposite edge. The edges shown A-A and C-C in the photo must be parallel and both must be exactly square to the front edge*

With the boards aligned, mark up for gluing.

Laminate the boards in the usual way...

...then clamp them up. PU glue should be set in an hour, depending on temperature and humidity.

Laminate the boards

Just as in previous lamination work, mark the position of the top board. This, of course, shows you where the glue is to be applied. Clamp up using the caul clamps and let the glue set.

Make and fit the fence supports

The fence supports give the shooting board a lot of rigidity, as they are wide, solid and well fixed down. They are going to need cutting off at 45 degrees so we'll just look at two ways to set your sliding bevel accurately.

I'm using a CNC machined miter square as a reference, and with this layout tool, I can set for an internal 45 degree measurement or an external 45 degree measurement. You need to do this in a well lit work area, as you really need to see the smallest fraction of a gap to set the bevel accurately.

TOP TIP: *It's useful to have two sliding bevels for this sort of work and have them set permanently, one internal and one external for the duration of the project*

I'm going to set two sliding bevels. Internal and...

...external angles are going to be required for the next steps.

Flush up the back edge of the fence supports and mark the bevel position with a sharp, hard pencil. I've cut this to an exact length so that the front happens to be flush as well.

Mark out and saw off both fence supports.

TOP TIP: *Use the miter shooting board to initially tidy up the saw cuts.*

TECHNICAL POINTER: *Mark up the fence supports, as* ***left*** *and* ***right****. You now need take a little more off the outside edges of the angled saw cut, not a lot, perhaps only 1⁄16", as shown in the bottom right photo. When you place them back on the board, both fence supports should look like the bottom right photo. You should be able to see the gap towards the outside edge that I'm pointing at. This will prevent any breakout from the back edge, as your shooting plane takes a little off the fence supports from time to time.*

The 45 degree angle needs to be flush with the ½" plywood bevel.

The miter shooting board will tidy up the saw cuts nicely.

Chamfer the edges with a block plane, but...

...take a little off each mitered end as well, so as to create the little gap I'm pointing to just here.

Mark the width of your plane sole, as you need to cut the supports down to this mark.

Check you have planed up square!

Drill for the fixing screws, countersink the underside, clamp up again and screw the supports in place.

Using your plane as a guide (that's my No.5½ in the photo), mark the fence supports according to the width of your sole plate.

TOP TIP: *Clamp the fence supports in place so you can work without them moving. Notice the little packers nipped up in the clamp. These make sure the fence supports are square, held firmly against the plywood and don't slightly lean over.*

Saw or plane the supports down to the marks taken from your chosen plane, checking that you are planing square as you go.

Drill clearance holes into the base board to allow you to screw the fence supports in place. Countersink the underside to allow the screw heads to sit flush.

Again, clamp the supports tight against the plywood using little packers, and after getting the sloping faces perfectly in line with the beveled plywood, put screws in from underneath to secure them in place.

Make the top guide bar

The top guide bar needs to drop down below the height of the fence supports, so we'll mark and cut a shallow rebate on each end.

Mark and plane a bevel along the length of the bar, in much the same way as you did before (page 363), and finish the job off with a light sanding down.

Invert the bar and place it against the fence supports, using a knife to mark the exact positions to cut the shallow shoulders. (See photo, top right.)

TOP TIP: *The small knife nick provides a precise reference point, but I like to indicate the location of any small knife nick with a clear pencil mark. It's a habit I got into after repeatedly using such small marks that I was never able to find them again!*

Define the shoulder lines with a knife, and the rebate depth with a gauge set to 3⁄16".

Plane a bevel along the length of the bar.

Mark out the rebates with knife nicks, and...

...give yourself at least half a chance of finding the knife nicks, by using a pencil mark as well!

To create the rebate on each end, square the shoulders across, then...

...mark the depth at 3⁄16" on the end grain and the 90 degree edge.

Define the cuts by creating knife walls with a chisel. The hold down keeps the work held tight.

Saw the cheeks, and...

...the shoulders.

Saw the shoulders down to the gauge line with a dovetail saw. The beveled face is not marked in the photo (middle, left) and I'm working to layout lines on the other side, facing me as I'm sawing.

TOP TIP: *Alternatively, you could saw the shoulder line and then simply hold the job on the bench with a hold down and a wedge, while you chisel out the waste down almost to the gauge line.*

Clean up the chisel marks with a nice sharp router.

Press the bar into position, marking the protruding ends with a knife nick. Mark all the way round then saw off the waste with a dovetail saw.

A hand router will clean up the recesses, flattening them off nicely.

Use a knife to mark the right length, and then saw both ends to length.

Fitting the top guide bar

This requires a lot of care and attention to detail.

You'll need to use two brass screws in each side of the top bar to hold it down permanently. If you split the width into ⅓rds by eye, the screws need to be at the ⅓rd and ⅔rd marks.

Start off by clamping the top bar in place gently. Take your sliding bevel and set the top bar to exactly 45 degrees from the plywood bevel, as shown.

Once you are satisfied, tighten the clamps and drill a pilot hole through the top bar into the fence support. Follow this with a clearance hole for the brass screw, going ONLY through the top bar. Do this on both sides, and put the brass screws in.

A final check will reassure you that all is well.

To finish off, take a file and chamfer the edges of the top bar evenly. This will protect the potentially fragile corners during use and handling.

On the completion of all that sawing, planing, filing and screwing, the photo, bottom right, shows you where you should be up to.

Set up accurately with a sliding bevel, clamp the bar in place and drill pilot holes.

Check the top bar is at 45 degrees, and that it's perfectly parallel with the plywood bevel.

Place the work in your vise and file a good chamfer on the edges as shown.

Well, this is what you should have now, so it's time for the bottom.

The usual procedure for a perfect 45 degree bevel: Set your gauge to the thickness...

...and transfer the measurement to the face.

Knife across to define the saw cut position.

Start off with a tenon saw...

...then switch to a panel saw.

Make the plane runner

The design of the shooting board requires the bottom runner for the plane to be at 45 degrees (rather than the plane at 90 degrees and the wood at 45 degrees).

For this reason, there's just a bit more sawing and planing to do before you're finished.

Just as before, set the marking gauge to the narrow edge, and mark this distance down the wider edge, thus defining a perfect 45 degree plane to saw down. Use a sliding bevel to mark the end grain.

For an accurate and easy start to the cut, use a dovetail or tenon saw before switching to a panel saw.

TECHNICAL POINTER:
Repeatedly swap the work around in the vice so that you saw from one side and then the other. This really does reduce any tendency to veer away from the lines that you've marked.

TOP TIP: *Once you are over half way down, put a wedge in the saw kerf and flip the work piece over. You can then start sawing from the other end. Remove the last bit carefully*

The marks from the saw cut will need cleaning up with a plane and then, I suggest, with a cabinet scraper to produce a silky smooth result. Don't be heavy handed with the scraper or you will form a hollow in the middle, where it's easiest to work!

Check your work as you go with a sliding bevel. Make small adjustments using a block plane and scraper, or use your bench plane with a very fine set.

When you put the runner in place, you should have a perfect 90 degrees when you check it against the plywood bevel and the top bar as shown here.

A cabinet scraper will give you a smooth finish.

Make repeated checks with your sliding bevel.

Fit the plane runner

The runner you've just made is going to be held in place with screws. The 'gotcha' or 'catch' here is that you need to plan the screw positions so as not to end up with threads poking out of the wood. Stand a screw up and move it to where seems to be the best place, as shown below, bottom left.

I've put two lines on the base board. The left hand line indicates the position of the runner, and the line I'm marking is where the screws need to go.

With the bottom runner in place temporarily, check you have a perfect 90° as shown.

This is where I need to put the fixing screws, so...

...this is where I mark the line for drilling!

Drill clearance holes into a piece of scrap.

Clamp the runner in place, and then invert the whole set up.

Countersink the clearance holes and drill pilot holes into the hardwood runner. Watch the depth!

Drill from the top, right through into some scrap. These need to be clearance holes rather than pilot holes, so that when you put the screws in you don't jack the runner off the baseboard.

Before you turn the job over, clamp it in place, tight against the beveled plywood edge.

With the clamps in place, and after a final check, drill the pilot holes. Be aware of the length of the screws and the depth of the holes. Don't pop the drill out through the other side! As I mentioned earlier, screws going into hardwood must be driven into pilot holes. The huge torque from tightening without a nice pilot hole creates the risk of you snapping the screw head right off.

Screw the runner firmly in place.

Fit the fences

The sliding fences will now need cutting down in order to slide underneath the top bar.

First cut a 45 degree angle on both left and right fences, making sure that the recess for the screw and washer is facing outwards. Mark them up on the back so you always know which is left or right.

Saw or plane off equal amounts from the top and bottom of the fences, keeping the screw recess reasonably central, and shoot the sawn ends on your miter shooting board. The fences have to fit under the top bar, as shown, middle right.

Drill, saw and file the slots as shown on pages 327 to 329, and then file down the outermost edges to give them a good chamfer. With the top bar removed, mark the screw hole positions at the very front of the slots, as shown.

You are going to need pilot holes again, drilled into the fence supports, and the easiest way to do this may be to take them off the base board and drill the pilot holes with the work in your vise, as shown.

Cut a 45° on the ends of the fences, and shoot the end grain to tidy up.

Cut the fences down to fit under the bar.

Cut slots and chamfer the back of the miters.

Mark the screw hole positions, and then dismantle the device, as...

...this will allow you to drill the pilot holes for the brass screws in the vise.

The neat trick here is to pre-thread the holes for the brass screws using a similar steel screw.

...final assembly is easy!

To fit the stops, line up the fence of the miter shooting board with the fence of the small 90° board.

Mark up the stop positions accordingly...

TOP TIP: *This is a neat trick with brass screws that I've mentioned before. After drilling the pilot holes, select a hardened steel screw with the same thread pitch as the brass screw, and using a cordless drill, run the steel screw in and out a few times. Putting a little wax on it will help.*

The brass fence retaining screws should wind in and out with very little effort, which is exactly what you want. They are not in an easy position to be able to apply a lot of torque and unless they turn easily, you are always going to risk either damaging the heads or even worse, snapping them off! Rebuild the board and check that all components went back together correctly.

Fit the stops

As with the other shooting boards, a pair of battens are needed to stop it moving around in use. Use the 90 degree shooting board as a reference and line up the fences with a straight edge.

With the bevel shooting board still in place, mark off the positions for the front and back stops, and then chamfer, sand and fit them as before.

...on both sides of the bench top.

Finishing

The whole device now needs a final going over, so plane up any edges you need to on the base board, sand down any edges that need it and generally get it ready for a coat of sealer, brushing off any dust when you're done.

Leave the whole device assembled, including the sliding fences, and give it a coat of sanding sealer, thinned down to 50% so that it spreads quickly and evenly.

Sand the first coat down and give it a second coat. As the sliding fences are still fixed in place, there is no chance of thick globs of sealer kicking them out of line. The sealer will however, creep into the gaps by capillary action and so the first time they are adjusted, they will need a short, sharp tap from the back to break the weak sanding sealer bond.

Sand down ready for the sealer.

Two coats of sealer are better than one. Don't scrape your brush over any edges, or you'll end up with more runs than the West Indies on a good day!

Longer work pieces can be supported on the bench hooks, from page 379.

Using the bevel shooting board

Planing end grain requires a very sharp plane iron. I would strongly recommend you consider replacing the O1 standard iron with either a Lie-Nielsen D2 or Veritas PMV-11 iron. Support longer work pieces using a bench hook (page 379).

For mitering molded stock, such as a rebated plinth, always arrange the molding to be at the front of the stroke. In this way, the plane won't break out the unsupported fibers. Left and right parts of a plinth can be planed down easily.

The miter should fit together perfectly.

The sanding plane from page 323 can also be used with this device, although I don't recommend it for particularly wide stock as you'll be at your shooting board all day.

Always plane towards the profiled molding, using either left handed,or...

...right handed orientations of the shooting board.

There you go. What a lovely job!

Bench hooks

The bench hooks described here have two purposes. Firstly they are great for supporting the ends of longer work pieces when used in conjunction with the 90 degree and bevel shooting boards. Secondly, when you are dimensioning longer boards on the bench, they can be used as a pair to support the work at each end as you cross cut the stock into smaller pieces, using your 90 degree shooting board as a central support. Typically, you would mark out, cut a whisker over length and then shoot to the right length, preparing all your stock in one batch. These will probably be used several times a day so find somewhere to keep them handy!

"...cut a whisker over length and then shoot to the right length, preparing all your stock in one batch."

Bench hooks are typically made in pairs, and need to be the same thickness as your 90 degree and bevel shooting boards.

What you'll need

- Marine grade or similar quality plywood.
- 17" x 12" x ¾" -1pc
- 17" x 12" x ½" -1pc
- Hardwood for the stops
- ⅝" x 1" x 12" -2pcs
- 8 x Wood screws 1½" No.8's
- Sanding sealer
- Polyurethane (PU) or PVA Glue

Note, these instructions are for PU glue. If you are going to use PVA, lamination will take over night, as PVA takes this long to fully set. PU glue reduces the setting time down to perhaps less than an hour.

Two out of one

It seems sensible where possible, to get 2 for the price of 1 in terms of effort and procedure. For these bench hooks, we'll laminate the base boards as one, before eventually cutting it in half. The reason for lamination is simply to make the thickness of the device equal to that of the bench shooting boards, so the work will be supported flat and straight.

You should be familiar with what to do by now:

- Spread the glue and let it froth a while.
- Whilst still sticky, align the boards and press them together.
- Clamp up, and move the whole assembly out of the way so you can get on with making the stops.

The materials for 2 completed bench hooks.

As per usual, laminate the boards together...

...judging when the glue has stopped frothing.

The caul clamps come in handy for this sort of thing.

This is not a miter box, but it does prevent me from slipping with my saw and leaving saw cuts on my vise jaws or bench top.

Either plane down or file an even chafer on 3 faces of the stops.

Make your stops

As the glue is setting, cut the stops to length (in half, as you need 2 at 6" long) and chamfer the ends as before.

Chamfer the tops using whatever tool you prefer, a file or a plane.

About an inch from each end, drill a clearance hole into some scrap and countersink the holes so that the screw heads will be recessed.

Countersink to prevent the screw heads from damaging your work or your bench.

Cut the boards

Set up the large shooting board and check the base board. If the glue has set properly, run round the edges of the board with a sharp plane to true up the edges.

Check the orientation of the board on the bench top. The board needs to reach the back edge of the bench top and overhang the apron by 1½" or so. Mark the dead center of the board and square a line down. Clamp the board in the vise and saw down your line.

Tidy up the cut edges either on the large shooting board, or use the shooting stick as a guide with the boards held in the vise.

TOP TIP: *When clamping a work piece in one end of the vise jaws, have a large wedge on hand to put in the other side. This will counter the twisting force on the vise and really increase the clamping pressure (see photo, bottom right).*

Plane up the board edges square.

The board needs cutting into two pieces.

Cut down your line with a panel saw.

The shooting stick comes in handy, once again!

Here's a good trick to increase the clamping pressure and prevent twist.

The bench hooks need to match the fence on your 90 degree shooting board.

Use a square or straight edge to line up the back stop with the fence.

As these bench hooks are designed to work alongside the bench top shooting board, use this as a reference to position the stops. Mark the front stop in line with the edge of your apron.

And position the back stop dead in line with the fence on your shooting board.

Seal up to finish

Every time you get the sealer out, don't forget to get out some scrap plywood to work on, or you'll end up inadvertently getting a fair bit of cellulose sealer on your bench top. Keeping you bench top clean and smooth is essential, or any work piece laid on top will get marked or dented from blobs of sealer or glue.

Nip the screws up with everything held in place.

Apply a coat of sanding sealer after a good sand down.

Acetone 99.9% purity
Go Green
EVO-STIK
IMPACT
BRIWAX
Sanding Sealer
METHYL ETHYL KETONE
Rustins
EVO-STIK
NEW IMPROVED FORMULA
ADHESIVE CLEANER
COLRON
SWAN
Titebond
LIQUID HIDE Wood Glue
Geocel
JOINERS MATE liquid
COLOUR TONE
Treatex®
Hardwax Oil Traditional
LIBERON
BUTTON POLISH
RONSEAL
QUICK DRYING
DARK OAK
Clear Satin
Hardwax Oil
Camellia Oil
100ml
ANTIQUE BROWN
WAX

Section 6
Chapter 14
Glue, finishes, solvents and fillers

I've applied up to six coats of the same finish!

I've always been a mad keen chemist - fascinated by chemical compounds, reactions and material properties. My family is convinced I'm a mad scientist and it's probably why I have so much fun in the kitchen, always curious about combining flavors in different ways. Chemistry, cookery and wood finishing have a surprising amount in common - a good background understanding actually gives you a lot of confidence, and dramatically increases the likelyhood of getting the results you want.

A lot of folks are put off getting involved in any of the above because they are simply unsure of the results of their endeavors. If food is cooked properly and is not too salty or spicy, the chances are that your family will eat it and not desert you for the nearest chip shop (probably equates to a 'Diner' in the US). Likewise, with many wood finishes, providing that you prepare your surfaces well, work quickly and carefully, you can get an even color change or surface finish, and it's probably all going to be O.K. Have a go, make mistakes, learn and have fun! Does it really matter? Well, of course it does, on larger pieces that you've put a lot of time into, but you'd have to be mad as a hatter to *experiment* with wood finishing on anything large and meaningful!

The 'brush on, wipe off' finishes such as hard wax oil, are incredibly forgiving and easy to apply, so I'd recommend you try these out first.

I have covered a selection of useful glues, solvents, finishes and fillers, but it's a small cross section of the very wide spectrum available. Each one is included because it has a very practical application, or is just could be useful to know about.

Hide glue as it should be - hot, runny and sticks like toffee to a blanket!

Natural hide glue is the best for instruments.

"With a whiff of steam and a few hot sand bags, he carefully rebuilds instruments worth thousands..."

Glue

For centuries, glue has been prepared from a variety of natural products including tree resin, animal hide and boiled fish bones to name but a few. More recently modern industry has provided us with a dazzling array of synthetic adhesives with a wide range of properties and applications. There are now enormous sub-groups that fall within particular categories, but we're going to look at just a few varieties of glue, most useful for a cabinet maker.

Natural products

Some folks, wherever possible like to use 'natural' or 'sustainable' products, in favor of the modern (and often harmful) synthetic materials available. In luthier work, antique repair and restoration 'natural' is an absolute necessity, as hide glue, for example can be 'unstuck' sometimes with the application of heat and moisture. The brittle nature of the bond is very useful allowing instruments and antiques to be prized apart and then fixed up, good as new, with minimal intrusion into the original materials, and no damage at all.

My next door neighbor (known affectionately as 'Tony Violin') is an expert restorer of stringed instruments, and uses only hide glue. With a whiff of steam and a few hot sand bags, he carefully rebuilds instruments worth thousands with a skill and total confidence that takes decades to acquire. It's a fascinating business to watch (and learn) and I'm amazed at what he does in a workshop the size of a phone booth!

Tony recently made the point that hide glue was not a gap filler. He assured me that a violin made with half a teaspoon of hide glue was a good indicator of quality, as opposed to a violin stuck together with half a pint.

A good rub with a damp cloth will remove hide glue, as the joint is squeezed together.

Likewise with joinery, there are no short cuts to quality workmanship, and using a lot of glue is no substitute for a proper fit.

We will look at using hide glue in detail when we cover veneer work in a later part of the course. However, if you are interested in using hide glue before then, there is nothing to stop you. Go ahead and get yourself a few pounds of 'pearl glue', a cast iron double boiler and a stout brush. Prepare the glue and get it to the consistency of maple syrup - it should run quickly off the brush but still make patterns in the pot. If it runs off in a thick strand, and the patterns remain for a while, it's too thick or too cold. Either way you are going to be in trouble if you use it. A little hot water, a hotter temperature, or probably both will sort it out.

Just remember three things when you glue up furniture: Work very quickly and give the joints no more than a good dab and a wipe with the glue. Keep the clamps on overnight in a warm place.

Make sure you thoroughly research the use of hide glue before giving it a try. Don't approach it with optimism and ignorance: you can quickly become unstuck!

This glue is too thick and needs sorting out.

"...there are no short cuts,... using a lot of glue is no substitute for a proper fit..."

Liquid hide glue

This is a water based product and is a close relative to the real thing, i.e the hide glue we have just looked at. There is far less time pressure gluing up with this compared to traditional hide glue. Once set, the parts may be subsequently separated with the application of heat and moisture, in much the same way as it's traditional counterpart. Amongst other ingredients, it contains ammonium thiocyanate, so it is quite toxic. The joint strength it achieves is very good, particularly if the joints are a good snug fit. Don't spread it too thinly, as it does shrink a little as it dries. Coat both surfaces adequately, and then expect quite a long wait before you can take the clamps off. Overnight should be long enough providing the temperature is around 60˚F (15˚C), otherwise it will take longer.

PVA

In *Working Wood 1&2* we used PVA for some fairly simple assemblies; the most complex being a chair side table and the workbench. This is a very versatile glue and is used by most woodworkers. As your projects become more complex and assembly time during the glue up gets longer, you will be looking for ways to buy yourself more glue up time.

I recommend that once your assembly is ready to glue, clamps set and packers to hand etc., take a well wrung out wet cloth and dampen down all the surfaces of every joint, before you apply the glue.

Alternatively, dilute the PVA with a little water to thin it out a bit. Either way will give you a surprising amount of time for more complex assemblies and you'll reduce the chances of the joints setting before you clamp up tight and check for square.

In both of the above cases, leave the work clamped up for longer than usual, as the overall drying time will have increased proportionally as well.

Liquid hide glue is used just like PVA, except for the fact that it can be 'unstuck', like the real thing.

> *"Once set, the parts may subsequently be separated with the application of heat and moisture..."*

Depending on the ambient temperature, PU glue is about as viscous as honey before it reacts with the moisture in the air.

Polyurethane Glue

So far in this course, we have recommended the use of PVA glue, which is the most commonly used glue in general furniture making. However, as there is quite a lot of jig making to do in this part of the course, the slow (usually overnight) setting time with PVA is less than ideal. In the interests of getting the job done faster, for tasks such as laminating plywood, I like to use polyurethane glue (PU glue). It's a boat building glue, so not surprisingly it's highly water resistant and it immediately starts to set on contact with moisture.

The air around us has moisture in it and wood always has a certain moisture content, so it's no wonder it sets inside a joint or when left in the open air.

It will fill gaps and irregularities very nicely, although I'd never suggest you use it for gluing up furniture. It's more appropriate as a construction or structural adhesive.

The setting process

The process of setting is complex, in terms of the chemistry involved, so we'll just look at what happens, not why it happens. On initial application, it spreads like honey, and the more you work it, the thicker it gets. You can see in the right hand photo, that the consistency has become much thicker, just by working it a little.

The first stage is characterized by the formation of gas bubbles (carbon dioxide) within the glue layer. As it expands and froths, it will stick to nearly anything it touches.

If it's worked about with a spreader, it thickens quickly.

> *"It's a boat building glue, so not surprisingly it's highly water resistant..."*

This is the first stage of setting - it starts to froth as carbon dioxide is formed within the glue itself.

It keeps on frothing for a while, and can exert a lot of force when confined.

It's stopped frothing now and has gone tacky.

TECHNICAL POINTER: *The foaming and frothing can exert an immense force if confined during this phase. You particularly need to watch out for this when laminating wide, flat boards as it's difficult to get sufficient clamping pressure to withstand the 'jacking' effect. This is not too much of a problem if you are laminating, say 2x3's, as you just apply pressure with some heavy clamps.*

The next stage of setting after the frothing, is when the surface is still 'tacky'. For a short time after the froth has developed, the tacky surface reacts with the air and hardens to form a skin. In the short tacky phase, the glue will, if required, act like a contact adhesive and it will stick to itself very readily. You can see how it is forming fine, stringy threads as I lift the spreading stick away. It has now finished expanding and frothing.

If the bubbles are squashed at this stage no more will appear, which means that two surfaces coated in this glue at the same time, will bond instantly as they are pressed together.

In the tacky phase, you can squash the bubbles and they won't reappear. It will now act like a contact adhesive, and if two parts are pressed together...

...you get an instant bond that increases in strength as the glue hardens.

"...the warmth reduces the viscosity of the glue to the consistency of maple syrup..."

Other characteristics of PU glue

This glue has no instant 'grab' if you clamp up a joint straight away. Quite the opposite, polyurethane glue acts as a first class lubricant. Your work pieces will move and slide very readily if you are not careful, so if at all possible, have a means of registering the edges so that they coincide.

Viscosity is also a big issue. If you are working in a very cold workshop, you'll struggle to squeeze the glue out of the bottle, and when you do get some out you'll have to spread it with a palette knife as it will be like toffee. The converse is true in the middle of a hot summer. The warmth reduces the viscosity of the glue to the consistency of maple syrup, and the stuff will run all over the place, dribbling off boards in all directions. (Note: This only applies to US readers, as a British summer is usually just as cold, wet and generally miserable as winter!)

So just be aware and pay very careful attention to the storage temperature. I keep my bottles in the house during the winter, and only take them out to the workshop when the woodstove has warmed the place up to a tolerable level.

Partially set glue can be rubbed off with methylated spirits. It is NOT a solvent for this glue so it won't dissolve the glue and smear it all over your work.

TOP TIP: *A very useful property of this glue is that it will not stick to a waxed surface. If you give all your clamps a good rubbing with some furniture wax, the cured polyurethane glue will easily peel off, leaving them clean and ready to use again. I have made the mistake a few times of not waxing part of a clamp, only to find that a drip had welded itself to some part of the clamp and required a good scraping to get it off.*

Another good trick with this glue, which will save time later, is to clean any excess that squeezes out of a joint with a cloth and methylated spirits. You have to patiently wait until the glue is almost set, at the very end of the tacky phase. It will rub off forming lumps and little balls of semi-set glue, leaving a nice clean surface.

The solvent to use with this glue is acetone, although standard cellulose thinners work as well. Don't try to clean up your work with acetone or you will spread a thin layer over the whole surface you are trying to clean, making it impossible to stain up later without sanding off all the glue. However, for rough work of little consequence you can clean up with acetone once it's at the end of the tacky phase. Use the solvent sparingly or you'll risk it seeping into the joint and weakening the bond. I much prefer to use methylated spirits instead to clean joints at the end of the tacky stage.

Acetone is very good if you accidentally get it on your hands, teapot, door handles, carpets, clothes, pets or children. I have done all of the aforementioned, but not all at the same time.

A little goes a long way! Superglue is ideal for fixing small cosmetic chips and splits.

Superglue

Firstly, this is not a constructional glue in project terms, so don't use it on woodworking joints. It is for very small scale use, along the lines of 'sailing ship in a bottle' models. Think of superglue as a cosmetic glue not for structural applications, and you won't go far wrong.

In the workshop, this glue is really good for very quick fixes of chipped wood edges. For example, if you were to catch an end grain edge or corner by accident and split a flake off, you can immediately fix it back on with superglue and clamps, and carry on working. Small splits or cracked moldings can be instantly fixed, and fine decorative work can be assembled and fixed very efficiently. Keep a soft cloth and some acetone handy in case you need to clean up spillages or accidental smears on your fingers or your work.

None of the solvents I've listed in this section will remove the glue once set, but acetone and methyl ethyl ketone will both remove the glue while it is still liquid.

Small bottles are useful as you don't end up throwing so much away when it eventually solidifies through exposure to the moisture in the air. However, slightly larger bottles are much easier to squeeze and therefore allow much more care and accuracy of application.

When I'm in a hurry I use a 'spray on' catalyst which speeds up the reaction, setting the glue in around 6 seconds.

Using a 'spray on' activator reduces the setting time to a few seconds.

Wood finishing

Pretty much, without exception, every article made from wood needs some form of finishing product. Quite apart from the aesthetic considerations of enhancing color and appearance, wood needs protection to resist abrasion from use and it needs protection to reduce the ebb and flow of water molecules that would otherwise cause unwanted expansion and contraction.

The three steps:

1. Prepare the wood.
2. Apply a color.
3. Apply a finishing/top coat.

This is a sequence that applies to many oil and water based finishes. However, if you are using emulsions or shellac the color and top coat are one and the same thing.

In *Working Wood 1&2* we've looked at how vegetable oil can be rubbed onto bare wood to protect kitchen utensils, and how a few simple coats of colored shellac can both enhance the look of a project and seal the grain. Beyond these simple finishes there is of course a vast range of highly effective wood finishes that can add a depth of color tone, a luster and a beauty to even the most plain and uninspiring woods. Some products color and seal the grain in the first coat, whereas others may simply change the color, but lacking any kind of binder, require further coats to bond and seal the color into the wood. A basic understanding of the differences in the chemistry of wood coatings is essential, and that's where we'll start.

Sand every surface of your work down to an even finish.

Apply a colored coat using a cloth or a brush.

Choose and apply the top coat sealer - Matt, satin or gloss are the usual options.

The powerful brown stain from walnut trees put to good use in the form of 'Van Dyke' crystals. Just look at the variation in shades from the same jar!

Identify the type of finish

Wood finishes come in a variety of different forms: Ready-made liquids, pastes, powders and concentrates. Knowing what you are dealing with is the key to understanding the use of any wood finishing material.

Whatever you chose, it's a good idea to become reasonably well acquainted with the health and safety data sheets (MSDS- US). They fall into four broad categories, in terms of the chemistry of their constituents:

1. Water based - This type is dissolved in or will dissolve in water, and water alone. This is the oldest category of pigments and was historically based on plant extracts or crudely processed minerals.
2. Emulsion based - These products are fast drying and are an emulsified mixture of oil based materials and water.
3. Alcohol/shellac based - This covers all the different shades and grades of shellac.
4. Oil/solvent based - This is by far the largest category and includes many paints, varnishes, waxes as well as hard wax oil.

Water based

Water based products are the most simple in that their only purpose is to change the color tone of the wood. Van Dyke crystals for example are a commercially produced extract from walnut shells. The color can be built up in layers, gradually darkening the wood to the desired tone (see photo above). Although natural dyes from plant roots, ochre, fungi, tree bark and suchlike have been replaced with artificially produced dyes on grounds of economy, many natural wood dyeing materials are still available.

With all water based dyes and emulsions the top fibers of the dry wood first need to be wetted down, then allowed to dry, and finally sanded down with 220 grit sandpaper. This is commonly referred to as 'raising the grain', and is an essential step if you are going to use any finish containing water on wood. Once the fibers have absorbed water, crumpled up a bit, and then been sanded smooth again after drying out, the process need not be repeated.

A simple coat of Danish oil will seal in the color, permanently locking the dye to the wood fibers.

A water-based dye is usually going to need a light coat of sealer to bind the color permanently to the wood. This can be either clear or tinted, and could be a varnish, a finishing oil or a shellac. With the color locked in, a topcoat of the same can then be applied to enhance the color and increase the protection for the wood. Water based dyes dry quickly, and so can be sealed after an hour or two.

Powder dyes are readily available, and when mixed in water, several different tints can be added together to get the desired color tone. If you try this, then make sure you record the recipe. Take detailed notes of exactly what you are adding, and the quantity of water you are using, otherwise you may never repeat the same shade again!

"...Danish oil will seal in the color, permanently locking the dye to the wood fibers."

Painted furniture can look beautiful, so don't dismiss emulsion paint too quickly!

Fresh mayonnaise is a very tasty emulsion!

"Emulsion chemistry is very complex nowadays, but every product is based on one simple principle..."

Emulsions

These finishing products have been around for a while. They are usually marketed as 'fast drying' and/or 'water based' and can be found under an enormous range of different brand names. Emulsion chemistry is very complex nowadays, but every product is based on one simple principle: An emulsion is formed when two immiscible liquids are mixed in the presence of an emulsifying agent. In the same way that washing up liquid enables the grease and oil from cooking to lift off the cooking pots into the hot water, chemicals such as glycol esters allow oil based pigments and alkyd resins to form an emulsion in water.

Mayonnaise is a common household example. Oil, vinegar, egg yolks and mustard are combined to form an emulsion. The egg yolk will mix easily with oil and water, which makes it an edible, emulsifying agent.

Emulsion paint and water based varnish work on the same principle. Many exterior and interior paints, wood stains and varnishes are emulsion based. This is not a typical finish for fine furniture, rather for outside benches, or workshop equipment. However, beautiful examples of painted fine furniture have been produced throughout the ages, all over the world.

This exterior wood stain is a quick drying, water based emulsion. It's great for workshop equipment like the saw horses.

In practice

Compared to a finishing oil, emulsions tend to have a high solids content and need to be applied with a brush. My usual approach is to get the coating on quickly with a roller, and then finish off with a brush in the same direction as the wood grain. The high solids content means that with a translucent colored coating you are probably going to leave brush marks, even with a really good soft bristled brush (which I would recommend for all brush applied finishes).
On furniture, these brush streaks would be very noticeable, and the awkward to get to places will look particularly patchy. Some folks may be very confident with emulsion finishes on furniture, and with skill they can be used very effectively.

I have to say, for nice furniture (as opposed to something for the workshop), I would not recommend an emulsion based product, unless you are actually applying paint to completely cover the wood. If you are planning on seeing some wood grain, you may want to use something else, such as a shellac, a finishing oil or a hard wax oil.

If you do want to use an emulsion based wood protector then just follow the directions on the tin. You won't have long to wait as it will be untouchable in 5 minutes and probably dry in an hour. (Untouchable - what I mean is you need to get it on and leave it, don't go back and fiddle with it as you'll just mess it up!)

If you are using an emulsion varnish, apply thin coats and sand (220 grit) lightly between each coat. You can choose a matt, satin or gloss coat, but even the gloss coat will not have the highly polished shine of a solvent based varnish. For convenience and ease of use (fast drying and brushes washed in water), emulsions are great for certain applications.

"You won't have to wait long, as it will... probably be dry in an hour."

Shellac can be built up, layer upon thin layer.

Use accurate weighing scales to get the right proportion of solid shellac flakes, to industrial ethanol.

Alcohol/shellac based

Shellac is more commonly known as 'French polish', however a more accurate use of this term is as a verb, in describing the process of 'French polishing'. To 'French polish' a piece of furniture, is to build up a great number of coats of shellac, with each coat having a successively smaller proportion of solids dissolved in alcohol.

An interesting fact about shellac is that it's collected as a secretion from the female Lac beetle. The small red bugs create tubular structures on the bark of several different tree species found in India and some parts of Asia.

Shellac has been used for centuries, and is bought either as a pre-made solution, or as a solid in the form of flakes. The strength of the solution is a very important factor in the application process. The standard measurement for strength of solution is based on the number of pounds of shellac dissolved in a gallon of alcohol. This is known as the 'cut' and for example, a '3lb. cut' would be composed of 3lbs of shellac dissolved in a gallon of alcohol.

The process of French polishing a piece of furniture is lengthy and time consuming and if you want to read about the full process, I'd recommend a web page published by Luthiers Mercantile International, a notable supplier of musical instrument building and repair products. (See pages of www.lmii.com/french-polish.)

Shellac is a useful solution to have in the workshop, even if you don't intend to learn the old art of French polishing. I use it when I'm restoring old tools, for the handles of planes and saws, and the bodies of old wooden planes. It dries quickly and imparts a warm color and nice 'feel' to old tools.

Three wood dyes; "Antique Pine", "Victorian Pine", "Peruvian Mahogany". Until you try it on the wood, you won't know for sure what you're going to get.

Oil/solvent based finishes

There are thousands of very secret and complex chemical recipes, each having very specific properties. A study of the full range of solvent based finishes is way beyond the scope of this book, or possibly any single book for that matter. However, we'll look at a few examples, concentrating on the practical application of each one.

Dyes and stains

The differences between a stain and a dye are important to understand. Particles of dye are very, very small, even compared to the size of the pores in wood. A dye will penetrate the pores of wood with even the finest of grains, such as cherry or maple. A dye is also fairly translucent and will not cover up the wood grain, allowing all the rich patterns of the wood to show through despite the color change. A dye usually has no binder to lock the color in. This means that successive coats of dye can be built up to achieve the final color, with the particles in each coat settling into the actual pores of the wood. When the desired color is reached, a top coat of some kind of sealer must be applied.
This could be a shellac, a finishing oil or a varnish and so on.

"A wood stain usually contains a high proportion of opaque pigments..."

A wood stain usually contains a high proportion of opaque pigments suspended in, or dissolved in a carrier. In the formulation, there is usually some kind of binder which has the effect of sealing up the wood pores. This means that further coats of stain can only be layered on top of the previous, so the color change is more of a 'cover up' than a through and through color change.

Here's a list of tips which will get you started when it comes to changing the color tone of your wood using a wood dye:

1. Make sure your wood is sanded evenly. 220 grit is standard. If you sand to 120, the wood will look darker and more 'rustic', even if you use exactly the same wood dye. This is because the surface texture of the wood directly affects the 'take up' of the dye. A glassy smooth work piece, straight from a sharp hand plane, will take up very little color. Sanding roughens the surface of planed work pieces to give a very even absorbtion of color.
2. Test the dye on an off cut first. The off cut should also be planed and sanded first to give it the same surface texture.
3. To apply the dye use a soft brush and apply it fairly liberally, as this will allow the wood to take up as much color as it can. Cloth off the excess soon after brushing it on, and rub the wood until it has lost all wetness and feels dry to the touch.
4. If you are happy with the general color and tone go ahead and dye up your project. I'd always recommend that you do the fiddly bits first, leaving the easy, larger panels or sides until you're sure you've done the tricky detail completely.
5. Wear disposable gloves and an old jacket for all dyeing and staining work. You need to work quickly so the dye does not start to dry in patches.
6. As mentioned earlier, a wood dye will always need to be sealed in with a top coat of shellac, finishing oil, hard wax oil or some sort of varnish.

Just like the water based products (not emulsions!), wood dye needs to be followed by a sealer, in this case a clear satin, hard wax oil.

Finishing oils

A 'finishing oil' is used as a sealer to lock in the color of the previous coat, or to simply seal up the grain against ingress of water. The finishing oils here each have different properties.

Tung oil

This is a very old type of wood finish and apparently was used in China as far back as 400 AD. Initial extraction is by pressing the oil out of the seeds (nuts) of tung trees. The raw product is usually heat treated to prevent it drying with a wrinkled finish. It has a pleasant odor and when dry and provides a better barrier against water vapor transfer than any other pure oil finish. However, it is still not that good as a sealer, unless many coats are applied. Tung oil is usually thinned out with a solvent, usually white spirits, to make it easier to spread a thin coat and to reduce the drying time. It's usually wiped on with a cloth and then rubbed to remove the excess. It quickly penetrates the cell structure of wood to a good depth. Successive coats should have progressively less solvent until the finish coat is just the oil. Give it at least 24hrs between each coat, and a gentle abrading with wire wool once each coat is fully dry. It clogs up sandpaper very quickly. I don't recommend tung oil as a furniture finish by itself, but some folks will swear by it, so I guess each to their own as they say. However, it is the main ingredient of one of my favorite wood finishes, Danish oil.

Pure tung oil is readily available.

The unripe nuts of a tung tree. As the seeds mature, the shell covering dries out and splits, and the nuts fall to the floor.

Danish oil has superior properties to those of pure tung oil.

This is how flax used to be harvested. It's grown on an industrial scale now.

Danish oil

Over the years I have gotten through a great deal of Danish oil and I love it. On top of a wood dye it seals the color in very nicely. As with all finishing oils, it should be built up in layers. However, Danish oil contains a certain proportion of varnish, which means that only a few coats are required, quickly producing a tough and water repellent finish. I've experimented over the years with different recipes using Danish oil, and I've had a lot of success in mixing it with white spirits and solvent based wood dye. The products are compatible, but do be aware of one thing: Estimate how much you are going to need and don't mix up too much more, as you could end up throwing it away. The high proportion of tung oil in Danish oil can react with the dye over just a matter of hours and form a thick jelly, which is no use at all. If you are not on a deadline, I'd suggest dyeing the wood and sealing with Danish oil in a two stage process, with a day between the coats.

It will impart a lovely satin finish when built up in a few coats. Apply Danish oil with a brush, a cloth or a roller, but don't go too heavy with each coat, as you'll need to take the excess off with a soft cloth before it goes tacky. On a hot day it will go tacky within five minutes so always remove the excess in good time. Just like any other finish keep your work away from any dust until it dries!

Despite the fact that I really like the smell of Danish oil, I always make sure the workshop is well ventilated when using it (as with any solvent based product). This is not to be taken lightly, as you could end up with a headache, and find that your next meal, whatever it may be, tastes of Danish oil!

Linseed oil

This is a wood finishing oil of historic significance and has been used in Europe for centuries. It's extracted by cold pressing the seeds of the flax plant. As an industrial raw material, vast tracts of land are given to the cultivation of flax and it's processed on a huge scale.

As a wood finishing oil it has it's limitations. The raw oil readily soaks into the open pores of any wood and will slowly dry and harden. However, it does tend to leave a slightly sticky surface and nowadays, a product known as 'boiled linseed oil' is far more widely used. The conversion process does not necessarily involve boiling, but rather it is processed and oxidized, with additives to improve the durability, drying time, penetration and toughness. It is totally inedible and should be treated with the same precautions as any paint product. It's also a base product used in the manufacture of a range of wood finishes, paints and varnishes.

Given the choice of these two, I would chose Danish oil every time for any work rather than boiled linseed oil. It's applied just the same as Danish oil.

Teak oil

This is a traditional finish for outdoor hardwood furniture, and offers a good level of protection from the elements. Teak has been used for outdoor furniture for centuries and this finishing oil enhances the color tone, especially as many coats are built up. It has a similar composition to Danish oil, only with a certain amount of boiled linseed oil thrown in. It's a good choice for external hardwood joinery.

Hard wax oil

This is not a simple finishing oil, like the ones we have covered so far, but is instead a very complex formulation. It's a pleasant 'eco' alternative to a lot of synthetic dyes, stains and finishes. It has a faintly eucalyptus smell to it, and I really like walking into my workshop in the morning, after using it the day before.

As the name suggests, this product is a solvent based mixture of finishing oils, various plant oils and waxes. This is one oil based product that has truly green credentials, save for a small solvent percentage, and may be built up in layers of color. The topcoat may be a matt, satin or glossy finish, but make sure that it is fully compatible with the colored coats applied previously.

Hard wax oil is a versatile finish that can be rubbed on and wiped off. It's important to use enough product to allow you to get an even covering with no bare patches, for every coat applied. The drying time does depend on temperature, but generally the work needs to be left overnight between coats. As a wood finish, it has to be one of my favorites as it's very easy to apply evenly and you can choose the sheen of the top coat with absolute confidence. The top coat will remain tacky for hours and needs to be left two days before it sets hard enough for use.

Teak oil has it's uses for outside furniture.

I love the smell of this natural product! You'll be seeing a lot more hard wax oil in the next part of the course, as it's lovely stuff to work with.

Sanding sealer is great for workshop jigs and devices. It soaks into the wood and hardens the surface, drying very quickly.

"Apply it with a brush, fairly liberally, and let it soak into your work... it will dry in a matter of minutes..."

Cellulose sanding sealer

Cellulose sanding sealer is another favorite of mine. It is definitely not a natural product and has no 'eco' credentials whatsoever. I use it for jigs and fixtures because it penetrates very well and sets hard in minutes. To be quite honest, you never really know what you are getting when you buy a tin of this stuff, unless you check the data sheet first. The main reason for this is that different companies use a range of ingredients with little or no standardization. The solvents used are the most noxious that I ever want to go near and can include acetone, xylene, ethanol, methanol, methyl ethyl ketone and a whole load more I won't mention. I have a particular dislike of anything containing xylene and toluene, although some think it smells wonderful. Regardless, it's a known carcinogen so avoid the fumes, or better still just avoid it all together! Before buying any particular brand, check the MSDS (data sheet) and find a brand that does not contain carcinogens. 'Mylands' US and 'Rustins' UK are both suppliers that make a point of using as few nasty ingredients as possible.

I like to thin down cellulose sanding sealer with between 30-50% standard thinners, as I find that for a lot of applications, it's a bit too thick straight out of the tin. Apply it with a brush, fairly liberally and let it soak into your work, brushing it out to a consistent finish quickly but with care, as it will dry in a matter of minutes. I say this because you have certainly got less than a minute to deal with any runs.

The liquid has a very high proportion of volatile organic chemicals (VOC's), usually between 80-90% and the solids dissolved are a type of synthetic plastic, usually nitrocellulose. Using this stuff is in some ways like plastic coating your work. This is great for plywood and jigs, but not so good for furniture. I use it for the ultra fast drying time and the hard protective coat it provides for things that are going to get a lot of everyday use. Clear shellac is a good alternative.

Polishes

We've covered the use of a good wax polish in the last book, so I'll just mention for the record that it can be useful to have a few different colored waxes in the armory, just in case after all the dyeing and sealing, you just want to go a shade darker, redder or browner. I don't think anything beats traditional beeswax polish. It's easy to use and smells lovely. Who could ask for more?

Solvents

I like to have a good range of solvents on hand in my workshop. The reason for this, as you may have noticed in the previous section, is that different finishing products can be removed or thinned down using the appropriate solvent.

This is the range (bottom photo) that I keep in stock, but I should make the point that if all you are ever going to use is PVA glue, a few different colors/grades of shellac and a tin of wax polish, you will certainly not need any of these solvents, except just a bottle of industrial ethanol for the shellac.

For polyurethane glue - ACETONE

For cellulose sanding sealer - STANDARD NITRO THINNERS

For spirit based dye and finishing oils - WHITE SPIRIT and METHYL ETHYL KETONE

For shellac - METHYLATED SPIRITS or INDUSTRIAL ETHANOL

Contact adhesive needs a very particular solvent. This maker (red tin) actually supplies a special solvent for sale alongside the adhesive.

For emergency cleaning I use a solvent based cleaner, formulated for cleaning UPvc plastic windows. It is a powerful concoction containing ethyl acetate and takes grubby finger marks off wood like nothing else. It's a good de-greaser for old hand tools, and I use it on my bench top occasionally.

Lighter Fluid - Petroleum based naptha is used as a cleaner and lubricant for french polishing.

Beeswax - It makes the best polish you could ever hope for, and it smells great.

This is my range of most useful solvents.

Rub in the shellac and pumice paste to fill the grain.

On large flat areas, using a sanding block would be the better way of getting a flat surface.

Use a thinner paste for the second coat.

Fillers

I always keep a few wood grain fillers on hand, as even top dollar wood can have fine surface checks and splits that need some attention. Some folks claim never to make mistakes, but I find this hard to believe. Simple human error can result in the need for a quick fix, and providing it's only cosmetic, fillers can be useful for the rare occaision we need to 'make good', as they say. One such memorable event was during the last stages of fitting a cabinet to a wall for a very well to do customer in Winchester. I drilled the first hole for the door handle on the hinge side, instantly knowing that I may have just halved the value of my work. It just so happened that I had some quick-dry powdered filler on hand and a jar of instant coffee by the kettle. It was a quick fix and thanfully, totally invisible!

There is no need to be unprepared for such eventualities as there is a fine range of quick dry fillers, in a range of wood shades at your local hardware store.

The only caveat here is this: If there is a chance that the use of filler may be obvious, you need to decide if making the part again is the better alternative, if you are aiming for high standards.

Pumice powder

This can be used as a very easy grain filler for woods with a large open grain structure like oak and mahogany. Take a few tablespoons of extra fine (320 grit) pumice powder and mix it with a little shellac (3 or 4lb. cut) to make a thick soup/paste. Rub this mixture into the wood thoroughly and wipe off any excess.

After 24hrs, sand down with a 220 grit carbide paper, using a small dash of naptha (lighter fluid) as a lubricant.

When it's dry and dusted off, repeat the process, using a thinner mix of pumice and shellac. Sand right through the shellac/pumice filler until you reach the wood itself. Any imperfections will be filled in beautifully, and then leveled off with a fine sanding.

You may be able to see a small dink in the wood (middle photo) just past the end of the pencil. This has been completely filled and sanded smooth.

When you are done, you should be able to run your finger nail across the grain without feeling the ridges.

This process is the first stage of a French polish application method that is exceptionally well documented on the website mentioned on page 399.

In the bottom photo, I've used a garnet shellac to build up many coats on the wood that you have seen being filled and sanded in the previous photos.

Conclusion

I hope that this brief introduction to wood finishing will give you the confidence to try out a whole range of different methods. The process of wood finishing can undoubtedly transform the most uninspiring wood into something stunning, adding a richness and warmth to any project. Once you've had a go at a few different finishes, you may settle on a favorite. I was astounded the first time I used a strong solution of Van Dyke crystals, the transformation was incredible, as the wood was a very plain, and slightly mottled, locally grown ash. I think that for simplicity and versatility, I'm sold on hard wax oil and I'd like to thank the fellas from Treatex for getting me hooked on the stuff! After 22 years of wood dye and Danish oil, I'm more than happy to switch to a fine smelling, environmentally friendly product, but you can make your own mind up, there's a lot of choice out there, and a lot of fun to be had!

Sand right through the shellac and pumice filler, right down to the wood.

The dust is very fine, and the surface is very, very smooth. (This fine dust also makes a good filler!)

Many coats of garnet shellac later! Seen on the right are flakes of garnet and blond shellac.

GRIPFILL
Wood Adhesive

Conclusion

It never ceases to amaze me what a little confidence can do for someone. With teenage children, I've seen the sparkle that lights up in their eyes when they are confident about having the knowledge and skill to 'get the job done'. Whether it's sharpening a chainsaw, making origami rabbits, cooking up a good pan full of spaghetti carbonara or creating a 'mind map' to help with wtheir studies, the particular activity is of little consequence. What really counts is the smile that grows at the thought of doing something you enjoy, and to have the confidence to tackle the job.

There is nothing sexist about the previous list of interests, as it's actually my son, Matt, who would make a good spaghetti any day of the week given the chance! It often takes a while to get confident in a particular area, and it can be a tough journey to get there, but we all started somewhere, and today, we can all choose the path we take.

If, through reading this book (as many times as you need to!) and having a go, you gain enough knowledge and skill to allow you to successfully tackle the methods and techniques shown, your woodworking confidence will be moving in the right direction. You'll also forge that strong link between confidence and the unashamed, sheer enjoyment of pursuing your interests. It's not so much the 'Where you are' that really matters, and it's definitely not the 'What you've got', but rather it's all about 'Where you are going'. If you've decided that making beautiful wooden furniture is something that you want to plow some time, effort and a little money into, I hope that this book and the following volumes will inspire and motivate you to forge ahead, having the confidence that sufficient sound teaching and guidance will be at hand for you to get you to where you want to be.

There is one last aspect of working wood that you should not dismiss or neglect - Camaraderie. Find neighbors, friends, relatives who are geographically close enough to spend time with, working wood, chatting and drinking tea with. Sure, you could be a member of a dozen online forums and have a lot of informative fun, messaging folks, reading comments, uploading photos of your work, and simply learning from others, but you can't beat actually getting together with people. Join a local club or even start a club. Get out there and make contact with like minded people.

The next part of this course is well underway and will be available for you very soon. I will cover detailed methods and techniques for making a range of cabinet doors, molded cornice, adjustable shelves and some variations of design which will turn a wall cupboard into the top section of a stunning Welsh Dresser (UK) or China Hutch (US). Until then, practice those rebates, grooves and moldings and get yourself a good set of workshop jigs and devices made - you're going to need them! Working wood can be hard work at times, but if it's not a whole load of fun, you're not doing it right!

Simon James

Index

Notes

Notes